Housing the Poor
of Paris, 1850–1902

Housing the Poor
of Paris, 1850–1902

Ann-Louise Shapiro

THE UNIVERSITY OF WISCONSIN PRESS

Published 1985

The University of Wisconsin Press
114 North Murray Street
Madison, Wisconsin 53715

The University of Wisconsin Press, Ltd.
1 Gower Street
London WC1E 6HA, England

First printing

Printed in the United States of America

For LC CIP information see the colophon

ISBN 0-299-09880-X

Publication of this book was made possible in part
by a grant from the Andrew W. Mellon Foundation.

For Michael, Daniel, and Julie

Contents

Illustrations

Figures and Tables

Preface

ID-NINETEENTH-CENTURY Paris was in many ways still a medieval city. Narrow, winding streets in poor repair turned to dust or mud depending upon the weather. Household garbage as well as the dung from 37,000 horses had to be carted away daily, while only 82 miles of underground sewers served 250 miles of streets. For the rest, wastes flowed in gutter streams to the nearest underground collector. Massive immigration from the provinces during the first half of the century doubled the population (from 547,756 in 1801 to 1,053,262 in 1851), straining the city's physical limits of accommodation.[1] Epidemic disease was chronic, spread by intense overcrowding and a contaminated water supply. Paris had become *une ville malade* in which the condition of the population itself increasingly suggested as grave a problem as did the filth and congestion of the environment.

For decades, public health activists had drawn a tight connection between the material setting and the physical, moral, and social well-being of the population. A. A. Tardieu began his dictionary of public hygiene with the statement that "the material conditions of life exercise so direct and so evident an influence on the moral dispositions of man that a well-organized society must constantly extend its efforts to improve the physical condition of the largest numbers of its citizens."[2] But more forceful than rhetoric were the lessons of immediate experience. The nearly simultaneous appearance of revolution in 1848 and cholera in 1849 dramatically confirmed the endemic pathology of the urban environment and the relationship between disorder and disease.

It seemed to contemporaries that the city was producing an enfeebled breed of men. Large numbers of military recruits were rejected due to physical disabilities, while the new statistical studies of Villermé and others showed considerably higher mortality and morbidity rates in the poorer districts. Medical topographies which had been so popular in the early years of the century no longer provided an adequate explanation of poor health. More and more, social reformers, hygienists, and politicians alike identified unsanitary working-class housing as the primary cause of urban ills.

All aspects of "the social question" seemed to converge in the issue of the worker's *foyer*. Bourgeois observers understood the miserable conditions in which workers lived as the source of moral laxness and political sedition as well as of poor health and disease. Underlying all discussion of the concrete problems associated with rapid, unplanned urban growth lay an intense, and often explicit, fear of the consequences of the geographic separation of the classes. Commentators warned of the danger of allowing Paris to be surrounded by impoverished enclaves hostile to the social order. Equally unsettling was the prospect that workers, deprived of the example of bourgeois *moeurs,* would slip into patterns of vicious or criminal behavior. The hygienist Du Mesnil voiced the chronic anxiety of his contemporaries that in the hovels of the poor "heroism was necessary in order not to succumb to hate for society."

The transformation of Paris during the Second Empire delineated the housing problem in sharper terms. Building activities continued to draw workers to the capital, while the incorporation of the suburban communes in 1860 added a poor population and a territory largely deprived of basic urban services. The development of the center city by Napoleon III and Haussmann exacerbated the disparity of conditions between old and new Paris and reinforced the working-class exodus to the eastern and southeastern arrondissements. By the early years of the Third Republic, workers complained of spiraling rents and abusive practices by landlords, while reformers noted an increase on the periphery of clusters of shantytowns — makeshift constructions with no sanitary amenities that escaped all public regulation. In contrast to the pattern of declining mortality in the western half of the city, mortality rates from contagious diseases remained persistently high in the east. The sites of poor health and unsanitary housing had become geographically more concentrated and hence ever more visible.

Clearly, the working classes, who were both biologically and politically suspect, had to be integrated more tightly into the social fabric. The agent for this task was to be improved housing. Housing reform promised nothing less than to reduce social tensions, moralize the working classes, promote public health, and create a more acceptable alignment between social space and geographic space. In the service of such laudable goals, the government took the first public step to regulate unsanitary dwellings with the Melun Law of 1850, which opened the interiors of private lodgings to public surveillance for the first time. It remained in effect for a half century until superseded by the comprehensive public health law of 1902. Together, these two pieces of legislation define a prolonged period in which the problem of housing the poor lay at the center of social debate.

The early consensus on the need for improved working-class housing did not, however, translate into a single strategy or a unified policy. Contemporaries approached housing reform from several different directions. Initially, Napoleon III and Haussmann expected that public health and political stability would automatically emerge through a program of public works. As the inadequacy of this traditional panacea became readily apparent, Le Play's social scientist followers instead defined the problem in moral terms. According to their analysis, the social question would best be addressed by transforming the "dangerous classes" into settled petty proprietors, that is, by making home ownership accessible to workers. If the worker could be secure in his own foyer, they claimed, family life would be restored to the alleged stability of an earlier time, the worker would regain his lost physical vigor, and the "chimerical fantasies" promised by political dissidents would fall on dead ears. Presumably, the hierarchical order of the family, dominated by the *paterfamilias,* could be projected onto the whole of social life, eliminating the disruptions and conflicts of an urbanizing society. To this end, then, they promoted the construction of model dwellings, *cités ouvrières,* which provided, in their eyes, the necessary environment for the assimilation of the requisite bourgeois values.

Working from different perspectives but sharing a less chiliastic mentality, both hygiene professionals and socialist spokesmen demanded, in contrast, a wide array of immediate specific reforms. Speaking with the reflected authority of science, hygienists lobbied to secure tighter regulation of existing properties. They pressed for more precise and comprehensive public health laws, more stringent enforcement, and expanded power for public health professionals. On the other hand, socialists incorporated housing issues into a more general attack on the inequities of capitalism, calling for the regulation of rents and the control of speculation, direct construction of new low-cost housing by the city, and, on occasion, the expropriation of buildings which were to be turned into workers' lodgings. Alarmed by this challenge and wary of losing control of the issue, the property-owning class determined to initiate its own solution to housing shortages. Municipal authorities began to consider a variety of schemes to encourage the construction of inexpensive lodgings within the city center, juggling the fiscal complexities and the political implications of public subsidies and tax incentives.

In sum, the housing reform campaign included disparate groups of activists, each operating with its own particular reform agenda. If contemporaries were unduly optimistic to believe that housing reform encompassed

all others, it does seem that the reform campaign itself captured some of
the most significant developments of the second half of the nineteenth century. An examination of reform activities serves, in fact, as a window through
which to view a society in the midst of profound demographic, political,
and cultural readjustments. Between 1850 and 1902, Paris became a modern urban agglomeration. And for the first time, the problems of inadequate urban services, severe overcrowding, and sharp polarities of wealth
and poverty, health and disease, had to be negotiated in the political context of a mass democracy. As traditional conceptions of public assistance
became ideologically obsolete and grossly inadequate, representatives of
the established classes strove to devise new mechanisms for assuring that
the material deprivation of the lower classes did not seriously threaten the
entire society.

Housing reform strategies — all promising to guarantee public order,
public health, and social peace — raised corollary issues which forced contemporaries to reexamine accepted dogmas and cherished assumptions.
Most important, the issue of working-class housing posed broad questions
about the appropriate role of government. Not only did it require a reas-
sessment of the acceptable level of government responsibility for the general welfare, but it challenged conventional wisdom on how to balance rights
of privacy against the public interest, and on the proper use of public subsidies and finance policy to manipulate the free market. Moreover, as housing problems undermined current understandings of the connections between public works and public health, hygienists challenged politicians for
authority over health problems. At stake was a possible transfer of power
from traditional political offices to new groups claiming their rights as
technical experts. And, at the most basic level, the persistent problem of
working-class housing called into doubt optimistic forecasts of continuing
economic advance and the progressive *embourgeoisement* of the lower orders, bringing the established classes face to face with an enlarged and increasingly politicized working class with pressing material needs. In addressing the question of working-class housing, the bourgeois society of
the second half of the nineteenth century was forced, in effect, to engage
in a complex process of self-examination and redefinition. It is the purpose of this book to explore this process as housing reform strategies developed in a changing political, social, and medical framework.

The study of urban housing is of interest to scholars in a variety of disci-
plines. Social and urban historians, sociologists, students of architecture
and urban geography, and historians of medicine and public health have
all explored the consequences of nineteenth-century urban growth, yielding a growing body of specialized analyses of different aspects of the urban

experience. Adeline Daumard has studied bourgeois proprietors in Paris during the nineteenth century, while Gérard Jacquemet has written on changing patterns of property ownership in the largely working-class section of Belleville.[3] The urban studies of David Pinkney, Anthony Sutcliffe, Norma Evenson, and Pierre Lavedan have examined in depth the decisions and priorities which governed the expansion of Paris.[4] The most comprehensive treatment specifically of housing is the work of Roger Guerrand, *Les Origines du logement social en France,* which is most nearly comparable to the excellent studies of London housing for the poor by G. S. Jones, Enid Gauldie, and Anthony Wohl.[5] Guerrand describes the social context of the housing problem from the utopians of the 1830s and 1840s to the conservative publicists of the Third Republic. He is interested primarily in the activities of bourgeois reformers and tends to neglect the changes that occurred over time and the specific political framework in which decisions were made. Scholarship on Parisian public health has considered the problem of housing only tangentially. Several studies treat the impact of cholera,[6] while George Rosen, Erwin Ackerknecht, Ann La Berge, and, most recently, William Coleman examine the overall development of the public health movement in France, particularly in the period before 1850.[7]

It is essential to integrate the perspectives suggested by the above studies in order to understand the meaning of housing reform in its nineteenth-century context—that is, as the touchstone for larger processes of political and social accommodation. It is my hope that this book provides that integration. Chapter 1 describes the changing character of the urban environment in the first half of the century, when contemporaries began to isolate working-class housing as *the* social problem most demanding of immediate attention. During the Second Empire, Napoleon III and Haussmann addressed health and housing problems by way of the accepted panacea of the times—public works—a strategy which dovetailed neatly with their aesthetic, economic, and strategic concerns (Chapter 2). Their unwillingness to rehouse those displaced by demolitions, coupled with the annexation of the suburban communes, exacerbated the shortage of working-class lodgings. Chapter 3 discusses the dimensions of the housing problem in the final three decades of the century in terms of construction patterns in the building industry, rent levels, the degree of crowding, and the incidence of morbidity and mortality throughout the city.

Through the closing decades of the century, conservatives rushed to retrieve the issue of working-class housing from the arms of revolutionary socialism through a variety of schemes to stimulate the construction of inexpensive dwellings. Chapters 4 and 5 describe these efforts. Chapter 4 examines the campaign of bourgeois reformers to create a regenerated class of worker-proprietors, an effort which was to emerge essentially through the private sector; while Chapter 5 analyzes the parallel attempts of the Paris municipal council and the national government to promote low-rent lodgings through public subsidies. By the end of the period, the most productive reform efforts were those of hygienists, who identified the housing problem primarily as a public health issue, and collaterally, as a problem of national security. Chapter 6 describes the activities of hygiene professionals in refocusing attention from stalemated questions of insufficient supply and exorbitant rents to more accessible issues involving the regulation, inspection, and disinfection of unsanitary dwellings. Of primary interest is the interplay between the demands of hygienists and specific political objectives formulated by leaders of the Radical party. In the end, the new political context, shaped in part by the ideology of solidarism, provided the framework for more comprehensive regulation of unsanitary conditions, while allowing public officials ultimately to divest themselves of responsibility for the housing market. In effect, the problem of inadequate working-class housing was redefined rather than resolved.

It is evident that different perceptions of the housing problem evoked significantly different responses; some of these were mutually reinforcing, while others worked at cross-purposes. Housing reform became, in the hands of different groups of activitists, a public works issue, a vehicle for the rehabilitation of the morally unregenerate working classes, a test case for monitoring the expansion of state and municipal responsibilities, a public health concern of quantifiable proportions, and above all, a means to preserve society from the dual perils of disorder and disease. An examination of the housing reform campaign reveals both the motives and the constraints within which nineteenth-century men operated as they sought to solve "the social question."

Acknowledgments

THROUGH each stage of its many transformations, this manuscript has benefited from the critical attention of caring teachers and supportive colleagues. I would like first to thank my dissertation committee at Brown University, who oversaw the earliest versions of this project: Burr Litchfield for his rigorous and invaluable criticisms which pushed me to refine and clarify the arguments of the thesis; A. Hunter Dupree for giving me the courage, the vision, and the tools to expand my conceptions of the history of medicine and public health; and Joan Scott both for her insightful comments and for being a model and mentor. In its second life, the manuscript was immeasurably improved as a result of the pointed questions and suggestions of Judith W. Leavitt and William Coleman. Other friends and colleagues, in both formal and informal ways, have helped to mold the final draft, especially Barbara G. Rosenkrantz, Kristen B. Neuschel, Peter Weiler, Kathleen Weiler, and Sandra Joshel.

I owe a particular debt to M. Roussier, chief librarian at the Bibliothèque administrative de l'Hôtel de Ville in Paris, who generously placed his extensive knowledge of municipal records at my disposal, easing my initiation into French archival sources. Mlle. Chambelland at the Musée Social similarly provided valuable assistance. I am grateful to Marie de Thezy, curator of photographs at the Bibliothèque historique de la ville de Paris, for locating a large selection of appropriate illustrations, which were reproduced by Jean-Loup Charmet. The staff of the Interlibrary Loan Office at Brown University also deserves special mention for their consistent helpfulness. Peg Cibes and Joan Barry typed the manuscript with patience and skill. The editors at the University of Wisconsin Press have been sensitive and helpful at every stage of the production process. It pleases me to be able to acknowledge the assistance of Peter Givler, Elizabeth Steinberg, and Carolyn Moser.

For helping me gain a room of my own, I want to thank my husband, Michael Shapiro, who seemed always to understand its importance. Daniel and Julie Shapiro have been waiting for this acknowledgement for what must seem to them an eternity. Their exuberant pride in my work continues to surprise, delight, and inspire me.

Housing the Poor
of Paris, 1850–1902

Ch. 1 Public Health and Public Order in the First Half of the Nineteenth Century

Paris was the center of a vigorous public health movement in the first half of the nineteenth century. For reformers, administrators, doctors, and politicians, the health of the population became a barometer for measuring the viability of the social and political order. The very destiny of the nation seemed to depend upon the healthfulness of its citizens. Medicine itself, however, offered few effective cures and even fewer explanations of the causes of disease. In the face of therapeutic impotence and in the absence of a specific etiology of disease, public health reformers concentrated instead on prevention, addressing a broad range of social conditions which, in contemporary minds, affected both moral and physical well-being. In medical monographs and treatises, they articulated a comprehensive definition of public hygiene which included such diverse topics as child labor, prostitution, factory and prison conditions, pauperism, food adulteration, and occupational health.[1] As the century progressed, general humanitarian concerns were replaced by more practical, technical objectives. Sanitarians in the middle decades of the century promoted improved water supplies and better sewerage, while later, in the postbacteriological era, hygienists lobbied for vaccination, mandatory disinfections, and a more rigorous regulation and enforcement of public health matters. But in its formative period, public hygiene claimed as its own almost all of the social domain.

The intellectual legacy of the Enlightenment and the reformist enthusiasms of the Revolution provided the context in which the public health movement developed. In his *History of the Progress of the Human Mind*, Condorcet had prophesied that in the rationally ordered society, efficient and just government would be accompanied by the disappearance of disease.[2] The *Encyclopédie* contained articles on the duration of life, foundlings, and hospitals with specific outlines of public assistance schemes, including old-age insurance and medical care.[3] Inheritors of this tradition underlined the social components of poor health and disease. J.-P. Peter's study of the Société royale de médecine suggests that during the Revolution, the new approach of the Société to the health of the nation (*la thérapeutique de la nation*) was conceived of as a scientific enterprise with a political parallel.[4] Health reform and political reform were to emerge together. Similarly, Michel Foucault has shown that in the years preceding and immediately following the Revolution, radical politicians considered doctors to be the midwives of the new order, ushering in an age of biological and social well-being. Medical professionals were to become a "therapeutic clergy" who would set normative standards of physical and moral health, and would ultimately become obsolete as the healthy society— physically and politically sound—emerged.[5] Political reform was to be grounded in biology.

In the 1790s, the Ideologues, a group of medical reformers led by Cabanis and Destutt de Tracy, systematized this tradition which elevated the function of medicine.[6] Inspired by Enlightenment rationalism and optimism, they made extravagant claims for the new, empirically based medical sciences. Most important was their commitment to treat the mind and body together, to see moral development as related to physical health. They therefore promoted a medical posture predicated upon an intrinsic connection between the development of man and the quality of his environment.

The logic of this perspective gave doctors a preeminent place in the expected advance of civilization and engaged their participation in the solution of social problems. In 1825, the hygienist F. E. Fodéré wrote that the solution to the problem of poverty "was especially reserved to three professions: the statesman, the jurist, and the doctor."[7] The editors of the new hygiene journal, *Annales d'hygiène publique et de médecine légale,* claimed similarly that "medicine does not merely seek to study and cure diseases, but has intimate connections to social organization":

> [Medicine] is able, by its association with philosophy and legislation, to exercise a great influence on the march of the human spirit. It must enlighten the moralist and undertake the noble task of diminishing the number of social infirmities. . . . The method of curing will never be more successful than when [doctors] extend the scope of their activity to the physical and intellectual aspects of man and when physiology and hygiene will lend their light to the science of government.[8]

Both the immature state of the social sciences and the loose definition of public hygiene encouraged cross-fertilization between the two. In such a climate, doctors in Paris could claim physiology as the basis for a science of man.[9]

In practice, health reform activities overlapped more general reform movements. Many doctors were, for example, Saint-Simonians. During the cholera epidemic of 1832, the Saint-Simonian journal *Le Globe* called for sanitary improvements of the water and sewerage systems while Saint-Simonian physicians staffed free medical clinics.[10] Improvement in health standards and health care were obvious goals for utopians seeking to restructure and rehumanize an industrializing society. Thus, the ideal communities conceptualized by both Cabet and Fourier contained extended proposals for community health care.[11] This connection between political organization and health received its fullest expression in the euphoric atmosphere of the early months of the Second Republic. Writing in the *Gazette médicale de Paris* during the spring of 1848, Jules Guérin described medicine as the logical and appropriate instrument by which a progressive government would foster the moral, physical, and political development of its citizens:

> The medical profession is in essence both liberal and republican. The physician by training and experience is conditioned to hate prejudice and to love progress. The intelligent cannot but perceive how medicine bears at many points upon communal, governmental, and economic life. Medicine, therefore, better than any other profession, can guide the social organism. In public hygiene medicine proffers the sovereign means for the amelioration of the lives of the poor, the workers, and of the entire human race. To attain this there is need for a liberal and progressive government, a widespread knowledge of the true significance of medicine conceived from its highest and widest horizon, and the harmonious cooperation of the medical profession. . . . Today when all the barriers of the past drop before progress, this ideal medicine can and must become a reality.[12]

Guérin's concept of social medicine was, however, less an outline for a specific program than the more ephemeral hopefulness generated by immediate political events. The context which sustained such expectations disappeared with the June Days, as did Guérin's column.

By the 1840s, in fact, the optimistic predictions of progressive change which informed earlier theorizing about social and biological health seemed increasingly out of touch with current realities. Contemporaries in Paris had begun, rather, to experience considerable malaise in the presence of a changing physical environment. The city itself had become suspect. Swelled by unprecedented in-migration, the population of Paris doubled between 1801 and 1851 within a static, and necessarily overstrained physical cadre. Not surprisingly, the literature of the period reflected a growing general alarm over the consequences of accelerating urbanization. One demographer concluded that such a pattern could only indicate "a serious trouble in the general conditions of society."[13] According to Louis Chevalier, contemporaries viewed Paris at mid-century as "suddenly darker and unhealthier, crushed by its mass, stifled by its own respiration, transpiration and excreta."[14] Victor Considerant condemned Paris in 1848 as "a great manufactory of putrefaction in which poverty, plague, and disease labor in concert, and air and sunlight barely enter. Paris is a foul hole where plants wilt and perish and four out of seven children die within the year."[15] Paris had become *une ville malade*.

In their treatise on urban hygiene, Monfalcon and Polinière observed that "large capital cities constitute an excessive agglomeration of people in a single place which deprives the individual of his right to a share of the sun, air, and clean water,"[16] while an anxious contemporary wrote that in Paris "one no longer lives or breathes except in the midst of a crowd, a mob."[17] In 1846, the Société royale académique de Nantes sponsored an essay competition having as its subject "the causes which produce the movement of agricultural populations toward large manufacturing centers and the means to remedy the situation." The jury received forty-nine memoirs on the problem from all over France.[18] Two years later the National Constituent Assembly ordered an investigation of labor problems in order to find a means to stop the emptying of the countryside into urban centers, and in 1851–52, the Académie des sciences morales et politiques heard two discussions of this ominous population shift.[19] The *Revue générale d'architecture et des travaux publics* repeatedly warned that engineers and architects could not by themselves solve the problems of growing urban congestion and urged the government to divert the flow of population through administrative decentralization and schemes to develop and embellish rural areas and small villages.[20]

It was the distribution of the population as much as the growth itself which caused concern. New in-migrants to Paris tended to concentrate in the central commercial districts on the right bank, especially in arrondissements IV, VII, and IX, where crowding became particularly intense. In the years 1801–46, the already densely populated center thus continued to draw new migrants even as the less populated periphery began to grow (see Fig. 1.1 and 1.2). In his study of the development of Paris in the first half of the century, Chevalier has noted that growth in the outlying quarters of the city was far less significant in social and demographic terms than the fact that growth rates in the older central districts fell only slightly or continued to rise.[21]

During this period, the western parts of the city, both the right and left banks, became comfortable residential areas, while commercial activities concentrated in the right bank center, and industrial enterprises were grouped in the eastern and southeastern sections of the city, which also contained the most homogeneous enclaves of working-class population.[22] Thus, arrondissements I and X were largely wealthy and residential; the aristocracy of commerce and finance and manufacturers of luxury goods located in the second and third arrondissements; and arrondissement IV, which included les Halles, the primary wholesale food market, was the most exclusively commercial district, populated by artisans, wholesale merchants, and day laborers who performed the multitude of menial tasks associated with a busy marketplace. Small-scale industry drew artisans and laborers to the fifth, sixth, and seventh arrondissements. Masons, construction workers, and day laborers tended to congregate in the poor districts around the Hôtel de Ville (IX), while industrial workers followed their employment into arrondissements VIII and XII.[23]

    It is important to recognize that before the rebuilding of Paris during the Second Empire, and before the annexation of the suburban communes in 1860, the arrondissements were, in general, more heterogeneous than they were later to become; poverty and comfort coexisted. For example, the eighth arrondissement included both unskilled laborers and the bourgeoisie of the comfortable Marais section; the quarters Mont-de-Piété and St. Avoie in the seventh were considerably better off than the more central quarters Arcis and Marché St. Jean; and the population of the eleventh arrondissement was mixed, bringing together bourgeois, professional, and working-class inhabitants.[24] Mixed housing in the center was characteristic, with bourgeois tenants occupying the larger lower-floor apartments and working-class tenants lodged in the smaller apartments above. By the end of the July Monarchy, however, the social and geographic polarization which characterized Paris during the second half of the century had begun in earnest. As working-class in-migration changed the character of the central districts, the bourgeoisie evacuated to the outlying areas of the first, second, and tenth arrondissements.[25] Figure 1.3 demonstrates this shift of population to the west, although the central districts remained, of course, the most densely populated.

    The growing crush of people was in itself menacing. But the greatest concern derived from the perceived changes in the character of the population. By mid-century, the working classes outnumbered the middle and upper classes by a ratio of three to one; middle-class Parisians were forced to acknowledge poverty as a persistent, pervasive phenomenon which could not be ignored, which in fact they brushed up against daily in the streets. Contemporary accounts typically referred to "unknown populations," "urban nomads," "veritable cave-dwellers who awaken as if by enchantment and cover our squares and our cross-roads."[26] The sense is inescapable that the city had been invaded by an alien breed who had penetrated and, even

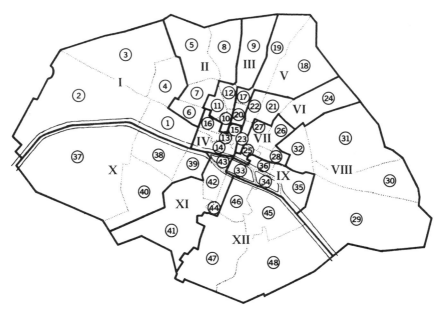

I	1 Tuileries	**V**	17 Bonne Nouvelle	**IX** 33 Cité
	2 Champs-Elysées		18 Porte St. Martin	34 Ile St. Louis
	3 Roule		19 St. Denis	35 Arsenal
	4 Pl. Vendôme		20 Montorgeuil	36 Hôtel de Ville
II	5 Ch. d'Antin	**VI**	21 Temple	**X** 37 Invalides
	6 Palais-Royal		22 Porte St. Denis	38 St. Thomas d'Aquin
	7 Feydeau		23 Lombards	39 Monnaie
	8 Fb. Montmartre		24 St. Martin des Champs	40 St. Germain
III	9 Fb. Poissonière	**VII**	25 Arcis	**XI** 41 Luxembourg
	10 St. Eustache		26 Mont de Piété	42 Ecole de Médecine
	11 Montmartre		27 St. Avoie	43 Palais de Justice
	12 Mail		28 Marché St. Jean	44 Sorbonne
IV	13 St. Honoré	**VIII**	29 Quinze Vingt	**XII** 45 Jardin du Roi
	14 Louvre		30 Fb. St. Antoine	46 St. Jacques
	15 Marché		31 Popincourt	47 Observatoire
	16 Banque de France		32 Marais	48 St. Marcel

FIG. 1.1   The Arrondissements and Quarters of Paris before 1860

From Louis Chevalier, *Classes laborieuses et classes dangereuses à Paris pendant la première moitié du XIXᵉ siècle,* map 1.

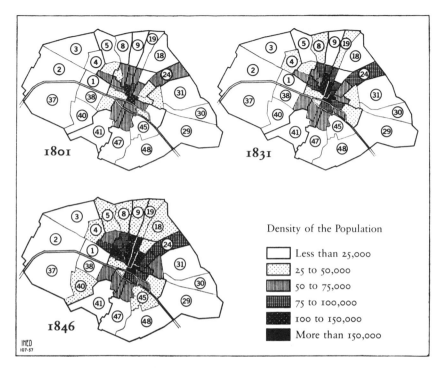

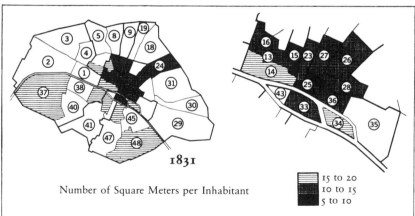

FIG. 1.2   Population Density, 1801–46

From Louis Chevalier, *Classes laborieuses et classes dangereuses à Paris pendant la première moitié du XIXe siècle,* maps 3 and 4. (To facilitate comparison, the quarters in Fig. 1.2 are numbered following the arrangement in Fig. 1.1.)

more, contaminated public spaces. Chevalier has found that the literature of the 1830s and 1840s became more somber, more serious, as the laboring classes were transformed into the dangerous classes in popular imagination.

Not only did romantic literature provide vivid descriptions of the depravity of working-class life, but a series of official and quasi-official investigations, all reinforced with statistical documentation, attested to a deteriorating situation. The Académie des sciences morales et politiques sponsored a series of inquiries into conditions of working-class life which produced frightening pictures of human decay. In 1840, Buret wrote in *De la misère des classes laborieuses en Angleterre et en France* that "in the very heart of the busiest centers of industry and trade, you see thousands of human beings reduced to a state of barbarism by vice and destitution. . . . The governments are rightly apprehensive. They fear lest formidable dangers may some day burst forth from amid these degraded and corrupted people."[27] In the same year, Frégier, head of an office in the Prefecture of the Seine, published *Des classes dangereuses de la population dans les grandes villes et des moyens de les rendre meilleures* purportedly to describe "the vicious and poor classes which swarm in the city of Paris."[28] The best-known exposés to emerge from the investigatory reporting were Villermé's *Tableau de l'état physique et moral des ouvriers employés dans les manufactures de coton, de laine, et de soie*, 1840, and Blanqui's *Des classes ouvrières en France pendant l'année 1848*. Both emphasized the close connection between physical and moral degradation. In social and political terms, the urban milieu was increasingly perceived as pathological, producing a population with withered bodies and corrupted *moeurs*—the human debris of a deteriorating environment.

By the 1840s, the preoccupations of hygienists coincided with those of nonmedical observers of urban conditions. Both looked to the immediate environment as the source of disorder and disease. In response to this understanding, hygiene monographs became less abstract and philosophical and more concerned with specific sanitation problems. Earlier in the century, in contrast, most experts subscribed to contagionist theories of disease, which identified the causative agent as the *contagium animatum*, a disease-carrying organism transmitted by interpersonal contact. This explanation translated into a public health policy based upon quarantines and *cordons sanitaires*.[29] Contagionism was attacked both by liberal economists, who saw quarantines as a threat to commerce, and by doctors, who disputed the theory on medical grounds. Gradually hygienists were won over to anticontagionist theories, which attributed the spread of disease to putrid vapors, or miasmas, produced by decaying animal or vegetable matter. Having been polluted by filth, the air itself became the medium which carried disease. Edwin Chadwick, England's premier public health

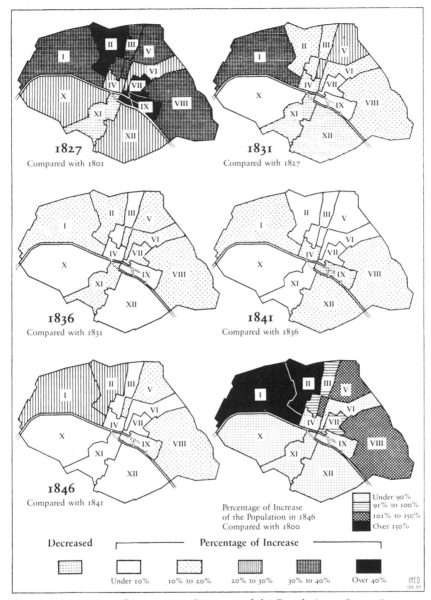

1827
Compared with 1801

1831
Compared with 1827

1836
Compared with 1831

1841
Compared with 1836

1846
Compared with 1841

Percentage of Increase
of the Population in 1846
Compared with 1800

Under 90%
91% to 100%
101% to 150%
Over 150%

Decreased   Percentage of Increase

Under 10%   10% to 20%   20% to 30%   30% to 40%   Over 40%

FIG 1.3   Percentage of Increase or Decrease of the Population, 1800–46

From Louis Chevalier, *Classes laborieuses et classes dangereuses à Paris pendant la première moitié du
XIXe siècle,* map 2.

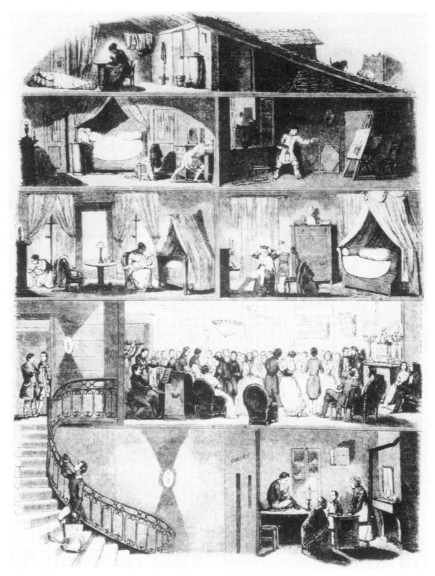

Mixed housing, characteristic of Paris in the first half of the nineteenth century.
Marc Gaillard, *Paris au XIXe siècle* (Paris: Editions Fernand Nathan, 1981).

reformer and an exponent of anticontagionism explained: "All smell is, if it be intense, immediate acute disease; and eventually we may say that, by depressing the system and rendering it susceptible to the action of other causes, *all* smell is disease."[30] Within this framework, most diseases were believed to be infectious rather than contagious, contracted by contact with deleterious air-borne miasma. Hence doctors and sanitarians insisted upon clear air and adequate ventilation and the removal of surface filth. They warned against living in close proximity to pestilential sites such as graveyards and collector sewers, or in areas with marshy or impermeable soil which created dangerous humidity.[31]

When Asiatic cholera arrived in 1832 and cut an erratic path through the city—"*une maladie tellement bizarre et capricieuse*"—doctors became convinced that contaminated air was the primary source of infection. Studies conducted during the epidemic of 1832 seemed to reinforce these convictions. In a hospital treating indigents and the insane, investigators alleged that cholera struck most severely the most crowded and most poorly ventilated dormitories, while the insane suffered higher mortality, it seemed, because it was not possible to open the windows in their quarters to "renew the air."[32] During the 1849 outbreak of cholera, the *Moniteur universel* published extensive advice on how to ward off and contain the disease. Dr. Réveillé-Parise maintained that although the cause of cholera was not known, "it had been demonstrated that the 'essence' of cholera exists temporarily in the atmosphere and in a more or less extended zone of the atmosphere. . . . The introduction of the choleric agent is by respiration, . . . therefore an essential hygienic measure is to secure pure, well-circulated air." He cautioned further that "cholera develops with greatest intensity in dark, humid, swampy locations, especially when the air is altered by the conglomeration of a mass of people."[33]

Hygienists subscribing to the miasmatic, or filth, theory of disease focused attention on conditions likely to vitiate the air, especially crowding, inadequate light and ventilation, excess humidity, faulty drainage, overflowing cesspits, and pools of polluted, stagnating wastes. Their wide-ranging concerns produced a public health movement committed to removing surface filth—the great sanitary awakening of the middle decades of the century. In fact, the concept of air as the medium for the transmission of disease was Hippocratic in origin and had been an accepted medical principle throughout the eighteenth century. But its acceptance earlier had focused interest not on sanitation particularly, but on topographical issues. Eighteenth-century medical treatises typically discussed the healthfulness of the site: the exposure, prevailing winds, contour and slope of the terrain, sunlight, and humidity.[34] It remained for anticontagionism in the nineteenth century to direct attention specifically to the character of the urban environment and to assert the importance of demographic rather than geographic factors.

The first cholera epidemic in 1832 had graphically demonstrated the connection between poverty, poor living conditions, and poor health. Sanitary committees urgently recommended cleaning up slum areas and removing external causes of insalubrity. In the absence of more specific knowledge, however, medical authorities tended to elaborate theories of predisposing causes, which included fatigue, intemperance, gluttony, and immoderate passions as well as the strictly environmental factors of filth, crowding, stagnant wastes, foul emanations, and impure food and water. Doctors advising a frightened population seemed to believe that personal and moral qualities triggered the pathological potential of the material setting. In 1849, Dr. Réveillé-Parise prescribed "40 doses of warmth, 5 doses of cleanliness, 1 dose of sobriety, 1 dose of activity, 1 dose of good sleep, 1 dose of healthy food, 1 dose of pure air, and 50 doses of spiritual tranquility—the anticholeric tonic par excellence."[35] Medical opinion clearly reflected preexisting moral convictions. Nevertheless, as alarming reports accumulated of the large numbers of military recruits from urban areas rejected because of physical infirmities, anticontagionist medical theory provided hygienists with a set of priorities which emphasized the need to clean up the streets and clear out the filth. It was then but a short jump from environmental to social explanations of disease.

The investigations of Villermé were most important in gaining credence for a social etiology of disease. Villermé was in touch with contemporary studies throughout Europe, all of which were using the new science of statistics to establish the relationship between morbidity and mortality on the one hand, and deteriorating urban working-class districts on the other.[36] In Paris, the first major official statistical collection, *Recherches statistiques de la Ville de Paris,* was compiled in 1821, subsequently permitting Villermé and his colleagues to reinforce their reports with convincing quantitative data. In 1830, Villermé undertook a study of the arrondissements of Paris to isolate the specific causes of differential mortality.[37] He attempted to correlate high mortality rates with traditional explanations of poor health which focused on ground elevation, type of soil, nearness to the river, degree of sunlight, prevailing winds, and population density.

With few exceptions, Villermé could not discover significant correlations using any of these standard variables. Instead, he found a direct, demonstrable connection between the degree of affluence and the health of the population; misery and high mortality appeared to be inexorably joined. In fact, in both 1841 and 1846 the two poorest arrondissements (IX and XII) had the highest death rates in the city, while the wealthy second and third arrondissements had the lowest. The same pattern appeared in the cholera death rate statistics of 1849: arrondissements II and III were the least severely struck, while the highest mortality rates obtained once again in arrondissements IX and XII.[38] The implications of these differences were not lost on contemporaries.

Hygienists, reformers, and philanthropists all identified working-class housing as the primary source of urban ills. More than any other factor, the congested and unsanitary quarters of the poor, surrounded by piles of garbage and excrement, appeared responsible for the condition of an entire class who seemed to pose such a visible threat to both public health and public order. Blanqui articulated the emerging consensus in the conclusion to his investigations: "I have studied with religious attentiveness the private lives of a mass of workers, and I dare to affirm that the insalubrity of their dwellings is the point of departure of all miseries, all vice, and all the calamities of their social condition."[39] Monfalcon and Polinière had written similarly in 1846 that one's *foyer*—one's home—was either a friend or an intimate enemy, a chance for illness or for health. In their minds, unsanitary housing degraded the worker morally at the same time that it profoundly altered his physical constitution. And, most importantly, they claimed a direct connection between domestic habits and political reliability: "Content with his dwelling [the worker] has respect for property and law and is committed to fulfilling his obligations."[40] Dr. Paul Taillefer suggested that poorly paid rural workers, whose lives were more difficult than those of their urban counterparts, were less recalcitrant, less dangerous politically, because they continued to enjoy the benefits of clean air and good health.[41] In Paris, that possibility had become increasingly remote. Bourgeois observers defined an urban syndrome: dark, humid, exiguous lodgings drove the worker to the cabaret; family life crumbled; the wife turned to prostitution, and the children to the streets; the city spawned a generation of vagabonds—pariahs living outside of social norms whose lodgings were sites of infection and sedition.

Pressure to take some remedial action continued to build throughout 1848 and 1849, intensified by political unrest and by the reappearance of cholera, the actual and symbolic representation of urban pathology. The formation of the Second Republic seemed further to require some tangible acknowledgment of working-class interests. Armand de Melun, a Catholic social reformer, wrote that the political question *and* the social question had become the order of the day. According to Melun, some form of government intervention was necessary in order to insure both the individual's right to work and his right to health.[42] At the same time, cholera once again opened the doors of the poor to administrative personnel, who published first-hand accounts of a degree of misery which, in practical terms, threatened the entire city. Victor Considerant noted that "the doctors who treated their patients at their homes during the cholera epidemic and ventured into the dens of the poor gave accounts at the time to make one shudder. . . . The rich did speak of the misery of the poor, but it was a thing for pity, not fear; they had no notion of this frightful contagious poverty; the cholera starkly revealed it."[43] Even more than Villermé's statistical studies on normal mortality, the incidence of cholera dramatized the consequences of poverty and overcrowding. The disease itself was terrifying. A syndrome of vomiting and diarrhea produced dehydration, giving the victims a ghoulish appearance; and those stricken often died within hours of the onset of the first symptoms. Social classes responded with mutual hostility and suspicion. The poor feared that their wells had been poisoned, while for the rich, cholera confirmed their sense that the lower classes posed an insidious, physical threat to their existence.[44] It seemed clear that infested working-class quarters constituted a general danger, and, more to the point, that the public works projects of the July Monarchy had clearly not protected the poorest and most densely populated sections of the city from disease in 1849. Monfalcon and Polinière urged that unhealthy dwellings be treated like adulterated food and removed from the market because "the worker is, in general, apathetic and extremely ignorant in sanitary matters,"[45] while hygienists increasingly sought the power to penetrate the interiors of private dwellings.

Provoked by the immediate danger, a variety of projects designed to improve working-class housing emerged during 1848 and 1849. On July 13, 1848, the Constituent Assembly passed a decree which offered a ten-year exemption from the doors and windows tax and from real property taxes on all buildings begun before January 1, 1849. In Paris, additional subsidies of 6 percent of the appraised value were offered to contractors building working-class lodgings.[46] Victor Considerant called for direct action in a proposal to the Constituent Assembly (April 14, 1849) by which the state would finance the construction of a collective (*commune sociétaire*) for 500–550 persons outside of Paris. The proposal was obviously too radical at the time to merit serious consideration, and the assembly did not discuss it.[47] In November of 1848, the Paris Health Council, an advisory body comprised of prominent hygienists, urgently recommended that the government take steps to regulate the salubrity of private dwellings and lodging houses which were notoriously unsanitary and overcrowded. As a result, a police ordinance was passed (November 20, 1848) which identified causes of insalubrity (including overcrowding, cohabitation with animals, unkept privies, stagnating household wastes, and the absence of windows), required the removal of household wastes, and set standards for the number of beds in relation to the size of the room in lodging houses.[48] No provision was made for inspection nor were penalties established for infractions (prompting a contemporary to note, somewhat ruefully, that "intent is not the same thing as execution"),[49] with the result that such regulations remained in practice a dead letter. On December 18, 1848, the government issued a decree authorizing the establishment of advisory councils on hygiene and salubrity in each department and arrondissement of France; these councils were to hold wide investigatory powers but had no executive authority to enforce their recommendations. Initially, the Paris Health Council resisted reorganization, claiming that it would be unwise to dilute its authority or to compromise the uniformity of standards which had been set for the city as a whole.[50] It was not until 1851 that health councils were instituted in each arrondissement of Paris under the direction of the prefect of police.

This flurry of activity culminated in the passage of the Melun Law of 1850, the first public health measure to supervise the interior conditions of private dwellings. In July 1849, Anatole de Melun, deputy from le Nord and brother to Armand, submitted a proposal to the National Assembly designed to regulate unsanitary housing. In its main provisions, the Melun Law established that

> in every commune where the municipal council deems it necessary, it may name a commission charged with investigating and indicating measures indispensable to the sanitary improvement of lodgings and outbuildings which are rented or occupied by others than the proprietor or tenant-for-life. Those buildings are insalubrious which are in a condition injurious to the life or health of their inhabitants.

The bill was favorably reported out of committee by Henri de Riancey and, following brief discussions, was passed on April 13, 1850. This landmark measure enlarged the scope of public responsibility for housing conditions and provided a necessary corrective to a health policy which had relied too heavily on improvements in public works.

Throughout the first half of the century, the administration of public health in France had largely been a local matter. The national government intervened only in a limited number of areas, taking particular interest in promoting vaccination against smallpox and in protecting France against the importation of contagious disease. Especially before the acceptance of bacteriological theories of disease, national health policy was understood as the defense of the nation against exotic illnesses, and, significantly, the bureau which supervised national policy was the Ministry of Agriculture and Commerce. The government thus confined its active role to the containment of major epidemics through extraordinary crisis measures, and even then, when cordons sanitaires and quarantines proved unsuccessful, ended by turning authority over to local officials. Beyond that, it sought advice on questions of public health from the Advisory Committee on Public Hygiene, which had been established in 1848, and, through circulars and memoirs, encouraged departmental prefects to supervise the health administration of their districts.[51]

In Paris, the prefect of the Seine and the prefect of police, who shared administrative responsibility for the city, also divided responsibilities for public health.[52] Large public works, such as the water supply, sewer system, and roads, fell within the jurisdiction of the prefect of the Seine, while the prefect of police had responsibility for legislating and enforcing most of the specific public health ordinances. The health duties for which the Prefecture of Police had primary authority included the surveillance of dangerous trades and industrial processes; the control of charlatans; the inspection of markets and slaughterhouses; animal diseases; the control of prostitution; the salubrity of public buildings and lodging houses; public lighting; the safety and circulation of public roadways; the stability of buildings and the cleanliness of their façades; the condition of stairways, corridors, and areas of common use; the construction, maintenance, and disinfection of cesspits; and the drainage and removal of household wastes from courtyards and alleys.[53] The Paris Health Council funneled technical and professional advice on these matters to the prefecture; however, the extent to which the recommendations were followed depended in large part on the personal interests of the chief administrator. Authorities typically adopted preventive measures in the face of an immediate problem, but let institutions and procedures lapse into disuse as soon as the danger passed. Without an acute crisis as a prod, prefects of police tended to find sedition more compelling than infection, and those health ordinances and administrative decrees which did exist received only sporadic enforcement.

The Melun legislation opened the doors of private lodgings to public officials for the first time. Even during the cholera epidemics, doctors had encountered intense popular resistance to allowing medical personnel into private homes. Workers typically saw doctors and pharmacists as government agents surreptitiously participating in a sinister conspiracy.[54] A good example of this deep-seated reticence may be seen in the comments of the mayor of Clamecy in the department of the Nièvre regarding home inspection. He wrote that

> in order to avoid home visits, always wrongly interpreted by the population, who believe that a tax increase will inevitably be the final result, those visited hope to ward off everything by declaring that all is fine and they ask no change in their habitation . . . so great is the difficulty of leading people to believe that one is interested in improving their material well-being.[55]

The official stature of the Commission on Unhealthful Dwellings represented a significant step forward and opened the possibility for greater regularity in the enforcement of public health measures. By creating a permanent institution with ongoing responsibilities, the law formalized a system for the investigation and processing of all reported cases of insalubrity.[56]

The potential significance of the precedent introduced by the Melun Law was very much on the minds of health and housing reformers. In spite of both the obvious need for some sanitary reform and the example of recent comparable legislation in England and Belgium, the French approached the issue with considerable apprehension. To allow administrative personnel inside private dwellings was to challenge the inviolability of private property, the cornerstone of society. Contemporaries conjured up menacing images of the creeping absorption of the individual by the state. In the report of a special commission on political and social questions in 1850, Michel Chevalier cautioned against giving the state too much power with regard to private housing. He wrote that legislators could not be "too circumspect" or "too reserved" because "if the authority intrudes in housing other than by general prescriptions . . . why not become similarly involved in food, and then in clothing, in heating, and lighting? We will then be swimming in the thick of socialism: the state meddles in everything, presides over everything, invades everything, and the society becomes a convent or a barracks."[57] He noted that lodging which could accommodate a small number of persons might become unhealthful when inhabited by many, and asked rhetorically whether the state would give indemnities to those workers who could not afford more spacious dwellings. Proponents of the Melun bill were sensitive to this line of criticism and, in fact, shared the worries of the opposition. In his report on the bill to the legislature, Henri de Riancey wrote that "the matter is extremely delicate. It raises questions of private rights, of property, of the home, that must be approached with extreme reserve. The independence of the domestic foyer, the free usage, the free disposition of that which belongs to a citizen commands the highest respect; for these are the foundations of society, the first guarantees of human liberty."[58] Sponsors sought therefore to produce a bill which extended existing police powers within carefully circumscribed limits. The resulting legislation inevitably contained serious loopholes and ambiguities which mirrored the fundamental ambivalence of its authors.

Although the Melun Law was to serve as the springboard for a highly professional public hygiene movement in the latter decades of the century, in its conception and form it was intimately tied to the humanitarian reform activities of the 1830s and 1840s, and specifically to social Catholicism.[59] Both Melun and Riancey belonged to the Société de Saint-Vincent-de-Paul and the Société d'économie charitable, Catholic organizations

committed to ameliorating the lot of the lower classes through private philanthropy. As they pursued housing reform, Melun and his colleagues
combined Christian charity with a paternalistic sense of responsibility for
their social inferiors. Essentially, they conceived of the Melun Law as a
"progressive and conservative" measure whereby the privileged classes fulfilled their obligations to the poor in response to an acute material crisis
which threatened all of society. Riancey and Melun invoked the studies of
Villermé and Blanqui to demonstrate the physical and moral decay of the
working population. They spoke of rachitic and scrofulous children, tubercular women, and enfeebled men—"decimated generations"—unable to
provide industrial or military manpower. The cities were allegedly propa-
gating a deteriorating race of men who fled their hovels in search of immoral and criminal pastimes and bred new generations who were corrupted
from the cradle on. It was the responsibility of the government, according
to Riancey, to undertake a series of measures for "general order and public interest" on behalf of the most unfortunate. While acknowledging explicitly that government had neither the duty nor the power to provide each
individual with the satisfaction of his material needs—that misery was,
rather, in the hands of God—Riancey added that governments may legitimately act to soften hardships.[60] Melun echoed that the law must protect
those workers, neither the provident elite nor the freeloaders and malin-
gerers, who live on the boundary between poverty and indigence "as the
father removes from his children's path the stones on which they will in-
variably fall."[61]

Current sanitary arrangements could not assure the desired results.
The only existing regulations specifically for housing established maximum
building heights in relation to the width of the streets. Police ordinances
governing general external sanitation tended to arbitrary and sporadic enforcement. Clearly, more precise and more comprehensive legislation was
in order. Riancey described Melun's proposal as an extension of municipal
police powers which did not introduce new principles. He cited as precedents laws of public order and public health which restricted the sale of
adulterated foods, prohibited unseaworthy vessels from sailing, prevented
the keeping of animals inside the home, regulated the maintenance of privies,
cesspools, and wells, and ordered the demolition of unsafe buildings.

Riancey emphasized that the Melun bill would not produce an upheaval in current practices. By leaving both the power of initiative to establish unhealthful dwellings commissions and executive authority with the
municipal council, sponsors of the legislation sought to accommodate the
interests of private property, which were, of course, represented on the communal governing bodies. Riancey reassured property owners that their rights
would be respected: "The paternal authority of the municipal council will

stagger delays and distribute obligations. Far from wanting to alarm the population, we wish to lighten its burdens little by little, with understanding and with patience. We desire neither to overburden or upset instantaneously its habits, nor even to quarrel openly with its prejudices and routines."[62] He predicted, somewhat naively, that new regulations would neither force large-scale evictions nor intensify crowding, since most causes of insalubrity could be remedied by the enforcement of established sanitary procedures.

The French legislation was, moreover, less rigorous than its English counterpart. Whereas the Melun Law did not apply to proprietors living by themselves (thus preserving what critics called the "sad right to suicide"), the English legislation applied equally to buildings let to rent and to those inhabited solely by the owner. More important, the English law permitted authorities to order repairs automatically at the landlord's expense. In contrast, the French legislation deferred more openly to the sanctity of the private home by building into the law safeguards against a potential "excess of zeal" by commissioners. It limited the authority of the Commission on Unhealthful Dwellings to those locations *reported* as insalubrious, and it set a maximum on the number of commission members so as to preclude arbitrary infringements of privacy.

The government's representative at the deliberations, the minister of agriculture, commerce, and public works, supported the cautious, somewhat tentative version of the bill recommended by the legislative commission. There were, however, a few dissenting voices. Roussel, deputy from Lozère, proposed a series of major amendments which amounted, in fact, to a counterproposal. He maintained that the urgency of the legislation had been well demonstrated and that it made no sense to undermine its application by restrictions which vitiated the original intent. Roussel's proposal urged that the law extend to the countryside, that it be mandatory, that it be enacted within three months, and that proprietors who voluntarily agreed to make sanitary improvements profit from the exemption from the doors and windows tax for six years rather than three.[63] The assembly rejected all of these amendments.

During the same discussion, Wolowski proposed that the Commission on Unhealthful Dwellings assume responsibility for stimulating the construction of inexpensive housing. Melun's original draft had contained an article providing that communes so authorized by the prefect could impose an additional 2 centimes tax on direct taxes, to be used to encourage the construction of small lodgings.[64] The objective was to forestall increased pressure on the housing supply due to the interdiction of certain buildings. Riancey's report set aside the issue of subsidies and construction incentives for a later debate in the hope that private philanthropy

would make it unnecessary to deal with the principle of public intervention.[65] Wolowski, however, reactivated Melun's earlier suggestion and urged
that the municipal council levy an additional 5 centimes property tax to
provide resources either to subsidize sanitary improvements or to encourage builders. He argued that proprietors were often only slightly better off
than their tenants and needed help to make repairs. Money thus expended
would benefit the communal budget, according to Wolowski, by saving
sums spent on hospitals and prisons while at the same time promoting personal morality. He claimed that the spirit of association for philanthropic
causes was not sufficiently developed in France and required the catalyst
of municipal assistance.[66] This discussion was punctuated by repeated noise
and interruptions. In the end, the assembly concluded that public charity
inevitably destroyed the impulse for private generosity; as one speaker
quipped, "If one wants to give to charity, one must dip into one's own
pocket and not into that of others."[67] The issue was dead, and the bill passed
in its more limited form on April 13, 1850.

Like the local health councils which they complemented, the unhealthful dwellings commissions authorized by the legislation were to be investi-
gative and advisory bodies, as contemporaries tacitly agreed to move slowly
in introducing regulatory precedents which opened private buildings to
public scrutiny. Nevertheless, the Melun Law represents the first modification of accepted orthodoxies regarding the sanctity of property and rights
of privacy. It therefore also reflects the emergence, by mid-century, of a
consensus among hygienists, reformers, and politicians that the living quarters of the poor required some degree of public regulation. Ordinary mortality, as well as the abnormal mortality of the cholera epidemics, had
pointed to working-class housing as sites of infection, while the differential in mortality rates between the wealthy and the poor arrondissements
continued, menacingly, to increase. And as geographic distance between
the classes became more sharply delineated within the city, the slums of
the south and east clearly suggested political disorder as well. By 1850, the
climate was receptive to reforms which specifically addressed the problem
of unsanitary housing. Melun's bill became law on its third reading virtually without opposition. Its passage marks the beginning of a half century
of intensive efforts to improve working-class housing in the joint interests
of public health and political stability.

CH. 2 Working-Class Housing in the Second Empire

T HE identification of working-class housing as a problem of public hygiene in 1850 placed it in a context which attracted only intermittent attention throughout the nineteenth century. Public health reform for most of this period was intimately, and inevitably, connected to larger social issues and political transformations. The objectives of hygienists translated into public policy only when those objectives became identified with the general interests of the society. In the end, legislators and members of government, in response to popular pressure or, more likely, political exigency, shaped and limited public health policy, selecting among possible goals those which seemed to intersect broader, well-defined needs. This pattern is clearly evident in the uneven path of housing reform. When social and political priorities reinforced public hygiene demands, substantive changes emerged; conversely, when political considerations and economic convictions worked at cross-purposes to hygienists' plans, public health objectives became secondary. The Paris unhealthful dwellings commission, authorized by the Melun Law, was itself the product of political upheaval—an attempt by reformers to neutralize the physical menace of the working class by sanitizing its environment. In this instance, public health was invoked to serve public order. The effectiveness of such commissions was inhibited, however, by concurrent policies of the administration which failed to complement, and indeed undermined, the activities of hygienists. During the Second Empire, other needs overshadowed those of public health. Thus, in spite of the apparent urgency of the problem in 1850, a coherent and effective plan for the improvement of working-class housing did not materialize.

In the earliest discussions of the Melun bill, the legislator Wolowski had underlined the dual aspects of the housing problem, pointing to the need both to clean up unsanitary lodgings and to provide new, inexpensive shelters. Throughout the second half of the century, interest focused alternatively on one or the other of these objectives, depending upon the immediate situation. The most continuous efforts were those of hygienists working for more stringent regulations and more uniform enforcement; as the century progressed, this movement gained momentum and authority. In contrast, attention to problems of supply was more sporadic and typically required the catalyst of an acute crisis in order to sustain official interest. A precarious political equilibrium tended to evoke concern for the shortage of adequate housing by raising the spectre of a disaffected working class pushed to antisocial behavior by its deteriorating surroundings. But brief episodes of public arousal did not produce a long-range or enduring strategy for addressing chronic housing needs.

The Paris Commission on Unhealthful Dwellings, created by the Municipal Council, began functioning in 1851. It was composed of twelve members, including a doctor, an architect, and a representative from the relief committee (*Bureau d'assistance*) and from the conciliation board (*Conseil des prud'hommes*). The commission was to visit those locations which had been reported as unsanitary, to investigate the causes, and to file recommendations with the mayor, who would notify the interested parties. After a period of a month, during which the landlords could reply, the reports were submitted to the Municipal Council, which determined the improvements that would be required and the length of permissible delays. If the housing could not be repaired and was judged irremediably unsanitary, the Prefectural Council could prohibit its use as a dwelling, or, in a situation in which the insalubrity resulted from external and permanent causes, the commune was empowered to expropriate the property for reasons of public health according to the provisions of the law of May 3, 1841.[1]

Even as it developed into a significant and increasingly powerful professional lobby, the commission found itself stymied by conflicting objectives. If it forced evictions from unacceptable lodgings, displaced tenants crowded into similar poorly constructed buildings, only worsening health conditions. The same lodging which was adequate for a small family clearly became unsanitary when inhabited by too many persons. In almost every report, the commission warned that the gravest cause of insalubrity was excessive crowding. But it was, by definition, legally powerless when the unsanitary conditions were not inherent in the building, and could only suggest palliative measures to promote cleanliness and to remove external filth.

These contradictions were exacerbated by contemporary policies of urban development. With the relative political stability and prosperity of the Second Empire, official interest in working-class housing quickly dwindled, eclipsed by the primary preoccupation of Napoleon and his prefect of the Seine, Georges Haussmann, with the rebuilding of the center city. In official minds, working-class housing needs were to be met only indirectly, through the development and aggrandizement of the city as a whole. At the same time, however, the annexation of the suburban communes in 1860 further enlarged the city's working-class population and its stock of substandard housing, while the rebuilding of the center decreased the number of lodgings available to the poor. In the absence of either government involvement or popular engagement in health and housing issues, it is not surprising that the unhealthful dwellings commission found the scope of its task ultimately beyond its capacities.

THE PARIS COMMISSION ON UNHEALTHFUL DWELLINGS

In its initial phase of operations, the Paris commission attempted to strike a balance between its reform commitments and the caution which accompanies new directions in public policy. To a certain extent, it deferred to the restrained image implicit in the enabling legislation. Its first annual report concluded with an extended expression of conciliation toward proprietors:

> The commission has especially understood that it must bring a spirit of conciliation to the application of a law that creates an entirely new system which might offend numerous interests and might become irritating, if, instead of considering it a law of public order and humanity, it makes of it a law of severity and repression; if instead of calling forth the generous sentiments of proprietors, it wounds them by untimely lawsuits; if finally, one provides too easy a means for tenants who see in the law a way to cancel the conditions of their leases.[2]

Similar remarks appeared in succeeding reports, but increasingly, they seem to be stylized, formal statements which were more and more at odds with aggressive postures adopted by the commission.

In actual practice, the commission defined its area of responsibility broadly. It maintained that insalubrity existed wherever a foul odor vitiated the air, or wherever there was humidity, dirt, or the absence of light or air. The scope of its investigations was wide-ranging. During its early tenure, the types of sanitary improvements most frequently recommended included the repair of walls with whitewash or oil paint and the renewal of wallpaper; the use of wainscoting to reduce humidity; the opening up of additional windows, doors, and skylights; the installation of chimneys in areas insufficiently ventilated; the elimination of partitions and ceilings which divided a room in two and restricted the circulation of air; the rais-

ing of floors above ground level to inhibit the seepage of moisture; the repair of pipes and drains and the removal of stagnating wastes; and the proper
maintenance and disinfection of privies and cesspits. It paid particular attention to the special problems of cellar and garret apartments most often
inhabited by concierges and domestics,[3] and to the living conditions of the
thousands of ragpickers of the city.[4]

In each report issued during the Second Empire, the unhealthful dwellings commission deplored the absence of adequate guidelines or regulations for new constructions. The city's powers to intervene in the sanitary
condition of buildings were enlarged by the law of March 26, 1852, dealing
with the land and buildings aligning public roadways. It stipulated that
facades had to be scraped and repainted at least once every ten years; that
each new construction in streets with sewers provide for the direct evacuation of liquid wastes and that older buildings comply within ten years; and,
most importantly, that builders file a plan with the administration "and
submit to the prescriptions which may be required in the interests of public safety and salubrity." In spite of this legislation, the unhealthful dwellings commission complained repeatedly that it was necessary to insist upon
modifications in new buildings almost immediately following their completion. Apparently the part of the law which dealt with standards for public safety received more consistent attention than did that which related
to public health. The commission acknowledged that it had no authority
to intervene in new buildings until they were rented to third parties, but
it stressed that it would be less irritating and less costly to entrepreneurs
to have clearly defined construction codes which prevented health hazards
from arising. For example, one of the most persistent problems was an excess of humidity, which could be eliminated by controls on construction
materials.[5] In its reports for the years 1860–61, the commission set out
specifications for the construction of washbasins, rainwater pipes, gutters,
water closets, and courtyards. It urged, further, that buildings be inspected
before habitation to certify that the approved plans had, in fact, been
executed.

In 1860, for the first time, the Commission on Unhealthful Dwellings extended its definition of insalubrity to include uncleanliness resulting from the lack of water. It concluded that deleterious miasmas were
likely to result from latrines, cesspits, and drainage pipes which were not
cleansed with an abundant supply of water. According to the commission,
the home was like clothing—"a defense against vicious exterior agents."
Without proper cleanliness, the atmosphere became corrupted, producing
dangerous miasmas which compromised the health of all inhabitants.[6] It
therefore claimed authority under the law of 1850 to require landlords to
provide water for cleaning, especially in dwellings inhabited by several

families. In contrast to this broad interpretation of public health requirements, the Advisory Council on Public Hygiene cautioned that the provision of water was not necessarily a *right,* and further, that such a standard
was untenable because the burden would not fall evenly on all proprietors.[7]
The unhealthful dwellings commission held a firmer line in principle, although in its 33,167 investigations as of 1869, it prescribed water in only 211
cases, all except 26 of which were sustained by the Municipal Council.[8]

In his analysis of Parisian administrative structures, Alfred Des Cilleuls
emphasized the conservatism of the commission during the Second Empire. Because appointments were funnelled through Haussmann's office,
Des Cilleuls believed that members, recruited so as "to offer guarantees of
competence and moderation," prescribed severe remedies only in extraordinary situations.[9] To a degree, this was true. The vast majority of affairs
which came before the commission were settled without recourse to the
courts. On the other hand, throughout the first two decades of operation,
the commission consistently sought to extend its authority. In addition to
its investigation of specific complaints, it prepared special reports on a broad
range of hygiene issues which were annexed to the annual transactions. For
example, the general reports for 1862–65 included supplementary reports
on the maintenance and use of privies in schools and asylums, the sanitary
condition of schools, the ventilation and cleaning of water closets, and the
potential explosiveness of gases produced in cesspits.[10] It prodded the administration to promote additional sources of referrals, as interested parties were often reluctant to file a complaint,[11] and called for the appoint-
ment of special inspectors to follow up on the orders of the Municipal
Council.[12] In its most strident pronouncements, the commission criticized
the dilatory legal appeals procedures and claimed that the only practical
way to achieve results was by the automatic execution of repairs at the expense of the proprietor.[13] The most sensitive jurisdictional issue involved
the extent to which an individual proprietor living by himself could be subject to administrative interference. In 1860, the commission stated that the
original deference to private property written into the legislation of 1850,
which exempted the proprietor living alone from public scrutiny, was no
longer appropriate.[14] In an effort to expand its jurisdiction, it decided
that in houses inhabited by the proprietor but not rented, it would consider the concierge and domestics as tenants paying their rent in personal
services, hence bringing the building within the scope of the commission's
responsibility.[15]

The men who sat on the unhealthful dwellings commission were men
with official and quasi-official connections. Many held important positions
in the city's administrative departments, especially in those which supervised roadways, engineering, and public works. Others were tied to medi-

cal institutions and to judicial offices.[16] They were men of standing in the community who could be trusted to exercise their authority with restraint. It is clear, however, that their growing expertise in matters of hygiene and sanitation pushed them to take more aggressive positions. By 1864, the commission had been enlarged to thirty members to enable it to handle a heavier caseload, and it met once every eight days, after initially meeting once a month. As the commission increased its membership, the additional seats were filled by specialists. In 1869, engineers, architects, doctors, hygienists, and scientists held twenty-one of the positions while the number of office-holders, judges, and administrative personnel remained static throughout the period, filling only three or four seats. In its early meetings, the commission moralized over the habits of vice of the poor. It worried that tenants might abuse the law to harrass landlords. As time went on, however, moral judgments disappeared from the transactions of committee meetings. By its very functioning, it provided a training ground for sanitation experts and a forum for enlightened discussion of increasingly technical problems, becoming the basis of a powerful lobby for sanitary reform.

More important than the basic conservatism of its personnel in undermining the commission's impact were the ambiguities of the legislation itself. The timid language of the law restricted its application and left room for wide judicial discretion.[17] Particularly confusing were the courts' inconsistent interpretations of the meaning of "outbuildings," which produced extensive litigation over which *dépendances* could be regulated by the commission. Similarly, the courts vacillated over whether the absence of water could be considered a legitimate cause of insalubrity within the powers of the commission to remedy. In the original legislative proposal as reported by Riancey, the commission was empowered to deal with unsanitary conditions resulting from the interior disposition of the building or from the actions of landlord or tenant. But the final version of the law omitted reference to situations created by the tenant. Initially, the courts had held that the landlord was responsible for all constructions built on his property, assuming that such changes were executed with the knowledge and tacit complicity of the owner.[18] In a representative decision rendered June 20, 1866, the court stated that "the object of the law of April 13, 1850, is to assure the salubrity of housing rented by the proprietor to third parties. It is not appropriate to examine the question of who created the unhealthful conditions."[19] This interpretation was abandoned fairly early, however. In a definitive pronouncement which governed future policy, the Prefectural Council held, on November 10, 1868:

> Considering that . . . the conditions which cause the insalubrity are not created by the proprietor, Mme F____ and did not exist when she rented

the building, but are produced by the subtenant . . . that it no longer is a matter of an insalubrious dwelling rented out, but of a lodging in which the occupant has made various modifications of his own free will and to his personal convenience; that if these modifications have produced insalubrious conditions, the tenant who must endure them has himself to blame; that in consequence, the law of April 13, 1850 cannot be applied to the proprietor.[20]

It followed from this decision that if a tenant transformed a property to a use for which it was not originally intended—for example, by converting a workshop which might not have windows into a habitation—resulting unhealthful conditions lay outside the authority of the Commission on Unhealthful Dwellings.[21] The courts pointed out that recourse to the municipal police was available, especially in situations in which the abusive use of one tenant jeopardized the well-being of fellow tenants or neighbors, or in which a tenant violated the conditions of his lease.[22] Through such decisions, the courts subtly redefined the intent of the housing legislation, choosing to consider it a means to protect tenants against unscrupulous or negligent landlords rather than as a more general law to promote public health. The unhealthful dwellings commission disputed this interpretation, which would permit a building entirely rented out to remain ouside its jurisdiction. It argued that in order to sustain the original spirit of the law, the proprietor must be held responsible for any unsanitary conditions which would not disappear when the tenant left, regardless of who had made the modifications.[23] The loophole, nevertheless, remained.

Framers of the law of 1850 simultaneously gave and withheld power. The law stipulated that the Commission on Unhealthful Dwellings could visit only those locations *reported* as insalubrious, that is, those for which a complaint had been filed. Most referrals came from the Office of the Prefect of Police, from hygiene councils of the various arrondissements, from building inspectors (*architectes-voyeurs*), and from doctors charged with the verification of deaths, as well as from concierges and tenants. Critics of this requirement argued that some proprietors were subject to harrassment from their tenants while other landlords responsible for identical, but unreported, conditions escaped attention. For enforcement to be systematic and comprehensive, they argued, the commission had to be empowered to make street-by-street, house-by-house visits.[24]

The possibility of lengthy delays and minimal fines further emasculated the commission's operations. The law allowed the landlord a year in which to complete the necessary repairs, after which he was subject to a fine of Fr 16–100 for nonexecution. Following this condemnation, he then had another year of grace before he became subject to a fine equal to the value of the prescribed work, and possibly double that amount. One contemporary critic called such penalties "an incentive to resistance."[25] In fact, because the law made no provision for the automatic execution of repairs, some proprietors did pay fines rather than carry out improvements, while others evacuated their buildings until the prohibition expired, after which they reopened under the same conditions.[26]

Most landlords, however, did comply with the prescriptions recommended by the Commission on Unhealthful Dwellings. Because so many of the buildings in Paris visited by the commission were quite old, it was difficult to rigidly apply uniform sanitary standards which could entail substantial expenses for the proprietor. Thus, the commission tailored its demands to accommodate the physical limitations of the given property as well as the landlord's ability to pay. At the same time, the situation in Paris was unique in that property values were rising so rapidly during the Second Empire that proprietors were willing to invest in repairs which occasioned relatively little expense in light of the advantages to be gained. Regularly increasing revenues soon made up for more limited expenditures. The commission noted in most of its reports that it met with little resistance from landlords. In 1851, of 160 visits, only 8 required a court procedure. In the subsequent eighteen years, the commission was consistently able to elicit compliance in approximately three-fourths of its cases, without even invoking the authority of the Municipal Council as provided in the law. In the 25 percent of cases which required some intervention, the vast majority were settled by an executive order from the Municipal Council and were not appealed through the court system (see Table 2.1). Appeals, moreover, did not necessarily imply resistance, as many involved problems of jurisdiction and questions of responsibility between the landlord and a tenant-builder.

The unhealthful dwellings commission increased its caseload substantially in the first two decades of its operations. Between 1851 and 1859, the number of visits increased from 160 to 641, and following the annexation of the suburban communes in 1860, the average yearly number of cases was close to 3,000 (see Table 2.1). The government saw the commission as a tangible symbol of its interest in the fate of the working classes and encouraged its activities. In a circular addressed to departmental prefects on December 27, 1858, Rouher, the minister of agriculture, commerce, and public works, regretted "the excessive preoccupation with the inviolability of the home and property" and urged commissions to resist the ill will or ignorance of landlords and the indifference of tenants.[27] And yet, even visiting 3,000 lodgings per year, the immediate impact of the Commission on Unhealthful Dwellings could be only modest: Paris contained approximately 68,000 houses by 1869, including 600,000 individual lodgings, most

TABLE 2.1 DISPOSITION OF CASES INVESTIGATED BY
THE COMMISSION ON UNHEALTHFUL DWELLINGS, 1851–69

Year	Terminated by Commission	Submitted to Municipal Court	Appealed to Prefectural Council	Deferred to Court[b]	Total
1851	152	0	0	8	160
1852	122	3	3	0	128
1853	172	12	5	0	189
1854[a]	228	92	6	0	326
1855[a]	355	149	20	0	524
1856	354	81	43	0	478
1857	369	94	29	0	492
1858	355	114	12	31	512
1859	458	139	0	44	641
1860	3,925	514	18	114	1,656
1861					2,915
1862					3,020
1863					3,072
1864[a]					3,698
1865[a]					4,160
1866	2,854	643	32	82	3,611
1867	2,232	635	26	114	3,007
1868	1,867	442	18	92	2,419
1869	1,772	401	20	82	2,275

SOURCE: *Rapport général sur les travaux de la Commission des logements insalubres* (for the years 1851–69).

[a] Cholera years

[b] Tribunal correctionnel

of which escaped any form of inspection or regulation. Although the death rate began to register a decline in the 1860s, the improvement can be attributed largely to public works projects which demolished blighted areas in the center of the city and to an expanded system of sewers which reduced the virulence of cholera and improved surface sanitation, and not directly to the work of the commission.

Some of the commission's impotence derived from the lack of any strong support for hygiene measures among the general population. Health reformers repeatedly complained that the French were slow to recognize the value of proper sanitation and hygiene; and in the absence of public commitment to a vigorous prosecution of health infractions, many went unnoticed. One hygienist observed that the penal code contained the principle that every injury caused even involuntarily to another could be subject to criminal penalty if it were caused by carelessness, imprudence, or negligence. No one thought to apply this category of offense to sanitary matters in France.[28]

But to a greater extent, the commission was the victim of a *question mal posée*. It could not both proscribe unsanitary lodgings and assure the poor of an adequate supply of acceptable housing. Further, it saw that badly depressed areas could be effectively dealt with only by large-scale demolitions and urged the commune to avail itself of the power to undertake expropriations for reasons of public health.[29] In most cases, such action was simply too costly. Implicitly recognizing the weakness of its position, the commission expressed the somewhat lame hope that "thanks to the August solicitude of Their Majesties the Emperor and Empress for all that touches the interests and well-being of the working classes, the poorest part of the population will find more suitable lodgings."[30] The actual policies of the government made of such hopefulness an idle fantasy, obsolete almost before it was uttered. Napoleon and Haussmann did undertake massive demolitions in the oldest quarters of Paris, but the new city did not and could not offer its working-class population more adequate lodging.

REBUILDING AND ITS EFFECTS

With the rebuilding of the city, the administration succeeded in converting Paris from a medieval city into an imposing capital.[31] Applying on an unprecedented scale "the surgical method to the treatment of a sick city," Napoleon and Haussmann demolished slums and drove broad boulevards through congested areas of the center, opening up corridors of light and air. They improved circulation with a coordinated network of roads which simplified communication within the city and increased access both to the central markets and to the railway terminals on the outskirts. The addition of a major system of collector sewers and an enlarged supply of spring water enhanced public health and reduced the incidence of cholera. They embellished the city with public parks, landscaped squares, and grandiose monuments. Invoking the accepted remedy of the times, Napoleon and Haussmann used public works to eliminate some of the most highly visible afflictions of the urban environment.

But public works could not fulfill the extravagant expectations which they raised. Although some of the worst slums were cleared away, broad boulevards and open spaces created an illusion which belied the reality. The demolition of groups of houses produced increased crowding in the remaining buildings as residential locations were converted into streets and open squares. The added elegance of the center (today's gentrification) accelerated geographic polarization among the classes, forcing the poor to migrate to the southern and eastern periphery. In spite of the incorporation of the suburban communes into the city proper in 1860, Napoleon and Haussmann neglected to provide comparable services to these annexed territories. Problems of overcrowding, shoddy constructions for the poor, and the geographic separation of the social classes did not begin with Napoleon and Haussmann; these problems were nevertheless intensified by the scale of redevelopment during the Second Empire. In the end, the grand enterprises of this period shifted the geographic locus of urban problems, particularly those of the working classes, but did not solve them. The social and material consequences of the rebuilding of Paris instead created the framework in which contemporaries struggled with the issue of working-class housing for the remainder of the century.

Napoleon's commitment to street improvements derived from many sources. Anticontagionist medical theories insisted upon the removal of surface filth and the opening up of congested areas. In the interests of ventilation and sunlight, the administration created twenty-two enclosed, landscaped squares. David Pinkney suggests that perhaps Napoleon thought of these breathing spaces as a substitute for improved housing, a solution which would benefit public health "by presenting a happy contrast to crowded slums."[32] The opinions of hygienists underlined this expectation, as the first annual report of the Paris Commission on Unhealthful Dwellings concluded that public health could not be improved without public works.[33] Most importantly, at this juncture political needs coincided with the concerns of public hygiene. The dark, twisted streets of the central quarters had proved difficult to subdue in times of insurrection; strategic considerations dictated their elimination. Simultaneously, Napoleon sought to increase employment and diffuse the economic distress which had been growing through the 1840s by stimulating a boom with the expenditure of public monies. Contemporary popular wisdom predicted that "when building flourishes, everything flourishes in Paris."[34] The configuration of motives which fueled Napoleon's desire to aggrandize the imperial capital thus received solid reinforcement on many fronts. By the end of the July Monarchy, pressure to begin a program of public works had been increasing.[35] It remained for Napoleon to complete the plan and to find the appropriate personnel and the financial means to effect it.

Napoleon inherited several projects for the physical development of Paris. During the Revolution of 1789, substantial pieces of property had been nationalized, prompting the creation of a commission to plan for its disposition. The resulting Artists' Plan established an overall street scheme based upon an east-west axis from the Place de la Concorde to the Bastille.[36] Napoleon I, who set many of the precedents later adopted by his nephew, executed several of the projects elaborated in the Artists' Plan, especially the east-west artery between the Tuileries and the Louvre, which

he named the rue de Rivoli. During the July Monarchy, Rambuteau, prefect of the Seine, undertook the next major series of public works, at least
in part owing to the outbreak of cholera in 1832. He began enlarging the
water and sewer systems, and oversaw street clearance and development
in the crowded areas around les Halles, the central markets. Some of these
projects lapsed as funding ran out, while the Revolution of 1848 interrupted
others.

Upon accession to the presidency of the Republic, Napoleon III began to plan for the modernization of the city. The basis of his conception
was a large cross—a north-south axis across the river, intersecting near
Chatelet an east-west artery which continued the rue de Rivoli. He also
proposed a major boulevard through the left bank (the boulevard Saint-
Germain), several roadways cutting through the right bank center, the development of the Bois de Boulogne, and the enlargement of the central
markets.[37] Prefect of the Seine Berger repeatedly resisted such ambitious
schemes and proved unwilling to float the necessary loans.[38] In 1853, Napoleon replaced Berger with Haussmann, an imaginative and resourceful
administrator who worked closely with the emperor to evolve a comprehensive development plan.

Abandoning the piecemeal strategies of their predecessors, Napoleon
and Haussmann planned for the city as a whole. They effected the "great
crossing of Paris"—intersecting north-south and east-west arteries—and
continued street development in a three-stage process (see Fig. 2.1).[39] Their
administration was as bold in its financing as in its designs. Both Napoleon and Haussmann subscribed to the theory that they could borrow extensively against anticipated profits from urban development. Because
Haussmann fulfilled the functions ordinarily held by a mayor and council
(and, in fact, nominated the council which was then appointed by the emperor), he was able to carry through his projects with minimal opposition
until the final years of the Empire.

The extent of Haussmann's demolitions for street improvements and
the increased value of the new constructions combined to produce a significant upheaval in the availability of inexpensive lodgings. As the population of Paris increased by 261,549 between 1851 and 1856, swelled largely
as a result of in-migration, the number of houses actually decreased from
30,770 to 30,175.[40] Critics of the public works programs pointed to the
growing incongruity between the diminishing housing supply and the
thousands drawn to Paris by the promise of work in the building trades.
Haussmann countered with the claim that although 25,562 individual lodgings disappeared in the period 1852–59, new constructions provided an additional 58,207 lodgings, a net gain of 32,645.[41] He estimated that 117,552
families, or about 350,000 persons, had been displaced as a result of demo-

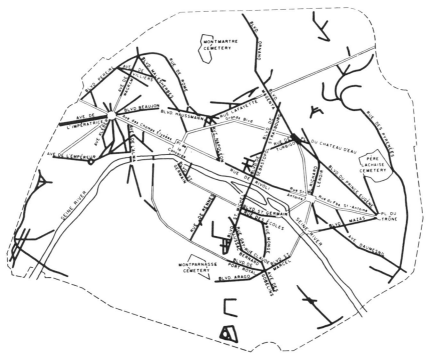

FIG. 2.1   Street Development, 1850–70
From Saalman, *Haussmann: Paris Transformed,* fig. 15.

litions, but considered this dislocation insignificant in light of the larger benefits provided by public works. In response to critics, Haussmann sanguinely noted that "it is not possible to accomplish this transformation without creating a general upheaval, the necessity of which cannot be appreciated by the masses, who become easily wearied, especially when [the upheaval] is prolonged for seventeen years."[42] Beyond the raw statistics, it is more important to assess the change in the relationship between the number of inexpensive dwellings and the size of the working-class population. Haussmann's policies are less benign when seen from this vantage point. The number of workers rose from 416,000 in 1860 to 442,000 in 1866, an increase of 25,000, with up to 70,000 more seasonal workers at a given period.[43] At the same time, the number of rents below Fr 250 increased more slowly: 101,909 in 1863; 104,619 in 1864; 109,634 in 1865; 114,169 in 1866.[44]

    The numbers of individual lodgings did not, moreover, necessarily indicate better living conditions. It is likely that the increased number of separate dwellings reflected the breaking up of old apartments into smaller units as well as actual new constructions, although the figures do not distinguish between new constructions and reconstructions. Building regulations of the time applied only to the height of buildings with frontage on the public street, fixing the allowed height in proportion to the width of the street. Because there were no controls on the height of interior floors, the size of individual rooms, or the quality of construction materials, builders frequently tried to squeeze an additional floor within the allotted building space. This practice produced apartments in which an adult could not stand upright, while partitioning created interior rooms with no direct access to light or air. In 1846, only the old fifth arrondissement had an average of more than forty persons per house. Ten years later, the density of the city had so increased that all but four arrondissements averaged more than forty inhabitants per house.[45] A contemporary critic observed that "too many defective, inconvenient, and unhealthy buildings have been erected owing to the owner's greed and the builder's inventive genius."[46]

The new constructions were significantly more valuable than those they replaced. In her study of houses and proprietors in the nineteenth century, Adeline Daumard has shown that during the Second Empire Parisian houses became progressively "more important, more luxurious, and more homogeneous" than in the past.[47] The average property tax paid per new house was substantially higher than the tax that had been paid by demolished buildings and, in fact, exceeded the average rate paid in the city as a whole.[48] In corroboration of this trend, Haussmann boasted that he had generated an increase in revenues from both real estate and personal property taxes from Fr 15 million in 1853 to Fr 18.6 million in 1860, and again to Fr 25 million at the end of the Empire.[49] After 1855, builders essentially abandoned the construction of middle-range dwellings in favor of more costly properties. Thus, as a certain amount of slum housing disappeared through demolitions, private enterprise did not provide substitute lodging for those forcibly evicted.

A steady increase in the price of land, accelerated by public works, both sustained the value of old buildings and elevated the price of new constructions. The average price per square meter of undeveloped land doubled in the 1860s, with substantially higher rates of increase in selected areas.[50] Louis Lazare, editor of the *Gazette municipale* and commentator on municipal issues, noted that in more extreme cases—for example in the sixteenth arrondissement—the price of land rose from Fr 25 per meter in 1845 to Fr 130–150 per meter in 1869, while land bordering the large avenues sold for as much as Fr 200 or Fr 300 per meter.[51]

The rapid increase in the value of land promoted a new conception of the use of urban space. Courtyards, originally intended for ventilation, came to be seen as too valuable to be left unproductive. Landlords conse-

Typical housing built during the Second Empire. Collection of the Frances Loeb Library, Harvard University.

quently enclosed courtyards so as to house small shops. The four-square-meter minimum courtyard space required by the ordinance of March 26, 1852, resulted in virtual airshafts which often became repositories for putrefying organic matter. As the facades on the broad boulevards improved, interior areas were gradually closing in upon themselves, becoming darker, more congested, and increasingly foul.

A Chamber of Commerce report in 1864 listed the three most pressing problems of Parisian industrial life as the situation of women, the length of the work day, and the difficulty of finding lodging.[52] Not only were working-class dwellings being replaced by bourgeois apartments, but rents had increased sharply throughout the city, rising anywhere from 40 percent to 100 percent.[53] In his description of working-class life in 1870, Denis Poulot wrote that "the term [rent day] is the sword of Damocles" for which the worker prostitutes himself, the married woman deceives her husband, the mother dishonors herself, and the husband sinks into vice.[54] Rent increases in working-class districts in relation to the value of the building were actually greater than in better-off quarters, as proprietors sought to compensate themselves in advance for problems of nonpayment and inconveniences resulting from the irresponsibility of working-class tenants. Two rooms which rented at Fr 170–180 at midcentury cost Fr 250–300 by 1855,[55] and the same single room which cost Fr 70–80 before Haussmann's tenure commanded a rent of Fr 150–160 by 1869.[56] Even those dwellings occupied by indigents sustained rent increases. Reports from the Public Assistance service indicate that the average rental price of indigent lodgings—66 percent of which were one-room dwellings—increased from Fr 113.45 in 1856 to Fr 141.27 in 1866.[57]

In 1855, the minister of agriculture and commerce authorized an investigation by the Chamber of Commerce to determine whether increases in earnings over the preceding three years had kept pace with increases in the price of food and lodging.[58] The report concluded that wages had not, in general, risen enough to offset the rise in the cost of living, producing "a certain malaise in the workers' lives." Throughout the city, rents had reportedly increased on the average by 25 to 35 percent. In the twelfth arrondissement, a worker's lodging which rented for Fr 120 in 1854 rose to Fr 140 in January 1855, and rose again to Fr 160 by the end of the year. Similar conditions were reported in arrondissements VI, VII, VIII, X, and XI. The situation was particularly acute for workers employed in the manufacture of small luxury items (articles de Paris), for jewelrymakers, and for workers in bronze and precious metals, who needed to be easily accessible to their places of work and could not quit the quarter in search of less costly lodgings. It was a well-understood axiom of the time that the Parisian worker rented the district even more than the individual dwelling. Married workers with families were in the most precarious situation. The Chamber of Commerce estimated that in 1855 a single worker required Fr 182.50 more for food and Fr 30 more for rent each year than he had needed three years earlier, totaling an additional obligation of Fr 212.50. If he earned between Fr 1.00 and Fr 1.25 more per day—that is, between Fr 300 and Fr 375 per year for three hundred work days—he would be left with a surplus. On the other hand, a married worker with two children would have to dispense Fr 328.50 more for food and Fr 40 more for lodging (a total of Fr 368.50 more) in 1855 than in 1852, which forced him to operate at a deficit.[59] Haussmann tended to dismiss the implications of increases in the price of lodging and subsistence with the rationale that both were due to spurts of economic development which added to public prosperity and would be compensated for by higher wages.[60] However, a report from the prefecture of police in 1855 echoed the findings of the Chamber of Commerce and concluded that "in sum, the worker is in a distressing situation."[61] An anonymous pamphlet compared the worker's fate to that of Jeremiah in Babylon, who found palaces but no shelter. The modern Jeremiah, "Haussmannized," cried out that although the city glittered, its people could not afford to live there: "Babylon, Babylon! You are a superb city and your enemies themselves proclaim you queen of the world and fall in admiration before your magnificence, although your own sons rest, exhausted, at the borders of your crossroads asking where they shall sleep the night."[62]

Demolitions, forced evictions, and rent increases heightened the antagonism between landlords and tenants. The prototypical avaricious landlord, Monsieur Vautour, became the focus of abuse in pamphlets and ballads. With his finger on the popular pulse, Daumier issued a new series of satirical lithographs in 1854 entitled "Tenants and Landlords." In one, a proprietor witnessing a demolition exclaims: "Good! They are tearing down another house. I will raise each of my tenants 200 francs!" A play from the same period displayed a sign offering lodging on the river, between Pont Neuf and Pont des Arts, "in the Chinese fashion," while the refrain of a popular song urged that "if you want to be happy, hang your landlord."[63] Proprietors were described as "greedy, pityless, cynical, insolent, and vain," idle parasites reaping huge profits without investing any productive labor, at the expense, always, of the working population.[64] The landlord countered with a defense of the social utility of his role. In 1857, Victor Bellet wrote: "It is proprietors who possess traditional habits of order, moderation, and thrift, the solid, if not brilliant, basis for public and private prosperity, and who each year contribute considerable sums to the public coffers through direct and indirect taxes, fees for registration, and transfers of ownership, and taxes of all sorts." He continued: "We say

Demolitions and rising rents produced a continuous pattern of evictions followed by the renewed search for lodgings. Marc Gaillard, *Paris au XIXe siècle* (Paris: Editions Fernand Nathan, 1981).

to tenants: if the demand for houses, shops, apartments, and lodgings exceeds the supply, and if prices are high in general, resign yourself to pay the elevated prices . . . and do not accuse an entire class of which many of you will soon be members, and which has its own difficulties as well as advantages."[65]

Real grievances confirmed the image of the landlord drawn by popular mythology. According to the Office of Tax Collection in 1850, the existence of 59,000 vacant lodgings forced landlords to reduce rents and to offer substantial lease concessions to prospective tenants.[66] In the succeeding twenty years, tenants rapidly lost this favored bargaining position. By 1860, the Office of Tax Collection reported a negligible number of vacancies, most of them appearing for one term, and rarely for two. It was accepted practice for landlords to demand six months, or two terms, payment in advance, giving each lease the character of "a new occasion for usury" by the landlord.[67] Since proprietors did not pay taxes on unrented property, there was no incentive to lower rents.

Alexandre Weill summarized tenants' complaints against proprietors in two pamphlets, *Paris inhabitable* and *Qu'est-ce que le propriétaire d'une maison à Paris*.[68] He argued that it was the high price of rents which forced up the price of other articles of subsistence and not the other way around, and that high rentals were the necessary consequence of customs which assured the privileged status of landlords above all other groups. Whereas various conventions regulated the activities of bankers and mortgage operations, as well as industrial and agricultural practices, rents and leases remained bound only by outmoded custom. Weill claimed that, in modern times, to protect real property in large population centers was "to push the water in the streams and to carry it to the sea."[69] The merchant paid for unsold goods, but property remained vacant at no expense to the proprietor. Weill called for a new definition of obligations in the relationship between tenant and landlord and suggested the formation of conseils des prud'hommes in each arrondissement to offer advice and to arbitrate in rent and lease disputes. Instead of permitting the landlord to enrich himself from the use of the two-term advance payment, he recommended that the money be deposited with a savings society which would pay interest to the tenant.

Popular indignation identified the real estate speculator, along with the landlord, as the source of spiraling rent prices. There was a general suspicion that those with personal access to Haussmann speculated in land and buildings later expropriated by the administration, for which high indemnities were paid. In his chronicle of Parisian life, Maxime Du Camp illustrated the kind of evidence which supported such charges.[70] He told of fraudulent legal operations which furnished clients with phony account books so as to raise the indemnities paid to expropriated merchants. Du Camp recounted the vicissitudes of a typical expropriation negotiation as follows: the proprietor is offered Fr 75,000, which he accepts; a decree of expropriation for public utility is issued; the proprietor then rejects the initial contract and appeals to the courts for Fr 1.8 million; in settlement he obtains Fr 950,000, more than twelve times the original offer. In a familiar anecdote of the period, a newly wealthy gentleman is asked: "How have you made your fortune?" He replies simply: "I have been expropriated." Lazare concluded similarly that the prospect of earning profits through indemnities would inevitably perpetuate the construction of substandard housing.[71] Daumard's recent investigations indicate that Haussmann probably was not actively involved in enriching his friends. Although many transactions were made through intermediaries in order to conceal the names of interested parties, there was no increase in voluntary sales prior to large-scale expropriations in several key districts.[72]

Nevertheless, real estate was, in fact, the source of windfall gains during this period. According to a decree of December 27, 1858, land which had been expropriated for public works but which was not fully incorporated in the new construction was to be returned to the original landowners. In the process, the original land appreciated considerably. Before 1860, foreign railroad development had attracted the bulk of large-scale speculation, and individual entrepreneurs, who were often connected to the building trades, bought land essentially for their own use. This pattern reversed itself after 1860, when investors began to pour their capital increasingly into real estate, and building societies gained a progressively larger share of the market.[73] By the end of the Second Empire, the mixed social composition of Parisian proprietors had been replaced by a more homogeneous class of wealthy *rentiers*. Ownership of land in the interior of the city became virtually inaccessible to small merchants, artisans, and members of the lower middle class.

The development of the center of Paris forced the working class to the peripheral districts in the north, east, and south as the middle and upper classes moved westward. Class polarization was reflected in growing geographic isolation. Corbon wrote that "the transformation of Paris has forced back the laboring population from the center to the extremities. They have made the capital into two cities, one rich, one poor. The latter surrounds the other. The poor are like an immense rope hemming in the comfortable classes."[74] Workers concentrated in the faubourgs du Temple, Saint-Marceau, and Saint-Antoine and in the quarters bordering the old *octroi* wall: Belleville, Menilmontant, Ternes, Montrouge, Vaugirard, and Grenelle. Between 1861 and 1872 the ten central arrondissements lost 33,000 in population as the ten outlying arrondissements gained more than 200,000.[75]

The social composition of the city, by arrondissement, may be seen in Figure 2.2. More and more, the working class turned over the upper floors of buildings in the center to domestics serving bourgeois tenants below in favor of the less expensive, less congested, but also less accessible lodgings in the suburbs.

Improvements in the suburban communes lagged badly behind developments in the center and west of the city. A contemporary critic claimed that "in cleaning up the poor quarters of Old Paris, misery was not suppressed. . . . It was, rather, placed out of our sight and unhappily, perhaps, also beyond our preoccupations."[76] Even before 1860 and the annexation of the suburban communes, the mayor of the old eighth arrondissement and a committee of proprietors from the old twelfth made formal protests to Haussmann charging official neglect of their areas.[77] The Lazare brothers widely publicized the unequal development of the east and west of Paris. Louis Lazare recounted a conversation with a cabinetmaker who had been forced out of the center of the city as a result of public works.[78] The worker told of material privations which constituted, in effect, a declining standard of living. Formerly he had been accustomed to drawing water from a public street fountain. In the east, however, he was obliged to purchase water from a commercial water carrier. Similarly, his wife had economized

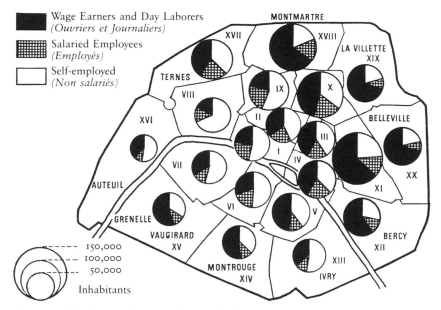

FIG. 2.2   The Social Composition of the Population, 1872

From Braudel and Labrousse, eds., *Histoire économique et sociale de la France*, vol. 3, *L'Avènement de l'ère industrielle, 1789–1880*, 799.

By the end of the Second Empire, old Paris had been encircled by irregular housing erected on the open fields of the peripheral arrondissements. Church of Notre Dame de la Croix and its environs (arrondissement XX), by Marville, 1868. Collection of the Musée Carnavalet.

on food by shopping in the central markets after the closing bell sounded and merchants had reduced their prices rather than repack their goods. She no longer had easy access to markets. There were few in the eastern parts of the city, and the administration made no attempt to remedy this situation until 1865, when plans were drawn to build markets in eight of the suburban arrondissements. Lazare complained that although the administration erected new theaters with city money, it did not follow through on its obligations to less favored parts of the city and turned these construction plans over to financial companies.[79]

Before 1860, workers typically chose to live in the suburban area between the octroi wall and the fortifications in order to avoid the tax on goods coming into the city through the octroi gates. (See the map of the city boundaries in 1833–48 and in 1860 in Fig. 2.3.) Both Lazare and the Republican Deputy Jules Simon argued that once this territory was incorporated into the city limits, so that the inhabitants were taxed equally with those of old Paris, it became necessary to provide comparable services to the new communes. In a speech delivered to the legislature, Simon described areas in the east in a state of viability which would not, he said, be tolerated by the most backward communes of France. East of Père Lachaise there were a large number of unpaved roads without even gutters; in Bercy and Montrouge there was no gas service, nor were there oil lanterns to light the streets.[80] The suburban communes had not, in fact, been included in Haussmann's three-phase network of street development, nor was the token money which had been allocated to the outlying areas efficiently used. One critic compared the "municipal fantasy" of developments in the east to the "false luxury" of central Paris as Haussmann opened up avenues in the midst of fields while bypassing the more congested areas of Montmartre, Batignolles, la Chapelle, la Villette, Belleville, Bercy, Vaugirard, and Grenelle.[81] (See Fig. 2.4.) Simon claimed that the Fr 200 million spent in the peripheral communes tranquilized consciences without improving conditions. Walks and parks like Buttes-Chaumont were a superficial luxury which obscured the absence of the real necessities of water, pavement, gas, and sanitation services.[82]

The annexation of the suburban communes presented a whole new array of problems for the Commission on Unhealthful Dwellings. These arrondissements included many of the industrial establishments which had been classified by the Conseil d'Etat as "dangerous trades" presenting particular health hazards to neighboring persons and property and therefore required to locate away from the densely populated center. Although these peripheral suburbs were less densely settled than the older sections of the city, the housing was more haphazard and often without any sanitary amenities at all. The open fields were dotted with makeshift dwellings built with

1833-48

1860

0 100   500   1000 m

Fig. 2.3   The Boundaries of Paris in 1833–48 and in 1860
From Rouleau, *Le Tracé des rues de Paris: Formation, typologie, fonctions*, 92–93.

46

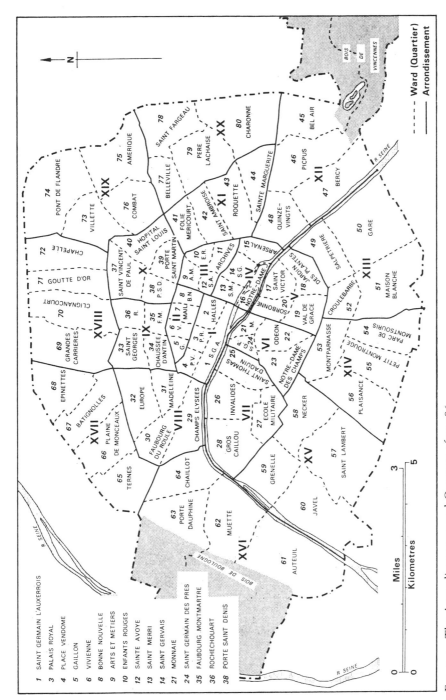

FIG. 2.4   The Arrondissements and Quarters after 1860

From Sutcliffe, *The Autumn of Central Paris*, xvi.

1   SAINT GERMAIN L'AUXERROIS
3   PALAIS ROYAL
4   PLACE VENDOME
5   GAILLON
6   VIVIENNE
8   BONNE NOUVELLE
9   ARTS ET METIERS
10 ENFANTS ROUGES
12 SAINTE AVOYE
13 SAINT MERRI
14 SAINT GERVAIS
21 MONNAIE
24 SAINT GERMAIN DES PRES
35 FAUBOURG MONTMARTRE
36 ROCHECHOUART
38 PORTE SAINT DENIS

the refuse and debris from construction sites. Because they did not align public roads, these buildings escaped even the minimal standards set by the 1852 decree. In addition, such housing was often inhabited solely by the proprietor and therefore outside the jurisdiction of the commission, while landlords who rented out lodgings in these shantytowns were frequently unable to afford even modest repairs.[83] The commission acknowledged that it was necessarily more lenient in its prescriptions for properties in the annexed territory.

While the government officially encouraged the regulatory activities of the commission, it had a blind spot for the conflict between its urban policies and the specific question of housing reform. Napoleon and Haussmann responded selectively to problems of urban development. They remained committed to street improvements as the primary instrument of an urban social policy and tended to address directly only those issues which could be resolved by public works measures. They saw improved sanitary conditions where slums were newly demolished but not the growing squalor of the outlying quarters.[84] Haussmann hoped to sidestep the problem of rehousing those evicted through demolitions by stimulating a building boom. He believed that "in such a case it is best to leave to speculation, stimulated by competition, the task of recognizing the people's real needs and of satisfying them."[85] He did not see that private enterprise was committed to profit and not to identifying social needs. In 1861, Haussmann objected to an "odious project to establish a maximum for rents" and to the "other chimerical idea of the city as house-builder."[86] Yet both Napoleon and Haussmann were self-conscious propagandists who worked hard to cultivate popular approval. Public pronouncements reiterated "the profound and tireless efforts of the Imperial government to ameliorate the conditions of the working population." The housing policies of the Second Empire reflect this tension between a basic commitment to laissez-faire economics and a propaganda campaign which required conspicuous public philanthropic action.

Official housing policies

Initially, Napoleon shared the feeling, particularly prevalent in the early 1850s, that more and better housing had to be provided for the working class—that workers adequately housed would turn away from politics in pursuit of the comforts of domestic life. The Société des cités ouvrières de Paris, founded by Chabert in 1849, was conceived of as a means to "pacifically disarm resistance."[87] Proponents of working-class cités typically saw housing as a means to render the worker "inaccessible to the seductions of politics," to transform him from an instrument of disorder into

Boulevard Masséna in arrondissement XIII (Porte d'Ivry), by Atget, 1910. Collection of the Bibliothèque historique de la ville de Paris.

a reliable *père de famille*.[88] They drew lessons from English experience to support this conclusion. For example, a report presented to the Académie des sciences morales et politiques claimed that although the population of Birmingham had increased by 50,000 persons in twelve years, the number of policemen necessary to maintain order had actually declined, from 420 to 327, following the construction of working-class housing.[89]

On several occasions Napoleon allocated government funds for the construction of complexes of workers' housing. None of these projects proved successful. In 1849, a private society began the construction of a *cité ouvrière* on the rue Rochechouart which later received a government subsidy and its name, Cité Napoléon. It included four buildings of three and four stories, with 170 individual dwellings of two rooms and a kitchen and a number of single rooms. The ground floor housed shops and workshops, and inhabitants had the use of common meeting rooms, washing rooms, baths, and a day nursery. Workers quickly dubbed this construction "La baraque," the shanty, and refused to become residents.[90] By the 1880s, the cité housed bourgeois tenants. Napoleon abandoned plans to erect a similar cité in each of the twelve arrondissements.[91] In 1852, the government earmarked Fr 10 million raised from the confiscation of Orleanist property for the improvement of conditions of working-class life. Of this sum, Fr 2 million were used for the construction of seventeen houses for workers on the boulevard Mazas,[92] and Fr 2,130,000 (representing one-third of the cost) were given as subsidies to builders who would erect working-class housing under government supervision.[93] In spite of low rents, tenants appeared only reluctantly.

Even with government assistance, it was difficult to build working-class housing which would be both inexpensive to rent and profitable for the investor. In 1853, Emile Muller, a prominent architect, appealed to the government for a subsidy to construct a complex between the boulevard Saint-Antoine and the boulevard Mazas (near Gare de Lyon). He planned individual units with access to common facilities for classrooms, washing, drying, and bathing. The tenant would pay 1 franc per day rental, and for an additional 49 centimes daily for fifteen years, he would eventually become the proprietor of his own home.[94] Yet, even the basic rent of Fr 365 exceeded the budget of the Parisian worker. Housing such as Muller's built through private speculation was most often beyond the range of all but a tiny elite of the working class.[95]

It was not simply workers' resistance to communal lodging and the financial problems of builders which produced such a record of failure. Rather, the profound ambivalence of both official and unofficial parties toward housing workers collectively inhibited any significant movement to construct cités ouvrières at this time. Contemporaries reacted with instinctive fear to any plan which increased regular contacts among workers in the absence of supervision from conservative men of property. In his criticism of the burden of the octroi, for example, Lazare expressed the fear that taxes had forced the *petits rentiers* out of Paris, removing the class which served as an intermediary between the well-off and the working class and represented a "permanent school in the benefits of sober economic life."[96] The report of the Chamber of Commerce in 1855 articulated a similar malaise in the face of growing separateness among the social classes. It claimed that the migration of workers to the periphery had had adverse effects on both the worker's conduct and morality, depriving him of "the bridle" provided by neighboring bourgeois. It spoke sentimentally of the former solidarity among members of the same house, who came to each other's aid in times of sickness and unemployment, "positive contacts" between worker and bourgeois, and of "a sort of human respect which imprinted a character of regularity on the habits of working-class families."[97]

Even Villermé, whose description of the conditions of working-class life had stimulated housing reform, recoiled before the concept of cités ouvrières.[98] He feared that separating workers from society in general would reinforce their jealousies toward the rich, to whom they already attributed "so many imaginary wrongs." According to Villermé, the immoral and antisocial worker corrupted the rest and produced a general lowering of the moral tone. In bourgeois imagination, common rooms became incubators of conspiracy and sedition, and dark corridors and stairways, the sites of prostitution and moral decline. Villermé advised that houses be built on the same alignment so that communication between neighbors would be less frequent, and that windows and doors be situated so that neighbors did not have a view of interiors. He felt that those workers whose "natural vice" led them to perpetual misery could not always be excluded from large common buildings and hoped that "the real working class" would shun such accommodations.

The bourgeoisie in Paris particularly feared the influx of unattached, unskilled provincials. Between 1833 and 1861, the percentage of native-born Parisians declined from 50 percent to 36 percent.[99] The provincial worker cut loose from the moralizing influence of his family seemed the quintessential bad seed which spawned disorder. Villermé claimed that single workers must not share the same buildings and courtyards with families. He argued against constructing special housing for bachelors, who were not likely to conform to rules and whose economies would only make available additional funds for orgies and intemperance. Common lodgings allegedly excited "socialist folies" and reinforced immoral predispositions. Instead, Villermé expressed the vain hope that private industry would house its own workers.[100]

Early interest in cités ouvrières thus turned quickly to disillusionment. A letter from the minister of the interior to the minister of agriculture, commerce, and public works in 1861 is especially revealing. The minister wrote:

> I will end by pointing out, Monsieur Minister and my dear colleague, that the principal goal of the Minister of the Interior was not to have a large number of lodgings built for the working class and at the same time to compete with private industry; but rather to create model houses presenting the best lay-out, the best ventilation, and the best sanitation. This goal seems to have been accomplished. Also, it has not been necessary, in pursuing this objective, to use more than a portion of the grant of 10 million.[101]

In the space of a decade, the administration progressively redefined its level of responsibility for housing. Competition with private industry was clearly out of the question. Napoleon abandoned his original idea of building a complex in each arrondissement for the more comfortable goal of setting a standard and providing a useful example. Similar ambivalence can perhaps be seen in the fact that a charitable society formed in 1853 to convert old houses throughout the city into workers' housing complained in 1863 that it had not yet been officially approved.[102] Hygienists as well had mixed feelings about housing set aside exclusively for workers. In its general reports for the years 1849–58, the Council of Public Hygiene and Salubrity for the Department of the Seine indicated that it seemed advisable in Paris to return to the concept of mixed housing rather than to adopt the model of large common dwellings, which bred immorality and disorder and hence insalubrity.[103]

In those complexes which did exist, owners sought to defuse the attendant dangers by controlling admissions and regulating the behavior of tenants. Frégier, head of a bureau at the Prefecture of Police, suggested that only married workers with a certificate of morality signed by their employers and the mayor of the commune be admitted.[104] Not surprisingly, Villermé echoed this recommendation.[105] Regulations for the Cité Napoléon, rue Rochechouart, contained no less than 100 articles.[106] Typically, such regulations included provisions for the maintenance of hygiene and order; the requirement that inhabitants return home before a certain hour, usually 10:00 P.M.; and often, the requirement that children attend school.[107] In his request for a government subsidy, Muller sought to conform to the "moralizing intentions" of the emperor in stating that "our enterprise addresses itself exclusively to upright, hard-working, and orderly workers. We have resolved to admit for occupation or ownership only those respectable family men who present every guarantee of morality."[108] The houses built with the help of government funds on the boulevard Mazas did, in fact, have a manager in addition to a concierge who visited each morning to inspect.[109]

Workers shared in the rejection of large communal dwellings in which tenancy represented diminished personal autonomy. The Parisian poor saw these so-called barracks as a type of poorhouse for small households. The imposition of paternalistic supervision made such accommodations totally unpalatable. Only the most desperate would consent to live in housing where conduct was regulated by bourgeois administrative personnel. Financial benefits and improved material conditions could not compensate for the implied loss of status. One disgruntled philanthropist complained that "in Paris, the worker, exhibiting a hateful defiance toward the propertied classes, flaunts the defects of his habitation" and refuses to install himself in newer, healthier quarters.[110] Blanqui noted in 1850 that, in contrast to London, where housing for the poor required that inhabitants wash their hands daily, French workers would never consent to such controls.[111] Several of the working-class delegations to the Universal Exposition of 1867 added their disapproval of the concept of cités ouvrières. They suggested that philanthropists and building societies were beginning to relegate the laboring population to special quarters as in the Middle Ages, and urged instead that the government tax vacant apartments to force down the rental price and make available more lodgings in the center of the city.[112]

Within a decade of the first experiment with high-rise communal workers' housing, the concept had aroused nearly universal dislike. The government, the propertied classes, and moralists alike feared the increased physical communication among workers, while hygienists deplored working-class habits of uncleanliness and resultant unsanitary conditions. The *casernes* came to be seen as harbingers of disorder and disease. Workers, for their part, refused both regulation and ghettoization. At the same time, the administration persisted in a noninterventionist housing policy as demolitions of low-rent dwellings continued to exceed their replacement.

The problem of working-class housing thus remained something of an abstraction during the Second Empire. Few observers held a realistic conception of large-scale, chronic mass poverty. Villermé expressed the common opinion that "those workers who earn the least will be forced, inevitably, to inhabit uncomfortable, insufficient, and unsanitary lodgings. . . . It is the fate of the poor, the harsh law of necessity."[113] For the rest of the laboring population, contemporaries shared a vague hope that workers would "level up" so as to eventually occupy the vacated dwellings of the upwardly mobile bourgeoisie.

In this context, the initial appeal of complexes of workers' housing within the city quickly turned to disaffection in both official and unofficial circles. At bottom, Haussmann saw himself as the mayor of a modernized capital and scarcely noticed the pattern of haphazard and incomplete development in the suburban communes. Nor did government officials, builders, or architects systematically consider the problem of housing as an integral part of a broader network of urban systems including transportation, drainage, and water supply.[114] Roads were driven through the eastern arrondissements without careful planning for the needs of the population. Napoleon and Haussmann were interested primarily in the circulation problems of the center, and were not particularly concerned with the viability of the suburban areas. While reformers commonly linked the issue of transportation to that of housing, no actual policy was generated to that end.[115] Those workers who chose to live at the extremities of the city because of cheaper rents faced a minimum of two to three hours of travel per day. Alexandre Weill noted that once the traveler reached the railroad stations of the city, it might take him up to two hours to reach his ultimate destination, and he might not find a seat on the buses.[116] Travel across the city was expensive, and lack of service early in the morning or late in the evening made bus transportation impractical for the working class.

Encouraged by the stability and prosperity of the time, administrators were able to ignore the shortage of acceptable working-class housing. They made little headway in evolving a realistic strategy appropriate to the needs of a modern urban agglomeration. Critics have attacked Napoleon's and Haussmann's policies on aesthetic and financial grounds.[117] While acknowledging that street improvements did remove unsightly slums and open up congested areas of the center, they have deplored the classical rectilinear pattern attempted in the new boulevards and the grandiose style of the public buildings. Haussmann's progressive disregard for sound financing has similarly come under fire. But perhaps the most valid and most obvious criticism which can be directed against the grand design of the Second Empire lies in the legacy which it conveyed to the Third Republic. Increasingly the city divided into a comfortable west and an impoverished east. The development of the center was achieved at the expense of the periphery. In succeeding decades, the shortage of inexpensive lodgings in the center and the problems of unsanitary working-class housing in the outlying arrondissements would only become more acute.

Ch. 3 Health and Housing Issues Redefined

NEITHER the sporadic philanthropic paternalism of Napoleon nor the regulatory activities of the Commission on Unhealthful Dwellings substantially improved conditions of working-class housing in Paris during the Second Empire. In fact, these small meliorist gestures were eclipsed by the physical transformation of the city, which served to heighten the urgency of the housing shortage. The annexed territory added a working-class population of approximately 350,000 to the city, in what Georges Duveau has called the proletarianization of Paris.[1] And the enlarged capital continued to draw massive waves of in-migration from the countryside. According to the census of 1881, only 36 percent of the population had been born in Paris or in the department of the Seine;[2] by 1886, only 25 percent of all heads of households had been born in the department of the Seine, while 70 percent came from the provinces and 5 percent from foreign countries.[3] The greatest increase in population, which occurred between 1876 and 1881 and added 280,000 inhabitants, prompted an anxious contemporary to note that it was as if a city the size of Orleans (60,000) had to be incorporated each year into Paris.[4] Such growth inevitably placed severe strains on the physical cadre.

Most of the new population, which was largely working-class, located in the peripheral arrondissements. (See the maps of post-1860 Paris, Figs. 2.3 and 2.4) For example, of the 280,000 persons added during 1876–81, 78 percent of this growth (218,009) occurred in arrondissements XI–XX. At the same time, the embellishments in the center had raised rents beyond the means of the working class and discouraged the construction of modest buildings, thus accelerating the removal of workers to the periphery. Between 1861 and 1896, the population of the city as a whole increased by 840,693, or 49.6 percent (see Fig. 3.1).[5] More importantly,

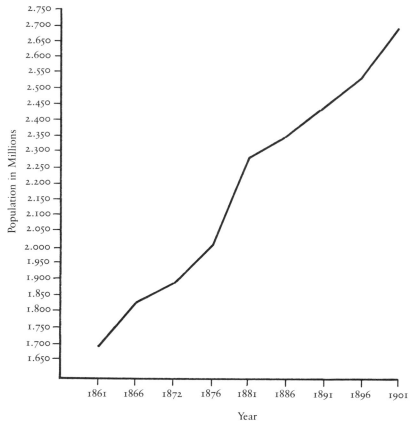

FIG. 3.1   Population Growth, 1861–1901
Data taken from *Annuaire statistique de la ville de Paris et du département de la Seine.*

during this period the first ten arrondissements grew by only 7.1 percent, in comparison with the monumental increase of 103 percent in the outer ten arrondissements.[6] Even after the initial evacuation of workers from the center—that is, after the 1860s—the pattern of pronounced growth in arrondissements XI–XX persisted. Between 1872 and 1896, the population of the outlying arrondissements increased by 62.3 percent, far overshadowing the negligible increase of 10.9 percent in the central districts. In contrast to the demographic patterns of the first half of the century, the locus of change had moved from the dense center to the fringes. In order to evaluate the impact on housing conditions of this population growth in the poorer sections of the city, it is necessary to look more closely at patterns of construction during this period.

Following larger trends in the economy as a whole, construction sustained erratic periods of boom and slump. Between 1830 and 1880, building activity was generally expanding, characterized by a significant peak in 1865–67 and occasional short periods of depression, particularly in 1872–75, after which recovery continued until the mid-1880s. The years 1881–84 were boom years in which construction exceeded demand, especially for bourgeois and luxury dwellings. Following this expansion, the long-term trend was one of decline, with stabilization at a lower level in the 1890s.[7] The number of new constructions per year may be seen in Figure 3.2.

The building industry obviously responded to the rapid growth of

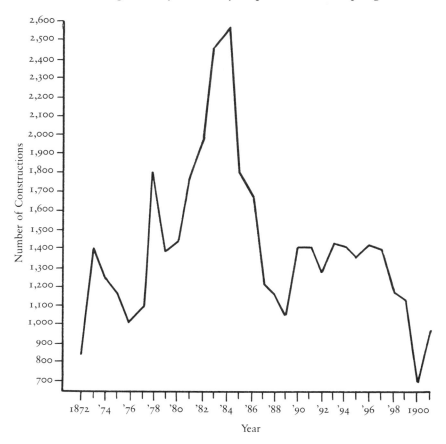

FIG. 3.2   New Constructions, 1872–1901

Data taken from *Le Livre foncier de Paris*, pt. 1, *Valeur locative des propriétés bâties en 1900*, graph 14.

the population in the early 1880s. But it is crucial to determine for whom the new constructions were built. Evidence from a wide variety of sources indicates quite clearly that middle-class and luxury construction far exceeded the building of modest or working-class lodgings. This preference was evident during the boom years of 1878–84 and became even more pronounced during the periods of slump and stabilization in the 1890s.

The data collected for tax assessments confirms the predominant pattern of building to satisfy the needs of the better-off segments of the population. Between 1878 and 1889, as Table 3.1 indicates, the supply of housing increased faster than the size of the population in the wealthiest arrondissements; conversely, increases in population exceeded increases in the housing supply in predominantly working-class arrondissements.[8]

An examination of requests for building permits further corroborates this trend. Most new building did occur in the peripheral arrondissements because, of course, it was there that large tracts of undeveloped land were available. Nevertheless, a substantial amount of this construction apparently took place in the better-off sections within these areas. For example, in both arrondissements XVII and XVIII, where two of the quarters were comfortable and two were more exclusively working-class, more constructions were planned for the wealthier districts. In 1891, contractors filed requests to build 381 floors (either new constructions or additions to constructions) in the two bourgeois quarters of the seventeenth arrondissement, Les Ternes and Plaine Monceau, in contrast to 211 floors in the poorer sections, Batignolles and Epinettes. Similarly, in the eighteenth arrondissement, builders sought to add 280 floors in the more comfortable quarters (Grandes Carrières, Clignancourt), and only 52 floors in the poorer districts (La Goutte d'Or, La Chapelle). The largest total number of applications for building permits was filed in the wealthy sixteenth arrondissement.[9]

TABLE 3.1 INCREASES IN HOUSING AND POPULATION IN
THE WEALTHIEST AND POOREST DISTRICTS, 1878–89

	Increase in lodgings (%)	Increase in population (%)
Wealthy arrondissements		
VIII	39.0	13.7
XVI	62.7	47.2
Poor arrondissements		
XIX	11.9	20.8
XX	21.9	32.8
XIII	29.0	41.6

SOURCE: *Le Livre foncier de Paris*, pt. 1, *Valeur locative des propriétés bâties en 1900*, Paris, 1900, graph 10.

Analysts of these construction patterns conclude that standard theories ascribing building booms to low interest rates and low building costs cannot sufficiently account for building cycles in the final third of the nineteenth century.[10] Gérard Jacquemet argues, rather, that construction is triggered by the needs of the most solvent sector of the population. It is thus most important to know something about the social composition of the anticipated tenants. Patterns of construction in Paris divide into two distinct periods. Before 1860, entrepreneurs who were often connected to the building trades bought land on which to build for their own use.[11] Increasingly after 1860, however, large building societies dominated the real estate market, buying up large parcels of land for speculative purposes. They found it more profitable and less troublesome to build for the middle classes—a predilection made practical by the emergence of a new social stratum in the final decades of the century who created a reliable constituency for middle-range housing.[12] Employees in the tertiary sector of the economy (e.g. commerce, banking, transportation, and service) enjoyed the prospect of relatively stable employment and opportunities for advancement—"les nouveaux locataires solvables"—even when starting salaries were inferior to those of some working-class trades. Proprietors need not depend upon the financially insecure and morally objectionable elements of the working class to fill their rental units. Hence, new constructions catered to the needs of this new stratum, pushing the working class into older buildings or outside of the city altogether.[13]

Jacquemet has documented the changing character of Belleville (in arrondissement XX) during this period. In 1888, for example, lodgings on the rue des Mûriers with rents of about Fr 200 for one or two rooms were occupied by working-class tenants: a painter in the building industry, a seamstress, a laundress, two shoemakers, two day laborers, two workers (undifferentiated), and a single salaried employee. There were few merchants or artisans except for those small businesses which serviced the district—i.e., wine-sellers, rag-pickers, second-hand dealers. By contrast, the new constructions erected in the 1890s along the avenue Gambetta and near the Parc des Buttes-Chaumont attracted tenants, new to the district, who were a socioeconomic step above their neighbors. Inhabitants of a new building on the avenue Gambetta included ten salaried employees, three merchants, three proprietors, two students, and only six workers.[14] The contemporary observations of the Pelloutier brothers concur with this analysis. They noted that, while numerous large roadways had been built in the working-class districts of Charonne and Belleville during the preceding twenty years, the newly erected buildings were expensive properties which compared favorably with the most comfortable quarters of the west and northwest sections of the city. The working-class population was obliged to withdraw to the small, sordid lanes and dark alleys flanking the new boulevards. In the end, according to the Pelloutiers, public works measures failed to benefit the class for whom they were, at least officially, intended.[15]

A combination of financial and psychological factors directed entrepreneurs to the construction of more expensive buildings which commanded higher rents. In the first place, the costs of increasingly stringent construction regulations for buildings aligning public roadways had to be borne by the proprietor. The Pelloutiers noted that every small modification in the streets presented a pretext for raising rents.[16] The prominent architect Emile Cacheux wrote in 1885 that

> the city of Paris distinguishes itself by its lack of encouragement to builders of working-class housing. . . . Thus, in the most deserted quarters, they build grand boulevards; the streets are laid without care for the embankments and excavations required by the bordering properties. . . . The City only accepts streets of 12 meters width, paved, with sidewalks, gaslighted, and provided with sewers. Such a street costs, at a minimum, 300 francs per linear meter, and it is the landowners of contiguous property who shoulder the initial outlays. As a consequence, it is impossible to build lodgings for a family along these streets at a price which workers can afford.[17]

At the same time, increasing prices for land in the city, particularly during the 1890s, discouraged the construction of inexpensive housing.[18] Clearly, rising costs outstripped the workers' capacity to pay comparable increases in rent.

In addition, taxes fell proportionately more heavily on inexpensive buildings. For example, on a house worth Fr 5,000, taxes totaled as much as an additional 20 percent on the initial expenditure: Fr 300 for octroi fees, Fr 180 for roadway charges, and Fr 540 for *taxes de viabilité*. In contrast, the charges for a house worth Fr 100,000 amounted to only 8.5 percent of the cost price.[19] Moreover, as properties changed hands, brokers' commissions of 2–3 percent and transfer and registration fees of 10 percent progressively raised the cost of a building, thus encouraging rent increases.[20]

In the search for a favorable return on their investments, building societies which had borrowed at high interest rates eschewed moderate constructions. Those contractors who shared in the Fr 2 million subsidy offered by Napoleon III in 1852 realized a gain of less than 5 percent after complying with the building regulations imposed by the architects of the Ministry of the Interior. By the 1880s, Cacheux reported that, after building twenty houses on the route de Charenton, M. Blondel found that the remuneration was too meager to warrant additional construction. Similarly, the Société coopérative immobilière des ouvriers de Paris earned only 3 percent on its investments and ultimately folded.[21] In 1888, the Société philanthropique de Paris undertook a major project to construct working-class housing with the aid of a gift of Fr 750,000 donated by Michel Heine. The society erected four buildings containing apartments of two or three rooms, a privy, gas, and direct plumbing, with rentals of Fr 150–300.[22] By 1897–98, the revenue from these buildings produced a rate of return of 2.21 percent, hardly sufficient to attract capital investments.[23] In assessing these attempts to build cités ouvrières, one reformer concluded that "those who undertake this work, which is certainly meritorious and worthy of encouragement, must recognize that if they wish to come to the aid not only of the elite workers, but of the poor, they must resign themselves to expect an extremely small remuneration from their money."[24] Such a prognosis discouraged further efforts.

Cacheux observed that investors lacked confidence in the credit of small proprietors and preferred to avoid the long and costly formalities involved in evicting or foreclosing those who failed to fulfill their contracts.[25] Speculators found, instead, greener pastures in foreign investments. For their part, landlords resisted placing themselves in a situation in which payments would inevitably be irregular and complaints numerous, leading one municipal official to conclude that "they no longer build for small pocketbooks and the problems which result for the workers exist without our being able to hope that this difficulty can resolve itself."[26] The inconveniences of dealing with tenants whose employment pattern was, after all, irregular at best, could not be ignored, and, as the socialist press broadcast the inhumanity of landlords, proprietors moved to defend themselves. In an article in L'Economiste français of April 16, 1884, the economist and publicist Paul Leroy-Beaulieu synthesized their arguments:

> Capitalists love their tranquility and their leisure; that is not a crime. If they have 500,000 francs to spend, they would prefer to build a house which will have four or five tenants bound by leases of six, nine, or twelve years, than to construct three or four buildings inhabited by 30, 40, or 50 households with tenancies of three months. In the first situation, they find peace of mind; it is a more agreeable proposition and, if we can use the word, more appropriate. They are not disturbed every instant by demands; they are dealing only with men of their own world; it is rarely necessary for them to evict their tenants or confiscate their property. In houses divided into small lodgings, in contrast, what difficulty! What care and what effort to manage in the midst of these tenants who do not always pay on schedule! What disagreements if they do not pay at all! A sensitive man does not like to throw his tenants into the street. However, if he is unwilling to do it at one time or another, he engages not in invest-

ments, but in ruinous philanthropy. If he does do it, besides the scruples
of his conscience, he runs the risk of being spoken of poorly, of being
held up to public obloquy as an inhuman proprietor.[27]

Leroy-Beaulieu concluded that entrepreneurs avoided the strain of walking
such a fine line either by investing in bourgeois housing or by refusing
working-class tenants.

Without substantial financial incentives, private enterprise had little
to gain by constructing low-cost housing; the profits were not great enough
to make such enterprises attractive in and of themselves, and the prospect
of unpaid rents, periodic evictions, and legal expenses further narrowed
the sellers' market for working-class units. Even with the incentives offered
by the Siegfried law of 1894, which sought to make funds earmarked for
low-cost housing available to contractors through *commissions des habitations à bon marché* (see Chap. 4, below), the industry continued to favor
more expensive buildings. As working-class housing deteriorated with age
and use, it was not replaced.

Thus, it appears that while the working-class population of the city
continued to increase in the final three decades of the century, the housing
stock accessible to workers did not keep pace. This construction lag resulted in higher rents as demand exceeded supply, in deteriorating structures and intense crowding, and in persistently higher mortality in working-
class districts.

RENTS

The discussions of working-class housing in the 1880s confirm almost
without exception that most workers could not pay more than Fr 300–350
annual rent, which usually meant one or two rooms and a kitchen. In 1887,
Arthur Raffalovich, the economist, estimated that only the elite (or 10 percent) of the Parisian working class (e.g., jewellers, stone-setters of precious
gems, engravers, and mapmakers) who earned Fr 20–30 per day, and a small
fraction of skilled laborers (joiners, carpenters, stoneworkers) who earned
Fr 8 per day, could afford rents above Fr 300.[28] As a consequence, Paris
was unusual in that as much as one-third of the population constituted
single-person households, 71 percent of whom lived in one room.[29]

The pressure on the housing supply, especially during the 1870s and
1880s, was reflected in a precipitous rise in rents. In a study of the cost of
living, Singer-Kerel found that from the early 1880s to the end of the century the scale of rents rose more rapidly than the cost-of-living index.[30]
Statistics provided by the cadastral service of Paris corroborate this increase.
In 1880, 67.6 percent of the lodgings in the city had an annual rent below

Fr 300. By 1889, the percentage of rents below this figure had dropped to 50.2, falling further—to 47.6 percent—by 1900. The increases between 1880 and 1889 were the most pronounced. During this period, the total number of lodgings increased by 104,836 while the number of rentals below Fr 300 declined by 69,093. In sixteen of the twenty arrondissements in 1880, more than 50 percent of the lodgings had rents below Fr 300, and in eight arrondissements more than 75 percent of the housing supply fell below this figure. By 1889, however, only nine arrondissements showed more than 50 percent of rentals below Fr 300, and only the thirteenth and twentieth arrondissements had more than 75 percent of their lodgings in that price range (see Table 3.2).

In 1882, the Prefecture of Police conducted an investigation of rent scales in the twenty arrondissements of the city which documents the beginnings of these changes.[31] Respondents indicated that on the average rents had increased by 25–30 percent during the preceding few years. Police commissioners in the fifth arrondissement cited average increases of 25–35 percent throughout the district, while reporting increases in the quarter Val de Grace of up to 40 and 50 percent. Apartments which rented for Fr 140 on the boulevard St. Michel in 1870 were Fr 200 in 1882. Similarly, on rue Soufflot, rue Gay Lussac, and rue Claude Bernard, apartments with annual rentals of Fr 300 in 1870 commanded a price of Fr 450 in 1882.

In arrondissement VI, the commissioner reported that workers employed in the printing and bookbinding trades of the district had been forced to move to the outlying areas of arrondissements XIII, XIV, and XV be-

TABLE 3.2 PERCENTAGE OF RENTS BELOW FR 300,
BY ARRONDISSEMENT, IN 1880 AND 1889

First group		Second group		Third group		Fourth group	
			1880				
XIII	93.2%	XII	83.0%	IV	62.9%	VI	53.2%
XX	92.9	XVIII	78.0	VII	61.7	II	46.8
XIX	88.7	XI	77.6	X	58.3	I	43.4
XV	88.2	V	68.6	III	56.9	IX	34.5
XIV	85.3	XVII	65.0	XVI	55.3	VIII	31.0
			1889				
XX	80.4%	XII	60.9%	XVII	43.8%	XVI	33.9%
XIII	77.3	XI	58.5	X	41.4	II	32.8
XV	69.8	XVIII	57.8	VII	39.4	I	26.9
XIX	68.7	V	50.2	III	39.3	IX	25.6
XIV	62.9	IV	44.9	VI	35.8	VIII	20.1

SOURCE: *Le Livre foncier de Paris*, pt. 1, *Valeur locative des propriétés bâties en 1900*, Paris, 1900, graph 9.

cause rents had risen so steeply. At the same time, new constructions in arrondissement VI contained larger apartments with rentals of Fr 600–4,000, thus attracting a higher socioeconomic stratum of senators, deputies, magistrates, and bureaucrats. The respondent in arrondissement XI reported similarly to the prefect that rents in the quarter Sainte-Marguerite had increased by 25–30 percent since 1878, so that a worker with a family might be expected to pay Fr 450 for two rooms and a kitchen, a figure well in excess of his budget. The commissioner in the quarter Plaisance (arrondissement XIV) stressed even more the short-term escalation in rents between January 1881 and June 1882. He cited as typical lodgings on the passage Didot (two rooms and a kitchen) for which the rent had climbed from Fr 300 to Fr 400 in eighteen months.

The police commissioners responding to the prefect in 1882 provided a variety of explanations for the dramatic increases in rents. Several reports mentioned rises in the price of land and the additional financial burdens generated by new municipal regulations that raised construction standards for sidewalks, sewers, and gutters. One respondent claimed that lower rents could be effected only by enacting "fiscal favors" to compensate the proprietor for his risk and his expenses. But interestingly, in the mode of explanation which characteristically blames the victim, most reports placed the responsibility with the workers themselves. They particularly pointed to increases in wages which raised construction costs and to strike activities which made it more difficult for the worker to meet his obligations. It followed, according to reports emerging from the fifth and ninth arrondissements, that workers habitually failed to make their payments, forcing an expulsion which involved considerable expense in legal fees (usually Fr 75) for the proprietor. The harrassed landlord therefore raised rents with each expulsion in order to recoup his losses. He also tended to require the advance payment of one or two terms (with three months being one term) in order to cover both the cost of an eviction and the possible dead time between tenants, during which no rent could be collected. According to one observer, tenants did not miss the opportunity to profit from the landlord's difficulties. In a typical anecdote of the period, Cacheux described the way in which a landlord could be held ransom by his defaulting tenants. The tenant states: "You spend 60 francs for our expulsion; give us 10, you save 50, and we will depart voluntarily."[32] The reports claimed further that socialist thought and "habits of luxury" had led the worker to regard his rent as a tax which did not necessarily have to be paid. Rent increases thus emerged in these reports as the necessary consequence of the difficulties borne by the proprietor.

On their side, workers were certain that the avarice of landlords lay at the bottom of rent issues. The mutual animosity between landlords and

Inhabitants of the territory near the old fortifications on the fringes of the city, 1900. Families with children were frequently pushed out of the center city by increasing rents and the refusal of landlords to permit children. Collection of Roger-Viollet.

tenants which had surfaced during the Second Empire continued, fed by actual abuses as well as by a rhetoric of heightened belligerency on both sides. The refusal of landlords to rent to families with children became a major source of conflict. In his investigations of slums in arrondissements XIX and XX, the hygienist Du Mesnil found that families continued to live in rat-infested quarters because proprietors of better dwellings had refused to allow children.[33] Other accounts indicate that expulsions were ordered after the rent had already been paid owing to the birth of a child, causing Georges Piart to write in 1882 of the "interminable martyrdom of tenants" created by practices which constituted, in effect, "an encouragement to infanticide."[34] He recounted the following incident which appeared in *La Lanterne*:

> Proprietor: "Are you a father, sir?"
> Tenant: "Not yet."
> Proprietor: "Do you intend to become one?"
> (Here the tenant smiles.)
> Proprietor: "Because if I see a child in my building, I will throw it out the window."
> At these last words, instantly overcome by a legitimate exasperation, and finding himself precisely in front of an open window, the tenant seized the proprietor by the leg and threw him into the void!

The tale concludes with an ominous warning from Piart: "Remember this, gentlemen and proprietors—the tenant was acquitted by the jury!"[35]

In fact, proprietors' rights were so extensive that ordinary practice, even without abuses, generated antagonism. The rights of the landlord to his tenants' property superseded that of all other creditors. Consequently, to protect against nonpayment of rents, the standard lease required as its first stipulation that the tenant furnish his lodgings with possessions of sufficient value to cover the amount of the rent.[36] The day after the landlord demanded payment of the rent, he was entitled to confiscate the tenants' furnishings (Code de procédure civile, art. 819) without a judicial order. At this point, the judge assigned a value to the confiscated property, and if the tenant did not pay within the succeeding eight days, his effects were sold. The rights of the landlord-creditor extended to those possessions which the tenant might attempt to hide with a friend, so that if the landlord could discover the deception within fifteen days, he was permitted to attach possessions held by a third party.[37]

Workers complained with some justification that the law conveyed rights on proprietors while saddling tenants with obligations. And the socialist press did much to reinforce the image of the landlord as the foremost villain of popular culture. For example, the journal *La Bataille* re-

_ Comment, madame.... j'ai l'imprudence de m'absenter de mon immeuble pendant quelques mois et voilà l'état dans lequel je vous retrouve ..... je vous donne congé dans les vingt quatre heures .... je ne sais même pas si je ne suis pas en droit de réclamer des dommages-intérêts à votre mari ! ....

—How can this be, Madam? . . . I take the liberty of absenting myself from my building for a few months and this is the state I find you in when I return. . . . I'm giving you twenty-four hours' notice. . . . I'm not even sure I don't have the right to ask your husband to pay for damages! . . . Honoré Daumier, *Locataires et propriétaires* (Paris: Vilo, 1977).

ported a typical encounter between a prospective tenant and the proprietor of a building on the rue des Martyrs in which the landlord refused to rent to the tenant because his furnishings were not sufficiently valuable, even though the tenant had offered full payment in advance.[38] Similarly, in an article in *L'Intransigeant* of July 27, 1882, Benoît Malon described the seizure of property worth Fr 1,000–1,200 by a concierge acting on behalf of an absent proprietor for an outstanding debt of Fr 31.[39] Piart reported that the proprietor of a dormitory for women factory workers refused to allow beds because the bed was not legally subject to confiscation. Instead, the proprietor insisted upon a divan on which a mattress could be laid so as to afford the landlord the necessary insurance against nonpayment which was his due.[40]

Tenants also felt victimized by the power exercised by the concierges.

In many cases, the owner of the building depended upon the concierge to act for him with regard to rentals and evictions. It was accepted practice for the concierge to receive a gratuity (*Denier à Dieu*), usually 5 or 6 francs, from the prospective tenant as a sign that an agreement had been reached. Tenants complained, however, that the concierge regularly broke the agreement when offered a larger sum, so that, in effect, the concierge was in a position to auction lodgings to the highest bidder. Tenants noted that it was in the interest of the concierge to maintain a steady turnover of clientele in order to regularize the flow of gratuities; hence the problem of unprovoked, random evictions.[41]

It is not surprising that associations emerged to provide assistance to workers escaping in the night with their furnishings (*déménagements à la cloche de bois*), but this could hardly provide a general strategy for dealing with rent increases or the use and abuse of landlords' rights. Proprietors countered by demanding payment in advance, especially of first-floor merchants, who had the best opportunity to slip away.[42] Piart argued, on the other hand, for a systematic effort by tenants to redress the balance of power in their favor. He claimed that tenants could, through coordinated action, combat harrassment and discriminatory practices by collectively refusing to pay rent increases and by compiling an index of acceptable and unacceptable landlords so as to orchestrate an effective boycott. He further sought to organize a tenants' society to defend tenants' interests in the courts and proposed arbitration committees of landlords and tenants to mediate disputes.[43] Increasing pressure on a limited supply of inexpensive housing, however, gave landlords a decisive upper hand. In 1879, Arthur Mangin wrote in *L'Economiste français* that

> formerly, the worker often had difficulty in paying his term; today he has difficulty merely in finding lodging; especially because proprietors are no longer content to require an enormous price for the least hovel; they impose on their tenants beyond that the most intolerable regulations: it is forbidden to have a dog, a cat, birds; it is forbidden even to have children; it is forbidden to bring up water after a certain hour; it is forbidden to hang laundry from the window; in certain houses, the tenant is admitted only on the condition that he not remain home during the day and receive no one. Is this to be at home?—to have to submit to such tyranny under the penalty of expulsion?[44]

Speculation, in addition to high levels of demand, forced rents upwards. Developers bought large parcels of land which they intended to hold, undeveloped, until substantial appreciation accrued. Critics noted, in fact, that even the land auctioned by the Assistance publique was sold

_ Vingt sous de denier à Dieu .... grigou va !... comme je leur z'y ferai encore vite fiche leur congé à ceux là !

—Two bits for the collection plate. . . . That skinflint! . . . They'll see how fast I'll give them notice to go to blazes! . . . Honoré Daumier, *Locataires et propriétaires* (Paris: Vilo, 1977).

Sleepwalking tenants. Honoré Daumier, *Locataires et propriétaires* (Paris: Vilo, 1977).

in large lots, which discouraged purchase by small enterprises and fueled, instead, the operations of large speculating societies.[45] In the expectation of considerable profits, these societies typically borrowed at usurious interest rates which further sustained high rents, while individual proprietors preferred to leave apartments vacant rather than lower their charges. In spite of the intensity of overcrowding in the early 1880s, the number of vacancies in the city continued to increase: 3,732 vacancies in 1880; 4,530 in 1881; 4,753 in 1882; 6,498 in 1883; and 10,099 in 1884.[46] Contemporary accounts indicate that entrepreneurs overbuilt bourgeois apartments and then continued to hold them vacant rather than convert them to working-class lodgings.

It was the high level of rents even more than the quality of the lodging which ultimately provoked resistance from tenants and made working-class housing a volatile political issue in the early 1880s. (See below, Chap. 5.) The immediate material consequence of higher rents was an increase in the number of overcrowded, makeshift constructions in the outlying areas of the city, which in turn prompted a growing public awareness of the numbers of people living in substandard conditions. Throughout the 1880s and 1890s, the protest voiced by hygienists, statisticians, and reformers increased in volume and intensity.

DETERIORATING HOUSING CONDITIONS

As rent increases produced evictions, workers did try to stay within their arrondissements when looking for new lodgings;[47] nevertheless, cheaper prices and lesser densities inevitably drew the working class to the outlying districts, especially to arrondissements XIII, XIX, and XX, where conditions were initially less crowded, but no less grim. Between 1876 and 1886 the number of people per lodging increased from 2.75 to 3.01 in the thirteenth arrondissement; from 2.86 to 3.08 in the nineteenth; and from 2.74 to 2.99 in the twentieth. In contrast, the fifth and sixth arrondissements, in the city center, witnessed a decline in the numbers of people per lodging: 2.99 to 2.97 and 3.14 to 2.88, respectively.[48] Du Mesnil observed that "although recently there has been a tendency for the migration of workers to the suburbs, the effects have not been significant or salutory. . . . The same exploitation has occurred in the suburban territories . . . the new housing built for workers often reproduces exactly the nuisances which with great difficulty were finally suppressed in older housing."[49] Many of the new houses in the peripheral arrondissements were plaster and tarpaper shanties hastily erected in the open fields and hence immune from the minimal regulations which set standards for housing aligning public thoroughfares (decree of March 26, 1852). The owners of these shacks typically held the parcel of land on a long-term lease and covered it with single-story shelters which could bring in profits of as high as 25 percent. The investigations of Haussonville and Raffalovich revealed that single rooms rented for Fr 140–200 annually, or Fr 2.50 per week, while the landlord sought to increase his revenues further by setting up a wine merchant on the premises.[50] Georges Picot complained that

> the more a house is poorly maintained, the more it is in ruins, the more profitable it is to the landlord. I have seen hovels in arrondissement XIII of Paris which yield 20 percent to their proprietor on the day before the Commission on Unhealthful Dwellings, citing the collapsing walls and the peril to the inhabitants, brings an injunction from the Prefect of the Seine to force an evacuation.[51]

Piart compared excessive speculation in lodgings to grain speculation in earlier centuries, suggesting that housing speculators had violated a principle of the contemporary "moral economy" and ought to be subject to legal sanctions.[52]

Investigators produced accounts of working-class districts on the periphery of the city which were truly horrific. Du Mesnil described the *terrains vagues* on which clusters of housing were erected as veritable sewers. Private roadways without any form of drainage turned streets into foul swamps in which the ruts and potholes were filled with decaying matter. Frequently liquid and solid wastes from clogged cesspits seeped into the first-floor living quarters of adjoining properties, while privies without covers overflowed into courtyards, and open gutters intersected walkways. "One can say," claimed Du Mesnil, "that here one breathes death."[53] The Pelloutier brothers echoed these findings. They wrote: "To enter into the houses is even worse. Dark, sticky with humidity and dirt which forms a paste, the corridors seem to be entries into underground passages or even into cesspits. The gas of ammonia and hydrogen sulfide expands as above a night-soil dump. . . . One lacks courage to climb the stairs and hastens to get out of the corridor."[54] Du Mesnil found, further, that in many cases two-thirds of the inhabitants did not have beds, five or six people might share the same bed, and others rented their beds during the daytime hours. During a cold winter, stair railings, doors, and windows had been broken up for firewood, and as rooms became uninhabitable, they increasingly became the repository for dirt and garbage. Rarely was there any water at all, either for washing or for cleaning. Fifteen to twenty people usually shared a privy, although there were examples of as many as fifty or sixty people using the same facility. In one such hovel in the thirteenth arrondissement the rent was Fr 3.75 per week.[55]

Boulevard Masséna, arrondissement XIII (Porre d'Ivry), by Atget, 1910. Collection of the Bibliothèque historique de la ville de Paris.

At the end of the century, Du Mesnil and Dr. Mangenot, a member of the Commission of Hygiene of the thirteenth arrondissement, conducted an intensive study of a small section of their district in the quarter de la Gare, bordered by boulevard Masséna, avenue de Choisy, and avenue d'Ivry.[56] They found, in general, cramped, poorly ventilated quarters with an overabundance of wine merchants and a scarcity of windows, privies, and water. For example, in one section of 160 houses with rentals below Fr 400, in 93 buildings there was no provision for water; 57 buildings had merely a fountain in the courtyard; and only 10 provided water in the building itself. There was no privy in 6 of the buildings, and 107 buildings had only one.[57] On the avenue de Choisy, the investigators found that of 38 shops, 27 sold wine and *eaux-de-vie*. Similarly, of the 61 small merchants occupying the *rez-de-chaussée* on the nearby avenue d'Ivry, 23 were wine merchants and 8 more were grocers who sold wine and eaux-de-vie.[58] Housing was frequently back-to-back with just one wall exposed to the air, while an unvented stove provided heat, and windows were most often kept closed. As land values increased, the courtyards between buildings shrank and were often covered over at the first-floor level, converting the street level into a commercial site and transforming the court itself into an air shaft of 15 meters depth on a four-square-meter base which received the emanations from privies and kitchens as well as the garbage strewn from above. Because population pressure kept demand high, there was little incentive to maintain the condition of buildings or to erect more solid constructions.

The official neglect of sanitary services in the outlying arrondissements which alarmed Haussmann's critics during the Second Empire continued into the final decades of the century. Although the Casier Sanitaire (sanitary survey of housing) reported in 1900 that only 11 percent of homes in the city were not provided with spring water, this statistic conceals the disparity between the wealthier central districts and the poorer periphery: while an average of 85 percent of the buildings in the first ten arrondissements were directly provided with spring water, the figures in arrondissements XI–XX varied from a low of 55 percent in arrondissement XX to a high of 87 percent in arrondissement XVII, which included two bourgeois quarters.[59] For the city as a whole, only 80 kilometers of public streets did not have pipelines for water in 1900. But there were, in addition, 900 private roadways, most of which had no water mains.[60] The burden of supplying water to the contiguous properties fell on the proprietor. The city could not compel him to act and could only close off access to the roadway. Increasingly the Commission on Unhealthful Dwellings assumed responsibility for the condition of private roads and lanes and could require a proprietor to hook up to the nearest water main. In actual practice, this power became a dead letter when the proprietor was himself too poor to undertake the expense. Consequently, significant numbers of buildings in the poorest districts had no water at all (22 percent of the buildings in the fifteenth arrondissement; 18 percent in the nineteenth; 15 percent in the twelfth; 12 percent in the twentieth; and 11 percent in the fourteenth and eighteenth), while comparable figures for properties in the central districts were negligible.[61]

Similar disparities are evident in the distribution of the various systems for the evacuation of wastes. In 1900, close to half of the buildings in the central arrondissements used the new system which provided for direct evacuation to a sewer (*tout à l'égout*). In contrast, this system was operating in only 10–30 percent of the buildings in the outer arrondissements.[62] The reliance on well water in these working-class districts, coupled with the presence of overflowing cesspits and poor sewerage, became increasingly alarming to contemporaries as they recognized cholera and typhoid fever to be water-borne infections.

Inadequate sanitary facilities became critical when accompanied by severe overcrowding. It is difficult to determine precisely the number of people poorly housed during this period. The most reliable measure of density is the number of persons per room; however, different districts will characteristically have different size lodgings, and some statistics will include the kitchen as a room if it is large enough to hold a bed (2 m × 1.5 m) while others do not. Nor is it necessarily specified whether or not the kitchen has been counted in the total number of rooms. Nevertheless, Jacques Bertillon, the head of the Bureau of Municipal Statistics in Paris, worked throughout this period to standardize the collection of data; his figures, collected in a uniform way over time, do give some indication of the scope of the housing problem.

In 1891, for the first time, the census contained questions designed to evaluate the housing conditions of the city, particularly the degree of crowding. Although room size was unavailable, Bertillon determined that overcrowding existed when there were more than two people per room. The census-takers thus concentrated on gathering data on the size of the household and the number of rooms. They defined "room" in its broadest sense, including kitchens, maids' rooms, antechambers, storerooms (as long as the dimensions were at least 2 m × 1.5 m), excluding only corridors and privies.[63] Bertillon found that 72,705 households comprising 331,976 people, or 14 percent of the population, lived in overcrowded conditions (see Table 3.3). Of greater interest is the distribution of the poorly lodged population throughout the city. The worst crowding obtained in arrondissements XIX and XX, followed by XI and XIII. The total picture may be seen in Figure 3.3.

Similar statistics were compiled in 1896.[64] The census found that 14.9

TABLE 3.3 BERTILLON'S TABLE ON OVERCROWDING

NUMBER OF HOUSEHOLDS	Number of Households Composed of:						
	3	4	5	6	7–9	10 or more	Total
			Persons				
who live in lodgings composed of							
1 room	28,475	10,429	3,462	1,161	490	14	44,031
2 rooms	—	—	13,931	6,026	3,711	98	23,748
3 rooms	—	—	—	—	4,575	173	4,748
4 rooms	—	—	—	—	—	178	178
Total households with excessive crowding	28,475	10,429	17,375	7,187	8,776	463	72,705
Multiply this last number by . . . . to obtain the number of persons living in overcrowded conditions . . .	3 85,425	4 41,716	5 86,875	6 43,122	8 70,208	10 4,630	— 331,976

SOURCE: Bertillon, *Essai de statistique comparée du surpeuplement des habitations à Paris et dans les grandes capitales européennes,* 5.

percent of the population (377,988 people) lived in overcrowded conditions, while another 36.3 percent (920,871 people) inhabited insufficient space — that is, less than one room but more than one-half room per person.[65] The arrondissements with the greatest crowding were XIX, XX, XIII, XVIII, XI, and XII (Table 3.4). According to the figures, more than one-half of the population of all of the ten peripheral arrondissements lived in less than sufficient conditions, except those in the wealthy sixteenth arrondissement and in the seventeenth, in which the figures are skewed because two of the quarters were wealthy.

Bertillon noted that in order to complete his research, it would be necessary to know the room size, a statistic not accessible through the census. He added, however, that "in the overcrowded lodgings, the rooms are generally very small."[66] An examination of the average rents paid throughout the city in 1900 supports Bertillon's conclusion: the arrondissements with the most people living in overcrowded conditions were also the ones

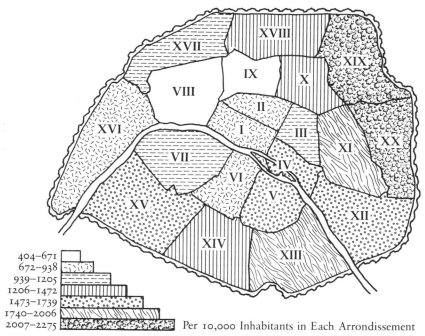

404–671
672–938
939–1205
1206–1472
1473–1739
1740–2006
2007–2275   Per 10,000 Inhabitants in Each Arrondissement

FIG. 3.3   Number of Persons Living in Overcrowded Conditions (more than two per room), 1891

From Bertillon, *Essai de statistique comparée du surpeuplement des habitations à Paris et dans les grandes capitales européennes,* 8.

with the lowest rents in the city, an indication that the apartments were probably quite small.[67] The lowest average rents were as follows:

Arrondissement	Average rent
XX	Fr 215.50
XIII	254.49
XIX	259.31
XV	281.63
XVIII	296.88

The unavailability of inexpensive housing swelled the rolls of indigents and increased the incidence of vagrancy. According to the census of 1886, registered indigents (including children under fourteen) constituted 12.9 percent of the population in arrondissement XX and 10.9 percent of the population in arrondissements XIII and XIX.[68] The Pelloutiers noted that prosecutions for vagrancy were increasing, accounting for 23 percent of

TABLE 3.4 PERSONS LIVING IN CROWDED CONDITIONS
IN THE SIX POOREST ARRONDISSEMENTS IN 1896
(NUMBERS PER 1,000 INHABITANTS)

Arrondissement	Overcrowded	Insufficient space	Total
XIX	253	407	660
XX	237	418	655
XIII	222	420	642
XVIII	139	477	616
XI	184	401	585
XII	175	396	571

SOURCE: *Résultats statistiques du dénombrement de 1896 de la ville de Paris et du département de la Seine*, xxx.

all misdemeanors in 1888 and 48 percent in 1892.[69] In response to these conditions, the municipality began to provide night refuges in the late 1880s and the 1890s. The Asile Benoît-Malon, which opened in January 1887, offered shelter for three or four nights to men and boys over ten. Work was optional, but it entitled the volunteer to a midday meal and to fifteen days additional residence. Following the initial stay, the individual had to wait two months before he could regain entry. In 1891, this refuge serviced 23,708 men.[70] A similar establishment founded in May 1889, the Asile Nicolas-Flamel, added workshops in 1893 and permitted residency of twenty days.[71] This refuge gave shelter to 18,913 men during 1891. In 1894, the Asile George Sand was opened to provide comparable shelter for women and their children.[72] This municipal response was, of course, only a palliative which could not appreciably affect the problem of insufficient housing.

MORTALITY AND HOUSING

Hygienists and statisticians identified high mortality rates in working-class districts as the direct consequence of deteriorating housing conditions. Villermé had conducted similar studies in the 1830s and 1840s and had reached similar conclusions; however, Villermé's work was laced with judgments of working-class morality and character as underlying, predisposing factors in the poor health of the population. In contrast, professionals in the postbacteriological period like Du Mesnil and Bertillon were concerned more directly with the specific conditions which fostered the spread of germs and disease. According to Du Mesnil, all infectious germs (including those which cause typhoid fever, smallpox, and diphtheria) found a conducive breeding ground in the quarters of the poor, while overcrowded conditions turned infections into epidemics. Where Villermé's anticontagionist theories had called for a general cleaning up of the environment, hygienists in the latter decades of the century focused on problems of contagion and on specific remedies involving the disinfection, demolition, and replacement of working-class housing. Dr. François Roques was typical in his observation that "an apartment recently inhabited by a person with tuberculosis, or typhoid, or diphtheria, in which the walls and floors contain millions of bacilli, is at least as unhealthful as an apartment in which the privies are overflowing."[73] The insidious image of multiplying disease-carrying microorganisms seemed, more than ever before, to provide a rationale for more careful supervision of working-class lodgings.

Throughout the second half of the nineteenth century, mortality in Paris had been declining, particularly after 1885 (see Fig. 3.4). For 1,000 inhabitants, the average number of annual deaths were as follows:

1861–1865	25.7	1881–1885	24.4
1866–1870	27.0	1886–1890	22.9
1871–1875	22.4	1891–1895	21.1
1876–1880	23.7	1896–1900	19.1

Bertillon attributed the decline in mortality to an attenuation in the incidence of typhoid fever, smallpox, measles, scarlet fever, whooping cough, and diphtheria, noting that this trend was similar to that of other large capital cities. Although this data basically traced an optimistic pattern, Bertillon's conclusions were not quite as positive. Rather, he cautioned that, in general, the city was actually less healthy than it appeared. Because the age distribution of the population was heavily skewed, comprising a disproportionate number of adults (20–40 years), he concluded that an under-representation of the ages which usually furnish the bulk of the mortality (i.e., children and old people) produced a more benign picture than was warranted by actual conditions.[74] Most important, the poorer districts remained significantly less healthy than the better-off sections of the city. If the arrondissements are grouped according to wealth, [75] the average death rate per thousand for 1896 was as follows: very poor arrondissements, 22.84 deaths per 1,000 persons; poor, 20.74; comfortable, 17.12; and wealthy, 13.44. Clearly, the poorest arrondissements sustained considerably higher mortality than did the wealthier districts. The same discrepancy appears for infant mortality rates, always a sensitive indicator of health conditions. These rates remained significantly higher in the poorest districts (Table 3.5).

Bertillon demonstrated further that all contagious illnesses constituted a more significant share of the causes of death in the poorer arrondissements.[76] He found that after 1880, the incidence of smallpox became localized in the eastern half of the city (particularly in arrondissements X, XI, XII, XIX, and XX), which typically sustained smallpox mortality rates

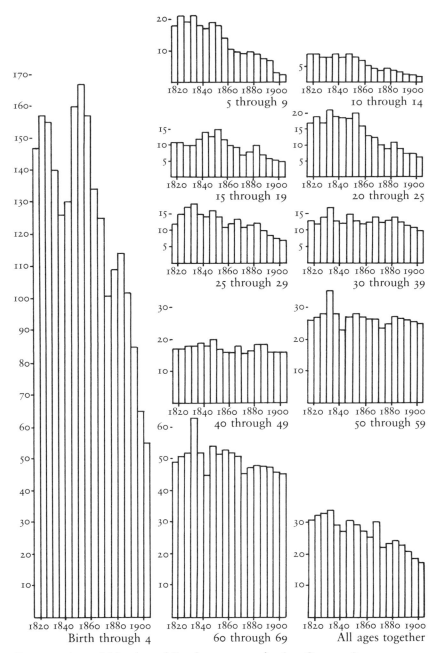

FIG. 3.4   Annual Number of Deaths per 1,000 by Age Group, 1819–1904

From Bertillon, *De la fréquence des principales causes de décès à Paris,* 116.

TABLE 3.5 COMPARATIVE INFANT MORTALITY RATES,
1893–97:
DEATHS PER 1,000 FOR AGES 0–1

Wealthy arrondissements		Poor arrondissements	
VIII	108.5	XX	252.0
XVI	135.2	XV	252.6
VII	153.4	XIX	259.8
IX	185.5	XIII	277.8
I	203.4	XIV	309.6

SOURCE: Bertillon, *De la fréquence des principales causes de décès à Paris*, 135.

of double or triple that of the citywide average.[77] Diphtheria, whooping cough, measles, and typhoid fever were similarly becoming rare in the central arrondissements while they continued to exact a toll in the periphery. It was increasingly clear that significant improvements in the health of the population would not result until something was done to ameliorate the miserable living conditions of the poor. Although the virulence of the major nineteenth-century scourges had diminished, contemporaries understood that the persistence of sporadic epidemics in working-class districts continued to be a threat to the entire city.

Hygienists noted that deaths from contagious diseases concentrated in a relatively small percentage of the houses of Paris.[78] This was particularly true in the case of tuberculosis, an illness which presented a notable exception to the pattern of declining virulence. The death rate from tuberculosis had, in fact, remained constant in Paris since 1865, even as it declined in other capital cities—a persistence which served for contemporaries as a measure of the fundamental unhealthfulness of the environment. Not surprisingly, consistently high death rates from tuberculosis obtained in predominantly poor working-class arrondissements; conversely, the wealthy arrondissements sustained the lowest tuberculosis mortality rates (Table 3.6).

The alarm over tuberculosis clearly directed attention to unsanitary housing. Robert Koch had isolated the tuberculosis bacillus in 1882, and continued experimentation demonstrated that the disease-carrying organism, usually ejected through spitting, could remain virulent for long periods of time in dark, poorly ventilated quarters. A study conducted by Juillerat, the head of the bureau for the sanitary census of houses in Paris, attempted to correlate death rates from tuberculosis with the height of buildings. He found that mortality rates rose in buildings without free space around them, and that the incidence of tuberculosis was greater in the lower floors, which

TABLE 3.6 ANNUAL NUMBER OF DEATHS IN PARIS FROM TUBERCULOSIS
PER 100,000 INHABITANTS, 1865–1905

Arrondissement	1865–1869	1870–1871	1872–1875	1876–1880	1881–1885	1886–1890	1891–1895	1896–1900	1901–1905
1 Louvre	358	443	381	344	327	315	289.0	264.4	258.1
2 Bourse	334	381	351	389	400	362	325.7	335.8	312.3
3 Temple	409	497	426	427	444	450	410.3	382.2	406.0
4 Hôtel-de-Ville	518	714	439	446	551	520	487.7	481.2	484.0
5 Pantheon	598	797	493	498	501	502	468.5	429.3	427.6
6 Luxembourg	392	480	339	334	329	314	297.5	284.6	276.4
7 Palais-Bourbon	407	768	361	354	333	315	273.0	246.1	238.3
8 Elysée	281	500	227	211	182	163	138.3	112.7	119.0
9 Opéra	257	351	295	274	265	253	229.6	209.1	186.3
10 Enclos-St.-Laurent	482	738	395	332	411	408	348.3	341.7	352.9
11 Popincourt	486	614	468	465	533	530	491.0	439.6	480.4
12 Reuilly	563	788	382	395	453	475	449.7	383.5	434.1
13 Gobelins	500	605	375	382	455	464	455.8	427.5	494.4
14 Observatoire	526	740	468	477	564	595	617.4	578.5	458.7
15 Vaugirard	375	975	470	457	497	508	476.5	445.3	431.1
16 Passy	240	284	306	268	285	265	216.7	159.1	210.5
17 Batignolles-Monceau	373	404	349	355	364	359	313.2	270.5	299.4
18 Montmartre	489	638	426	432	525	524	496.5	459.6	443.2
19 Buttes-Chaumont	521	703	447	440	487	528	517.4	516.7	486.8
20 Menilmontant	584	819	547	562	628	582	542.9	510.4	581.4
Men	480	683	433	452	—	—	—	—	—
Women	425	553	370	355	—	—	—	—	—
All of Paris	453	612	402	401	441	436	407.6	376.7	389.3

SOURCE: Bertillon, *De la fréquence des principales causes de décès à Paris.*

had poorer ventilation and less sunlight.[79] Henri Monod, director of public hygiene and assistance in Paris, wrote that the most important factors in the propagation of tuberculosis were the congestion and insalubrity of dwellings.[80] Monod offered a telling contrast of the situation in Paris to that in England, where, he claimed, tuberculosis mortality had been curbed because the battle against unhealthful dwellings had been fought more fiercely.

Thus, the inequality of conditions, both in life and in death, between the ten central arrondissements and the ten peripheral arrondissements which Jules Simon had lamented in 1869 became more pronounced during the Third Republic. High mortality in the poorest districts, underlined especially by the persistence of tuberculosis, identified working-class housing as the breeding ground of infection and disease. Not only were the garbage heaps and wastes surrounding workers' housing seen as a serious public hazard, but contemporaries had come to understand the very walls, ceilings, furniture, and clothing of the worker as presenting a danger which was largely immune to remedial public works policies. The unhealthful dwellings commission could attempt stricter enforcement of sanitary standards, but under contemporary conditions, increased rigor largely meant a policy of shoveling out the poor. Du Mesnil observed that the only remedy for buildings in a state of total decay and insalubrity was to tear them down. But demolition had to be countered with new construction. The housing situation was comparable, according to Du Mesnil, to the aftermath of a flood, fire, or famine—a crisis which called for immediate, positive action.[81] The mechanism of the free market did not supply the remedy. Rising land values and the prospect of substantial profits drew contractors to the construction of bourgeois and luxury dwellings and increasingly away from lodgings for the working class. While construction lagged, the population continued to increase by significant numbers through the end of the century. It remained for philanthropists, reformers, and politicians to attempt to manipulate the market so as to make the construction of working-class housing an attractive proposition for entrepreneurs who clearly believed that their best interests lay elsewhere.

CH. 4 Working-Class Housing and *les Classes Dirigeantes*

B y the opening years of the Third Republic contemporaries were writing in earnest of a deteriorating urban environment that seemed immune to remedial measures. Capturing the pervasive malaise of the bourgeoisie, Georges Picot observed that "the indefinite increase in the urban agglomeration is one of the most enigmatic problems of our time. The moralist and the economist are equally troubled."[1] It was indeed moralists and economists who took responsibility for the social question in the final decades of the century. They embodied that characteristically nineteenth-century combination of genuine, albeit paternalistic concern for the working class coupled with a thinly suppressed fear of the physical presence of the poor—of their living conditions and their lifestyles. Housing reform became, in their hands, the means to reverse current tendencies in favor of more acceptable social and spatial alignments.

Paris had divided into two cities—one rich and one poor, one healthy and one plagued by illness. Once again, in 1870–71, the simultaneous appearance of political revolt and epidemic disease (this time smallpox) had reiterated a familiar, disturbing pattern. The poverty and poor health which had become entrenched in the eastern half of the city seemed clearly to pose a general threat to the entire population. It was incumbent, then, on the traditional *classes dirigeantes* to rescue their world from the biological and political menace the masses of workers represented. Emile Cheysson, a prominent social scientist and philanthropist, pointedly warned his contemporaries that "we are obliged to deal with this problem [the poor] as much from the calculated egoism of self-preservation as from love of our fellow man and elevated sentiments of social obligation."[2]

Polemicists and reformers focused attention on the growth of the *population nomade* who crammed into furnished rooms, temporary shelters, and unsanitary hovels. One observer noted that it had become more difficult for the worker to provide for himself in Paris in the 1880s than it had been forty years earlier.[3] Another acknowledged that while the more comfortable classes might be able to adjust to the diet of the workingman, no such accommodation could be made to the worker's lodgings.[4] At the International Exposition of 1878 in Paris, Emile Trélat described workers' housing as *the* crucial issue of industrial society, the source of all modern misery. He noted that although wages were higher, order was missing, physical suffering grew, and morality was declining. According to Trélat, it was the unanimous opinion in Western nations that "hygiene as well as order, security, morality, and, in a word, the prosperity of industrial populations were linked to the character of the worker's habitation."[5] Jules Simon spoke for a broad spectrum of contemporary opinion when he wrote that the improvement of working-class housing "holds within it all reforms in a single one."[6]

No one doubted that the shoddiness of the physical setting produced parallel moral decay. Bourgeois investigators who visited the living quarters of the poor emerged with lurid descriptions of promiscuity, debauchery, and irresponsibility: the sexes mingled indiscriminately in cramped quarters, beds were shared, and the numbers of cabarets and wineshops in each block continued to grow. According to Picot, "fathers, mothers, daughters, and sons live together, pell-mell . . . their souls atrophy and their habits become corrupted."[7] The reports of the Comte d'Haussonville were similarly filled with dire predictions about the lives of immorality inevitably awaiting the children reared in such an environment.[8] More and more, bourgeois reformers were coming into contact with an alien culture, a population living outside the accepted social norms. Workers paid on Saturday were still sleeping off the effects of wine and alcohol on Monday, and these were often the better-paid elements of the working class. Middle-class conceptions of incentive and responsibility could not account for the perversity of such a situation.

It seemed apparent that moral issues lay at the bottom of social problems, that material improvement waited upon a spiritual renewal. Simon lamented the moral laxness of the working population, noting that the development of "le caractère" continued to lag behind national progress,[9] while even the Commission on Unhealthful Dwellings, investigating the poor in the old twelfth arrondissement, wrote that "it was sad to note the kind of pride which these unfortunates have in their abjection; they seem happy in the life that they have made outside of all the laws of society."[10] Simon's assumptions led him to conclude that "the evil is at bottom a moral disorder, and the problem to resolve is this: to help the worker to save himself. There is a greater service to render him than to give him work or money:

Interior of a working-class dwelling in 1900. Bourgeois reformers were particularly alarmed by the lack of privacy—the mingling of the sexes and the sharing of beds. Collection of Roger-Viollet.

it is to inspire in him the love of work and an inclination for saving. . . . The productive force and the domestic prosperity of a people depend, above all, on its *moeurs.*"[11] During the Second Empire, the issue of sanitary housing had largely been conceptualized in engineering terms as a public works problem. Once the focus shifted so as to emphasize moral development, an acceptable solution required the transformation of the worker's character.

LE PLAY AND THE MOVEMENT FOR MORAL REFORM

The established classes were predisposed to see the working population as morally degenerate. But it was the scholarship of Frédéric Le Play which provided them with a scientific framework from which to act on their beliefs. In 1856, Le Play founded the Société des études pratiques d'économie sociale to study social questions scientifically. Le Play and his school of investigators were committed to intensive empirical studies from which "social facts" and behavior patterns could be determined that would allegedly have greater validity than a priori conceptions and theoretical systems.[12] At the same time, they encouraged the establishment of *unions de la paix sociale,* local organizations which would popularize the conclusions reached by their scholarly task force. Le Play and his followers thus hoped to channel future social change in keeping with empirically verifiable laws of social evolution. Accordingly, they constructed a social philosophy which combined an interpretation of the past with a prescription for the future. In actual practice, they stimulated a movement that was grounded in the most cherished articles of faith of the bourgeoisie and moved toward social reform on the basis of backward-looking dogmas.

The careers of Emile Cheysson and Georges Picot, two of the most prolific propagandists of Le Play's circle, are illustrative. Both combined technical expertise with a style of social activism based in a conservative social ideology and laissez-faire economics. They insisted that private initiative, rather than traditional charitable enterprises or public welfare schemes, would resolve social problems. Cheysson had been educated at the Ecole polytechnique and the Ecole des ponts et chaussées.[13] He was recruited in 1864 by Le Play to work on the mechanical operations for the Universal Exposition of 1867, of which Le Play was commissioner-general. The distinguishing characteristic of this exposition was the prominence given to social issues, particularly in Group X, which included "objects for the material and moral improvement of workers." From 1871 to 1874, Cheysson served as director of the Creusot mines, supervising the enlightened policies of Schneider, the owner. It was at Creusot that he gained direct experience with the potential accomplishments of private initiative in such areas as schooling, housing, and insurance. In the 1870s and 1880s, Cheysson continued his technical career, working for the Service for the Navigation of the Seine and in various projects involving surveying and mapping. But increasingly, he devoted his attention to social questions.

In 1885, Cheysson became a professor at the Ecole des mines, teaching *économie industrielle,* a course designed to train industrialists to fulfill a social responsibility as an integral part of their business careers. Similarly, between 1887 and 1901, he taught a two-year course in social economy at the Ecole libre des sciences politiques. The first segment of the course concentrated on questions relating to conditions of work, including an examination of wages, production cooperatives, unions, strikes, and employers' institutions; the second half of the program addressed issues of working-class domestic life, focusing on crises in the working-class family and the necessity for some kind of social insurance. Cheysson frequently represented the government at international conferences on statistics, low-cost housing, and industrial conditions. In his academic appointments, civil service positions, and quasi-official functions, he was typical of the well-connected bourgeois reformers of the Third Republic. [14]

Picot, similarly committed to social activism, was a judge, an historian, and the director of the Railroad of the South. Throughout his career, he identified himself as an opponent equally of socialism from above and socialism from below. He campaigned unsuccessfully in the municipal elections in Paris in 1884 and in national legislative elections of 1885, 1893, and 1898, dubbed disparagingly by his opponents as "Monsieur the académician," "the candidate of dear bread." A sympathetic biographer explained these failures as the inevitable product of universal suffrage, "which does not bring forward superior men."[15] It is evident that in spite of his philanthropic preoccupations, workers did not consider Picot a friend of the working man. In fact, the programs sponsored by Le Play's followers failed to attract working-class adherents, undoubtedly because of the underlying paternalism which transformed programs of social reform into mechanisms of social control.

Le Play attributed contemporary ills to Rousseauian doctrines of equality, which had undermined social stability, generating "a dust which agitates the wind of revolutions."[16] He saw the Terror as the necessary consequence of Enlightenment ideology, which produced political chaos and reinforced social disintegration. To reverse these tendencies, Le Play sought to reinvigorate the authority of the Decalogue, particularly the commandment which established the preeminence of the father. According to Le Play's analysis, egalitarian theories had translated into policies, such as universal suffrage, which weakened paternal authority and hence the stability of the family, leaving the individual to confront the growing power of the state in isolation. Particularly culpable were the laws which established the sharing of inheritances, thereby aggravating poverty and making the worker's expectation of owning his home ever more precarious. Le Play noted that the dominant European tradition provided for the integral transmission of property, which was, not coincidentally, also the characteristic practice in France during her former periods of prestige and prosperity. He maintained that all the current symptoms of French decadence—sterility in marriage, depopulation, the desertion of the countryside, and the abnormal growth of urban centers—could be traced to the insecurity of the possession of the *foyer domestique.* Armed with these insights, Le Play hoped "to prevent our unfortunate fatherland from continuing in the path which leads it so rapidly to the abyss."[17]

Le Play nurtured an image of a hierarchical, rural society undisturbed by the dislocations of urban and industrial development. He saw in the older styles of economic organization, in which the home and the workshop were joined, a system which maintained family unity under paternal authority. By contrast, contemporary patterns of production destroyed the family's economic function and substituted materialistic bonds between employer and worker for the affectionate ties of an earlier day. Modern society, according to Le Play, disrupted the rapport between masters and workers established by the fourth commandment, which provided that superiors ought to love their subordinates as their children, while the subordinates, on their side, ought to love, fear, and respect their superiors as their fathers.[18] The order of family life was to be projected onto the whole network of social relationships. Instead of ineffective systems of public assistance, Le Play called for a return to the mutual rights and duties of the old patronage system. Presumably as the established classes resumed in full their charitable obligations, the lower orders would be restored to a posture of respectful obedience.

He looked to the countryside as the ultimate source of regenerative change, because it was there, in small neighborhoods, that people most readily, if not spontaneously, acknowledged the preeminence of an aristocracy based upon birth and fortune, but even more, upon talent and virtue. Le Play bemoaned the contemporary disorganization that obscured the benefits of a natural hierarchy:

> The suffering classes, which today dominate society by their votes, are generally incapable of comprehending the true interests of their families and even more, of their localities. They are not inspired, therefore, by sentiments which for ten centuries have pushed the peoples of the Norman race to constitute hierarchies. Sentiments of hate and envy, developed by the disorganization of the *foyer* and the workshop, cause the population to be suspicious of the natural authorities who would be worthy to govern the neighborhoods.[19]

He observed that successful societies had always been grounded in religion, the family, and property, all of which operated on the principle of inequality among individuals. The "catastrophe of 1871" was dramatic confirmation for Le Play of the need to reinstitute aristocratic control.[20]

Le Play offered an image of the future based upon a retreat from contemporary trends. The model he constructed was, in effect, Jeffersonian in its emphasis on small-scale production, rural dominance, and peasant proprietors. In spite of its increasing irrelevance in an urbanizing society, this concept retained a firm hold on the imagination of bourgeois reformers into the twentieth century. As late as 1905, Cheysson, one of Le Play's most energetic disciples, could write that "the first cause of all social malaise is the uprooting of men from their native village."[21] He maintained that all have "unconscious aspirations" toward the land, the forests, the sun, and the countryside, and hence concluded that the worker with a small home and garden was the most reliable guarantor of national well-being. Athough Rousseau remained the identified source of contemporary misfortunes, his detractors ironically preserved his sentimental attachment to the alleged harmony and morality of an earlier period when men lived close to the land.

The precondition for the regeneration of the habits and morals of the working class, then, was to be the establishment of a stable family life within the privacy of an individual home. In a single step, workers could be placed in healthful surroundings, tied to the political order, and separated from the unregenerate and criminal elements who populated the congested areas of the city. The value of le foyer thus transcended its importance in the immediate context of material necessities as it became the agent of social harmony. Simon predicted: "Because the influence of family life is irresistible, moral reform will inevitably follow domestic reform."[22]

THE WORKER-PROPRIETOR: FROM URBAN NOMAD TO PETIT BOURGEOIS

In the 1880s and 1890s, Le Play and his circle vigorously reinvoked the dream of the worker-proprietor which had first appeared during the Second Empire. Writing in the principal organ of the movement, *La Réforme sociale,* Edmond Demolins elaborated the articles of faith of his colleagues:

> The possession of his home creates in [the worker] a complete transformation. . . . With his own small home and garden, one makes of the worker the head of his family worthy of this name, one who is moral and provident, aware of his roots, and able to exercise authority over his family. He soon forgets the cabaret, whose principal appeal has been to remove him from his miserable hovel. The day when he possesses a pleasant healthful home, the home in which he is King, *his own* home which he loves, where the landlord cannot pursue him. . . . his life takes on a peacefulness, a serenity, a dignity characteristic of Oriental men which is nearly unknown among the nomads of our large cities. . . . It is therefore of immense social importance for the worker to possess his own home. Soon it is his home which possesses him; it gives him morals, it establishes him, it transforms him.[23]

Following this fantasy to its most utopian conclusion, Simon (perhaps the foremost publicist of the gospel of the worker-proprietor) prophesied that by forming his own cooperative building societies, the worker might even become a capitalist![24] The social question was to be solved, in effect, by causing the working class to disappear into the bourgeoisie.[25]

Like Napoleon III, the bourgeoisie rejected the casernes, large building set aside for the working class which had briefly been promoted by officials during the Second Empire. The prospect of large numbers of workers living under the same roof suggested every form of irregular behavior—"la réunion pour la débauche." Communal living was, according to Simon, contrary to the human spirit and to human destiny:

> What is this life which begins (in a crèche), only to continue in a workshop and to finish in an almshouse? It is a communal life from its first to its last day. Imagine the perfect example of each: an admirable, well-maintained nursery; an attractive school, neither too indulgent nor too severe; a large, well-ventilated workshop, where the job is tiring without being exhausting; an almshouse which lacks nothing of the necessities of old age. Is this really the life of a man? Is this the life of a woman? Perhaps the body will do well in this communal life, but is it for this that our souls were created?[26]

Echoing this same conviction, Picot spoke of a separate roof as the very condition of family life. His slogan became "one family, one foyer." Without his own home, the worker remained a drifter, a pariah of the established society.

The panegyrics of the period almost always referred to the need "to attach the poor, seminomadic population to the soil" and to endow the father with the appropriate framework within which he could be "an example to his children."[27] The actual physical mobility of workers seemed to disturb bourgeois conceptions of a well-ordered society. In discussing the social consequences of "the disorganization of the family," Ernest Passez complained, for example, that workers changed locations at will and, with only the bond of wages between employee and *patron,* were not reluctant to switch jobs and even trades.[28] Workers with permanent lodgings, it is implied, would be more stable, more dependable, more closely tied to their employers. Moreover, the privacy of a separate dwelling would presumably exercise a brake on the sexuality and promiscuity suggested to bourgeois investigators by working-class life. Simon wrote almost mystically of the garden as "the professor of morality" which "vanquished the cabaret."[29]

The community of workers' housing built at Mulhouse in 1853 by industrialist Jean Dollfus—the cité ouvrière—became the dominant model for housing reformers: single-family dwellings financed by private enterprise, grouped in units of four, each dwelling with its own garden, in which each tenant could become the owner of his lodgings after fifteen years of mortgage payments. It was, according to bourgeois analysis, the periodic excesses to which the worker succumbed which made his life so precarious. The economist Leroy-Beaulieu reported, for example, that workers in Lille exhausted yearly, on the festival of Broquelet, every bit of savings accumulated for medical insurance, permitting no carry-over from year to year. Moreover, in the last month before the holiday, they did not pay the butcher, the baker, or the grocer; they borrowed from friends; they asked for an advance from their employers. All of the money disappeared without a trace during the holiday, and the worker was left in debt.[30] It seemed clear to Leroy-Beaulieu and his colleagues that if the worker could focus his aspirations on a long-term goal which would make his day-to-day existence more orderly, the worker might then pull himself out from his debased condition. The possibility of property ownership and the habits which it engendered were to be the basis for the transformation of the working-class character. Contemporaries did not need to be reminded of the moral benefits conveyed by property. The litany was familiar: sobriety, stability, respectability, and thrift. In place of sinister images of drunkenness and unbridled sexuality, reformers substituted the pastoral vision of the responsible worker, surrounded by wife and children, tilling his garden in his spare time and conscientiously saving for the future — able, at last, to appreciate "this instinct of property that Providence has placed in all of us."[31] Through home ownership, the worker reentered the mainstream of social life, transformed from an uprooted nomad into a settled petty proprietor. In the most single-minded way, bourgeois reformers thus sought to remake society in their own image.

The concept of the worker-proprietor embodied a thinly veiled distinction between the deserving poor and the morally unregenerate, a distinction which underlay the program of Le Play's circle but which often surfaced quite explicitly. Cacheux pinpointed the sensitivities of bourgeois reformers when he urged the construction of low-cost housing because "poor but honest workers are forced to live among a population riddled with vice."[32] And, moving further toward acknowledging their real constituency, Brelay admitted that the goal of home ownership applied only to the elite of the working class and to the petit bourgeois, who shared habits of saving and foresight and were "adept at Anglo-Saxon self-help."[33] In a pamphlet on the ways to improve small dwellings, Picot began by identifying the need to create inexpensive lodgings for the poorest workers as the most pressing problem. Yet he immediately abandoned this issue and continued: "But all this brings us away from small houses with gardens, the natural dwelling for a man, the normal home for the family."[34] It is apparent that a normative conception of social life informed and focused the programs of Picot and his colleagues, despite its limited connection to actual conditions. Particularly in Paris, the père de famille with his individual foyer had little basis in reality. The statistical studies of Jacques Bertillon indicate that single-person households and households without children constituted a substantial segment of the population. In 1891, for example, 31 percent (272,431) of all households were single-person households, and another 27 percent (236,179) contained only two persons.[35]

The image of the worker-proprietor nevertheless dominated bourgeois reform activities. It was so compelling because it addressed simultaneously the most intense social, economic, and sexual anxieties of the propertied classes. Jules Siegfried, a committed disciple, asked rhetorically: "Do you want to create, at the same time, contented men who are true conservatives; do you want simultaneously to combat misery and socialist errors; do you want to increase the guarantees of order, of morality, of political and social moderation? Then let us create workers' housing!"[36] With the problem identified, the strategy seemed clear; the worker would have to have his own foyer. Le Play urged all parties to transcend their differences and focus their efforts on the one reform which incorporated both "individual well-being and national dignity." Not only did the cité ouvrière preserve the integrity of private enterprise, but it carried the implicit promise of a society without class divisions. The combination was irresistible.

Because shared lodgings did not have the moralizing potential of a separate dwelling, it followed that housing for urban workers would have to be constructed in suburban areas. Many urged the development of cheap and efficient transportation systems to make such a solution practical. But even in the absence of acceptable suburban transportation, reformers allowed themselves to enlarge on romantic fantasies associated with their vision of housing reform. Cheysson railed against the "artificial and pernicious conditions" of urban crowding and sought instead to give "the uprooted children a corner where they could see the sky, grass, and flowers." In keeping with this goal, he recommended the use of window boxes for flowers, as had been the practice in England, Germany, and Brussels, in order "to place within the austerity of lives bowed by incessant work a little poetry and an ideal of beauty."[37] Siegfried echoed Cheysson's hope that more genteel surroundings would help to resocialize the working class. He argued that misery is frequently the product of vice, which as often as not comes from idleness. To combat the unstructured leisure which dragged the worker fatefully to the cabaret, he offered "honest distractions" such as musical societies, concerts, gymnasia, and workingmen's clubs.[38] Similarly, Leroy-Beaulieu urged philanthropists and industrialists to provide agreeable dwellings which would keep the worker from the cabaret, where he became "envious, greedy, revolutionary, skeptical, and eventually communist,"[39] while recommending, at the same time, the salutary influence of good books, music, and societies for popular instruction and recreation. Picot, as usual, gave expression to these sentiments in their most basic form: "The great, the true duty of the employer of labor is to raise by degrees the intellectual and moral level of him whom he employs, not by submitting him to an inflexible rule, but by . . . teaching him how he should employ that most delicate of instruments, his liberty."[40]

The body of assumptions which informed this line of attack provided almost endless detours around the core problem of poverty. This was as true in a discussion of economic issues as in the more idyllic descriptions of pastoral regeneration. The work of Picot provides good evidence of this kind of selective blindness. He passionately pursued reform, arguing that social improvement in general depended on the worker's bettering his living conditions. At the same time, the precarious vacillation between poverty and indigence which plagued the lives of large segments of the working class could not be ignored. In the face of such intransigent contradictions, Picot rested all hope in the improvement of the moral character and habits of the worker, thereby closing off the discussion of alternatives which threatened current dogmas of political and social economy. Specifically, Picot noted the increased consumption of alcohol throughout France, but especially in the cities, and reiterated the familiar lament that alcohol had produced the degeneration of the race, the decline of the birthrate, exemptions from military service, and general physical enfeeblement. He concluded that this syndrome of deterioration would be reversed if the worker did not have to flee his home. In support of this thesis, Picot reported a conversation with a woman living at Mulhouse. He asked, "Where does your husband spend his evenings?" The proud reply was: "With us, since we have our home."[41]

Picot followed up this scenario with extensive calculations on the amount of savings which would result from greater sobriety on the part of workers. Making his inferences even more explicit, Picot suggested that if there were a magic wand in the world, it would be the notion of savings. Identifying his position with scientific truth, he claimed that Pasteur had demonstrated that small particles could have profound consequences, and as polyps and madrepores had formed continents, he urged even the small savings of 10 centimes per day.[42] On the other hand, he acknowledged that "suffering for a man who earns fixed wages is certain," and "for the worker who suffers, daily saving is an expression empty of sense."[43] In these perverse circumstances, Picot concluded (as a sort of law of moral experience) that "savings does not come from salaries, but from the effort in itself,"[44] and from "domestic virtues,"[45] from a stable family life and a wife skilled in the practice of domestic economy.

The difficulty of asking an impoverished worker to save was not lost on Picot's contemporaries. Responding to Picot's remarks in the Académie des sciences morales et politiques in 1884, Léon Say noted that "we turn in a vicious circle; the worker is certainly poorly lodged; he is counseled to surround himself with comfort, air, and light. It is as if one would order an indigent to Italy to regain his health."[46] In spite of this perception, however, Say in the end echoed Picot's conclusion, almost to the word: "With saving, if the worker wants to impose it on himself, one can achieve miracles."

The social scientists saw their mission as double-edged: to promote the construction of low-cost housing by private enterprise while effectively stealing the thunder from the socialists. Picot observed in 1885 that "politics will be about social issues."[47] He sounded the theme for Le Play's followers in maintaining that it was the responsibility of conservative parties to undertake reforms which would defuse the socialists' appeal and called his colleagues to immediate action: "In the face of socialism, which gives everything to the state, let us firmly plant the flag of private initiative; let us show what it ought to do; let us prove by the facts what it is able to do."[48]

The construction of working-class housing was thus to be the best defense against socialism—the way to put an end to "the chimerical dreams" raised by working-class agitators. Picot looked to the Republic of 1789, not 1793, as the model for controlled change initiated by the classes dirigeantes.[49] Similarly, Leprince emphasized that the issue was one of both social equity *and* social order, and that on the anniversary of the Revolution of 1789, it was necessary to rededicate efforts leading to the rapprochement of classes.[50] Contemporary socialists evoked, instead, threats to private property and political stability reminiscent of Jacobin excesses, and Picot did not hesitate to wave the red flag. In a typical tirade against state intervention, he charged that state regulations would create "a society in which all initiative would be banished, giving birth finally—to the great joy of the Jacobins— to a society with the most despotic organization that the world had seen since the ancient cities."[51] Never at a loss for the dramatic example, Picot retold an incident in which a socialist member of a large commission was asked why he opposed the formation of construction societies. The socialist reportedly answered that construction societies "satisfy the worker, . . . they kill the motive power for all action, that is, hate, because they deprive us of a combattant and make of him a bourgeois."[52] For Picot, whose message was anything but subtle, the fate of the political system rested on timely, but carefully chosen reforms.

Private enterprise and the cité ouvrière

The articles on workers' housing which appeared throughout the 1880s and 1890s in *La Réforme sociale* presented the construction of low-cost housing as a smart business venture which also served a social purpose. Proponents geared their campaign to assure economists that these construction enterprises were viable on their own terms and were not, in any way, acts of charity. Picot claimed that financially profitable English building societies had been founded on the strictest principles of political economy which guaranteed subscribers regular dividends of 5 percent on their investments.[53] Supported by the reports of hygienists and statisticians, reformers argued further for improved housing on the basis of a cost-benefit analysis, again using England as the model. For example, proponents of the cité ouvrière frequently cited a study of 50,000 workers recently installed in model housing in London which showed a reduction of 1,000 deaths per year and a decrease in the incidence of illness from 20,000 to 15,000 annual cases. The English sanitarians Chadwick and Farr estimated that the savings realized from the decline in deaths and illness, and even from reduced burial expenses, represented more than the interest on the capital expended for the new lodgings.[54] And, even more impressive were the estimated millions of francs which would be earned by workers whose lives had allegedly been prolonged for a decade or more while the state saved the funds normally poured into hospitals, poor-relief institutions, and prisons.

Le Play's social scientist followers were joined by political economists in promoting the cité ouvrière. Both groups emphasized the importance of single-family units, and both were committed to working through private enterprise. However, the economists—especially Leroy-Beaulieu, Ernest Brelay, Arthur Raffalovich, Henri Baudrillart, and G. de Molinari—focused more specifically on the flip side of the coin in setting out the reasons why such ventures could not be undertaken by public authorities. Like Le Play's group, the economists who became involved in the question of working-class housing were prominent men who moved in quasi-official circles. Leroy-Beaulieu, the foremost spokesman for liberal economics, founded the journal *L'Economiste français,* which carried articles throughout this period opposing public intervention in the housing market. He was a titular professor of finance at the Ecole libre des sciences politiques and a member of the Académie des sciences morales et politiques.[55] His colleague and collaborator H.J.L. Baudrillart enjoyed a similar career: he edited the *Journal des économistes,* taught political economy at the Ecole des ponts et chaussées and at the Collège de France, and was also a member of the Académie des sciences morales et politiques. Reminiscent of Picot, Leroy-Beaulieu tried without success to enter politics as a constitutional candidate in 1878 and as a monarchist in 1885, sustaining defeats by radical candidates. He was decorated by the Legion of Honor, as was his colleague Arthur Raffalovich, a descendant of a Russian-Jewish family of bankers who served as the agent for the Russian ministry of finances in Paris. Both Leroy-Beaulieu and Raffalovich were members of the English League for the Liberty and Defense of Property and its French counterpart, the Société pour la défense et le progrès social. The conservative credentials of this group of reformers were impeccable. They would mount, in the 1880s and 1890s, a vigorous campaign against the expansion of the public sector.

In the face of the apparent failure of private philanthropy, it had become "seductive," according to de Molinari, to entertain the prospect of "obligatory philanthropy" in which the municipalities and the state undertook the construction of inexpensive lodgings.[56] In the first place, Leroy-Beaulieu argued, the state must not become the competitor of private industry and thus discourage initiative on the part of individual entrepreneurs. He posited as a general rule that "where the state wishes to create abundance, it creates scarcity."[57] Baudrillart concurred, maintaining that by bringing "great distress to legitimate interests," public intervention would drive capital out of the building industry, retarding all progress.[58] Leroy-Beaulieu emphasized at the same time that it was unrealistic to believe that the state could build more cheaply and efficiently than could private enterprise. He claimed that profits on real property were not as dependable or constant as one might expect and noted that there was no reason to believe that public authorities would necessarily have greater wisdom or exercise greater circumspection than the multitude of joint-stock construction companies which had failed miserably. Public monies could not, he concluded, be put to such risk.[59] He argued further that it was unwise to enlarge the powers of municipal councils, which were frequently "incompetent, incoherent, and badly controlled financially," and supported his position with examples of the squandering of funds left in the charge of municipal authorities by a wealthy philanthropist.[60] Because the membership of municipal councils changed regularly, they tended to be more responsive to electoral pressures, leading, in the end, to unsound finance and arbitrary decisions.[61] Most importantly, Leroy-Beaulieu concluded, state enterprises inevitably were more costly, primarily because the state was so often moved by "the demands of the most turbulent of the electors" and was the first to capitulate to the wage demands of striking workers.[62] Political economists warned that state involvement in industrial activity did not sufficiently safeguard either the interests of the taxpayer or of the consumer.

Economic arguments were buttressed by moral ones. Workers who received assistance from the state would become, according to liberal economic theory, demoralized dependents. Arthur Raffalovich recited the familiar syndrome: government construction of working-class housing would raise taxes, demoralize workers, break their initiative, compromise their efforts to economize, and teach them to rely upon outside supports.[63] In speaking of municipal sponsorship of night refuges, Leroy-Beaulieu claimed that such institutions actually encouraged vagrancy and concluded that public philanthropy—that is, "legal charity"—when it became systematic and institutionalized, acknowledging assistance as a right, generated improvidence and misery for workers and blunted the sense of responsibility of the rich.[64] Baudrillart took this line of argument one step further, predicting that lazy workers who had become accustomed to state assistance would inevitably escalate their demands, ultimately threatening all property.[65] Leroy-Beaulieu also feared that rents paid to the state would increasingly tend to lose their essential character of a remuneration for services rendered and would come to be regarded as an abusive tax which ought to be resisted.[66] Frédéric Passy asked: "How can the law favor one group at the expense of another? . . . Where does this process stop? After having tried to secure lodging at a reduced price, why not free lodging; and after lodging, why not clothing, food, amusement, transportation, and the rest?"[67]

All of these concerns stemmed from deep convictions about the legitimate role of the state which were being called into question by the scope of the problem of working-class housing. Government intervention in the housing market appeared to be a form of state socialism—that is, a preparation for collectivism—and, as Leroy-Beaulieu intoned, "there is no good socialism, just as there is no good cholera."[68] Political economists recognized the state's responsibility to enforce existing legislation relating to unsanitary dwellings and acknowledged its authority to provide a sewer system and an inexpensive supply of high-quality water, while supervising the healthfulness of such public places as theaters, markets, and even lodging houses. But beyond these functions, public regulation became inappropriate. Leroy-Beaulieu observed that the state was, after all, simply the party in power, possessing therefore no special hold on the truth and, in fact, endowed by definition with vulnerabilities which rendered it eminently corruptible. He warned that its powers ought not, then, be enlarged: "The indefinite extension of the attributes of the state or of the municipalities is desirable neither for financial equilibrium and the clarity of budgets, nor for the independence of citizens and the impartiality of the administration."[69]

Although municipal and state cooperation to provide subsidies or tax exemptions to builders of low-rent housing emerged as a serious option in the early 1880s (see Chap. 5), actual construction by public powers was never a real alternative. It was left to private enterprise to satisfy the need for inexpensive lodgings, and numerous efforts were made to this end. Most projects failed, either because the constructions were too expensive for all but the elite of the working class, or because they were relatively unprofitable for the investors. One of the most frequently cited projects was the development built by the Société des habitations ouvrières de Passy-Auteuil, dubbed the El Dorado of its kind.[70] It consisted of small houses of four or five rooms with a garden in front and a courtyard in back, each selling at a cost of Fr 6,000. The rent was set at Fr 240 per year (4 percent of the cost), to which was added an additional Fr 240 for mortgage payments, totaling an annual expenditure of Fr 480, which would give the tenant possession after eighteen years.[71] It is clear that this scale of rent exceeded the budget of Parisian workers. Throughout the 1880s and 1890s, virtually all discussions of working-class housing acknowledged an absolute upper limit for rents of Fr 400 per year. Emile Cacheux, one of the founders of the Société immobilière de Passy-Auteuil, admitted that the models built were within reach of only a small minority of workers. He examined the budgets of 1,000 workers to determine who would be able to pay a yearly annuity of about Fr 400 and concluded "with regret that there were only a very few workers realizing any savings at all." Of the initial 1,000 households studied, only 129 enjoyed an annual excess of receipts over debts, and of these, only 33 would be able to accumulate enough savings to add to their annual rents (Fr 250–300) so as to reach the necessary Fr 400.[72] Haussonville noted, in addition, that the vast majority of savings accounts held small sums which would be quickly wiped out by unexpected illness or protracted unemployment.[73] Even Picot admitted the impracticality of the Passy-Auteuil project, stating that, whereas outside of London, small houses with three rooms and a garden cost Fr 222 per year (plus Fr 65 for transportation to the city), the Paris counterpart at Auteuil was considerably more costly because the land on which it was built was too expensive.[74]

A similar community built outside of Paris at Issy by E. Naud and Company was similarly irrelevant, in the end, to the problem of working-class housing. The first buildings, containing four rooms, were erected in 1883 and sold for Fr 7,000. By 1889, this company was building three basic models: some like the first; a second type including three bedrooms for Fr 11,000–15,000; and a larger model for Fr 25,000 with two or three rooms on the rez-de-chaussée, three bedrooms on the first floor, and one or two more on the second floor. Of the twenty-five houses sold or rented with a promise to sell, ten were occupied by bank clerks and employees in government and commerce, ten by merchants, three by persons from the liberal professions, and two by rentiers.[75]

The Société des constructions ouvrières de France did build modest housing in the largely working-class district of Buttes-Chaumont in the nineteenth arrondissement.[76] The houses cost Fr 6,000, and the worker became an owner by making a down payment of Fr 500 and paying Fr 389.64 for fifteen years (Fr 192.99 to the Société des maisons ouvrières and Fr 196.65 to the Crédit foncier). After fifteen years, the obligation to the Société would

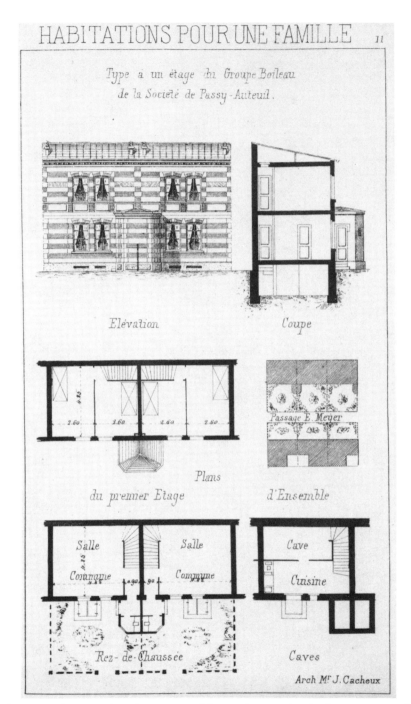

Type à un étage du Groupe Boileau de la Société de Passy-Auteuil.

Elévation Coupe

Plans

du premier Etage d'Ensemble

Rez-de-Chaussée Caves

Arch Mr J. Cacheux

The private home and garden promoted by Le Play's circle of reformers was realized in the cité ouvrière of Passy-Auteuil in arrondissement XVI. Emile Cacheux, *Etat des habitations ouvrières à la fin du XIXᵉ siècle* (Paris: Baudry, 1891).

be discharged, leaving payments of Fr 196.65 to the Crédit foncier for the next thirty-five years. Such a protracted amortization schedule assumed a stability in working-class life that simply did not exist. Cacheux remarked that he had been accused of building "for the aristocracy of misery," but he noted in his defense that inexpensive isolated dwellings were not feasible in the city.[77] It appears that, at least in Paris, projects which were economically viable for construction companies were beyond the resources of their targeted community.

In spite of this evident contradiction, the effort to stimulate private construction of individual houses for the working class persisted unabated in the final decades of the century, promoted largely by Le Play's followers.[78] Spearheaded by the efforts of Jules Siegfried,[79] reformers mounted a campaign to make the construction of working-class housing financially practicable. This effort culminated in the 1894 law on *habitations à bon marché*. The objectives of the legislation were to make credit available to construction societies, to favor low-cost housing with tax exemptions, and to promote the integral transfer of property to an heir on the death of the primary owner. Siegfried observed that home-ownership by workers had been inhibited primarily by two factors: French investors preferred government bonds and railroad stocks to real estate and construction, and the civil law provided that, at the death of the father, the inheritance be shared, a formality which generated so many fees and expenses that the heirs were often left nearly penniless.[80] According to the provisions of the 1894 law, builders were granted a five-year exemption from real property taxes and doors and windows taxes, and shares of construction societies were exonerated from the tax on revenues from stocks and shares and from lesser accessory fees. The measure further permitted relief committees, hospices, savings banks, and the Bank of Deposits and Consignations to place one-fifth of their funds in the construction of low-cost housing. At the same time, the law addressed the issue of the conservation of estates. It stipulated that the worker could pay a light tax each month in addition to the rent and amortization fees; this tax would be reimbursed at his death in order to guarantee uninterrupted mortgage payments. Article 8, called by *La Réforme sociale* "the most important innovation," revised the civil code so as to preserve the integrity of *le petit foyer de famille*. The new law provided that the inheritance be maintained intact until the children reached majority, at which time the parties could agree to award possession of the home to one member of the family. Local committees (*comités des habitations à bon marché*) were to be set up in each department, supervised by a Superior Council on Low-Cost Housing to study all facets of the issue and to facilitate the application of the law. In reporting on Siegfried's bill to the Chamber of Deputies, M. Vian observed:

> Today [the worker] lives in a city, in a collective house, in a single room, poorly ventilated, unclean, unsanitary, where his landlord charges him dearly, and where nothing holds him aside from the hours when he is sleeping or ill. . . . M. Siegfried's proposition is sincerely inspired by a democratic sentiment. . . . It aims to realize in the social order a progressive step which above all offers the workers an influence which is beneficent, elevating, and pacificatory.[81]

These auspicious goals notwithstanding, the Siegfried law failed to produce the desired results. One disappointed commentator noted that "the confidence placed in private initiative was misplaced. . . . Few committees function regularly with any appreciable results. Some claim that they cannot act because of lack of resources. Others are held up by formalistic preoccupations and questions of detail, and others (e.g., Lyons) claim that there is sufficient healthful, low-cost housing in their district so as to render the committee superfluous."[82] The reasons for the law's ineffectiveness are not hard to find. In the first place, the 1894 legislation made the formation of local committees optional, a loophole which was not closed until a new act in 1906 provided that one or two committees, with operating funds, be established in each department.[83] Nor did the law establish sufficient tax incentives to appreciably increase the appeal of building low-cost housing. Cacheux documented the heavy charges which encumbered real property in Paris. The roadway expenses (street, water, and sewer) were as much as Fr 400 per meter, while the taxes for a house with a rental of Fr 300–400 might be as high as Fr 120.[84] The advantages actually conferred by the Siegfried law were minimal: it extended the current two-year exemption of new houses from the doors and windows tax to five years (Siegfried had asked for a twelve-year moratorium), while the average savings on property taxes amounted to a mere Fr 8.90 annually.[85] The law did exempt societies for low-cost housing from mortmain taxes, licensing taxes, and stamp and registration fees for acts creating or dissolving these societies. But because few societies functioned regularly, these exemptions were irrelevant.

Perhaps most important in the end was the basic reluctance of the French to invest in working-class housing. The transfer of funds from charitable and savings societies to the construction industry simply did not occur in spite of the flow of circulars from the minister of the interior to administrative commissions reminding them of their options.[86] Siegfried lamented this intransigence: "It is curious to note," he observed, "how the French, so bold, so revolutionary even in politics, become reserved, prudent, even timid when it comes to the handling of funds."[87] It appeared that appropriate legislation and formal institutions could not, in themselves, generate the desired social progress.

Siegfried's contemporaries were not altogether surprised by the difficulties encountered by attempts to promote low-cost single-family housing. On the one hand, police and health regulations regarding the construction of roadways, sidewalks, gutters, and drainage pipes in the city added substantially to building costs, while the high price of land in effect mandated commercial enterprises for street-level properties.[88] On the other, suburban construction was not an acceptable remedy, since urban workers needed, above all, to reside near potential worksites. Du Mesnil repeatedly emphasized the very obvious lack of sanitary lodgings for the thousands of Parisian workers involved in the reception and marketing of food and in sanitation and maintenance in Les Halles, an area perennially surrounded by horrible slums.[89] In a perceptive study of overcrowding and low-cost housing, Henri Turot and Henri Bellamy criticized the sociologists and philanthropists who rigidly adhered to their image of the suburban worker surrounded by family and garden. They pointed, even beyond the obvious time and expense of traveling, to the material deprivation involved in an exodus from the city. Workers would lose the advantages of hospitals, relief organizations, crèches, and schools.[90]

The very prospect of home-ownership itself presented some serious drawbacks, particularly if the housing was connected to a suburban factory or mine. Turot and Bellamy argued that when a worker was paying off a mortgage to his employer and was locked into his residence, he placed himself in an inferior bargaining position regarding conditions of work. They concluded that the question of inexpensive lodgings had to be clearly separated from the problematical issue of proprietorship.[91] Affirmation of this point of view came from a surprising diversity of sources. The socialist Benoît Malon noted that, while cités ouvrières might be well intentioned, it was impossible not to recognize that by tying the worker to a fifteen- to twenty-year mortgage, the employer increased the worker's burdens and diminished his economic leverage, making changes of employment and strikes more difficult.[92] Police reports confirmed that workers paying mortgages to factory employers were the least able to sustain a strike,[93] while even Brelay in *La Réforme sociale* admitted that factory housing automatically became implicated in the level of wages and that the worker would inevitably find it distasteful to return to a home which suggested the pervasiveness of the authority of the patron.[94] Haussonville romanticized the worker's perspective: "For him, to be bound by a contract to live under the same roof for twenty years, to work in the same factory, to bury all economies in the same spot, is to rivet himself once again to the soil [glebe], to cut the wings of his hopes and to renounce the dreams of fortune and grandeur which haunt his imagination."[95]

In recognition of the difficulties of the Mulhouse model, Du Mesnil, along with other hygienists and with municipal authorities, urged that collective buildings containing inexpensive lodgings be built in the city. Yet Cacheux observed in 1891 that it had become impossible to reestablish mixed housing in Paris, that the division between bourgeois and worker had become too profound. The garrets and upper stories originally inhabited by the working class had increasingly been taken over by domestics serving the bourgeois families below, and the worker was too proud to inhabit servants' quarters.[96] On the other hand, urban cités ouvrières had frequently been preempted by tenants of a higher social class than that for which they were originally intended, or had deteriorated into overcrowded and unsanitary slums. At any rate, such collective dwellings aroused bourgeois fears and were unacceptable on both moral and political grounds. Their suburban counterparts were too costly and inconvenient. In the absence of a clear alternative, Le Play's strategy continued to offer a positive prognosis for an apparently insoluble dilemma, based at least upon a coherent, if flawed, vision of the direction of social change.

A RETREAT INTO ENLIGHTENED PATERNALISM

As the program of the social scientists became in practice as chimerical as that of the socialists, financial conservatives continued to warn against the adoption of heroic remedies. Leroy-Beaulieu argued that the abuses accompanying the system of private property must be accepted because the system itself was so beneficial and, in fact, necessary to general prosperity.[97] Increasingly, the writings of the political economists conveyed a mood of resignation toward poverty, which had apparently become a permanent and intractable social fact. Baudrillart observed that industrialization, with all its material benefits, also brought "destructive socialism, strikes and violence, and unhealthful housing."[98] This was simply the dark side of contemporary life, the unfortunate concomitant of progress. It seemed unrealistic to expect to be able to satisfy all the needs of the undeserving poor—the residuum. Raffalovich drew the inevitable conclusion; "Against extreme poverty there is no remedy; pauperism is incurable";[99] Passy concluded that "it is better for the worker to have a cramped, somber, humid dwelling than none at all."[100] Echoing this conclusion, Leroy-Beaulieu noted that "what is to us a hovel is for the lowest class a sort of Eden" and criticized the "superficial philanthropy" which engineered the destruction of the legendary Cité des Kroumirs, removing a slum but forcing its poor inhabitants to seek even more precarious shelters.[101] The poor would have to continue to be inadequately housed because of the meagerness of their resources. There appeared to be no alternative.

This resignation was rationalized by a moral judgment. Rarely did these writers discuss poverty as a cause of miserable living conditions,[102]

and some implied that the worker would choose his slum rather than be-
have more responsibly. Leroy-Beaulieu stated: "It is said that a decline in
the number of unhealthful lodgings will force the worker to spend more
on housing and less on drink. . . . But there is always an element which
considers housing only as a shelter against weather." Brelay was even more
explicit: "No one compels workers to live in unsanitary housing. They do
so by choice and are free to leave." According to Brelay, poverty could be
the result of circumstances, but was certainly also connected to laziness
and intemperance.[103] Passy rushed to second this explanation. He claimed
that the causes of great miseries are often not what they seem. For example, an investigation of the grim plight of English handloom weavers indicated that these unfortunates who chose not to enter factories and to
continue weaving by hand did so because it was an easy trade; they were
without ambition or perseverance. According to Passy, indolence, improvidence, and ignorance were the most frequent causes of misery.[104]

It seemed clear to Leroy-Beaulieu and his colleagues that the worker
was largely responsible for his circumstances. Poverty might dictate modest lodgings, but bad habits and uncleanliness, according to bourgeois observers, turned lodgings into slums. Leroy-Beaulieu stated: "It is necessary
to guard against sentimentalism. Unhealthy dwellings come most often from
the lack of care and cleanliness of those who inhabit them. . . . Real progress, then, is the progress of hygiene, of its popularization."[105] Brelay argued in a similar vein that before putting workers into new housing, it would
be necessary to instill habits of discipline and cleanliness, respect for neighbors, and punctuality in meeting obligations.[106] Baudrillart claimed that
among the most significant factors inhibiting housing reform were the inertia of the workers themselves and their long-standing habits of uncleanliness. He expressed some distress at the same time that reformers were not
always well received—"a strange situation for friends of the working class."
In Baudrillart's words, "Sometimes the workers exhibit an excessive resignation while at other times, they express impatient and unreasoned demands
which reject the best solutions in favor of chimerical desires."[107] Whether
the difficulties lay in external factors or in the perversity of the working
class, the conclusion was the same: "The intervention of the state cannot
provide a remedy for either the insufficiency of wages or for the depraved
habits of the poor."[108]

The acceptance of the status quo implicit in this perspective did not
reflect an entirely pessimistic viewpoint, however. On the contrary, Leroy-
Beaulieu insisted that the intensity of the social and material crises of the
preceding half-century was in fact subsiding on the basis of its own inter-
nal dynamics. Critics of capitalism had claimed that urban real property
ought to be held in common, or, at the least, profits from real estate ought

to be regulated because the growth of the city and municipal building projects had enriched a class who profited while contributing nothing. Answer-
ing these charges, Leroy-Beaulieu maintained that the dislocations of 1840–
80 were unique, part of a transition to a period of slower growth and shrink-
ing profits in real estate which would narrow the gap between the fortunes
of landlords and tenants. The operation of long-term economic trends would
theoretically produce an economically more balanced society; the housing
situation would remedy itself. He wrote in 1883:

> We are leaving what I have called "the chaotic period" of large-scale in-
> dustry, a period of transformation, agitation, suffering, groping. Sis-
> mondi, Villermé, the elder Blanqui were right to be alarmed at all the
> misfortune which accompanied this age of transition. These misfortunes
> are all, by nature, temporary: if they have not yet disappeared, they are in
> the process of disappearing. Modern society is moving toward a state
> which will be characterized by a smaller inequality of conditions. The
> social question, to the extent that it is resolvable, will resolve itself, gradu-
> ally, by the continuous action of large economic forces which have been
> operating for several years. Any revolutionary action of the state to hasten
> this movement will only impede and retard it.[109]

More specifically, the housing market provided economists with a case
study of the operation of the laws of supply and demand. Passy articulated
the harsher directives of laissez-faire principles: "Crisis is the only remedy
for crisis."[110] But from a more positive point of view, there was a general
expectation that sluggishness in the construction industry would discourage provincials from coming to the city or cause an exodus of the unemployed, while overdevelopment of bourgeois dwellings would force builders to turn their attentions to working-class lodgings.[111]

Although economists denied the state any role in this process, they
did encourage public authorities to manipulate the tax structure so as to
reduce the cost of basic necessities for all classes. The principle defining
legitimate tax policy was that it not be "class legislation" favoring one group
of citizens over another or penalizing one segment of taxpayers. Leroy-
Beaulieu wrote: "The state and the cities are not obliged to sacrifice in order
to make human conditions more equal; they do not even have the right
to do so. But neither are they prevented from coming to the aid of the working classes by loans or by other measures which cost taxpayers nothing."[112]
He claimed that the problem of workers' housing could be substantially
alleviated without direct expenditures or subsidies simply by "well-ordered
public finance." Especially important would be the elimination of the octroi tax on construction materials, which added 5 or 6 percent to the cost
of a house in Paris, and the reduction of transfer and registration fees, which

raised the selling price of a house by 10 percent and hence increased the likelihood that the new tenant would be of a slightly higher social class than his predecessor. [113] He further recommended reducing to a minimum the cost of sewers, water, and lighting, and decreasing transportation costs by reducing licensing fees on public vehicles. [114] Beyond tax measures, economists frequently mentioned the need to change the custom requiring rent payments for the trimester in advance, in favor of payment by the week or month. [115] All of these propositions represented an effort to tinker with small mechanisms within the system while scrupulously avoiding any challenge to the system itself.

In the final years of the century, the writings of both the economists on the one hand, and Picot, Cheysson, Siegfried, and their colleagues on the other, exhibit a subtle shift in emphasis. The hopeful predictions of the 1860s, 1870s, and 1880s had failed to materialize; the working class had not become homeowners, respectable pères de famille, living side-by-side with the established classes. In fact, an increasingly politicized working class had become more articulate, better organized, and more threatening. The classes dirigeantes met the situation with a solution which was perhaps even more anachronistic than the promotion of worker-proprietors and equally as naive. Echoing the rhetoric of solidarism, they called upon the wealthy and the privileged to extend their protection to the worker. In the face of the persistence of poverty, in the end all that was left was an updated paternalism and the hope for peaceful coexistence.

In the last year of the nineteenth century Leroy-Beaulieu acknowledged that his earlier analysis of the social question, expressed most completely in *De l'état moral et intellectuel des classes ouvrières* in 1868, had been inadequate. The material problems of the working population had not been relieved through moral education. [116] He observed that the worker of 1899, "so turbulent, so hostile to society, so openly communist," had been amply provided with primary education without its having produced a moral transformation. He noted once again that the least docile workers were also the most skilled and the most literate, that the groups most taken with socialism were the ones whose futures were most secure. Anticipating modern theories of revolutionary behavior based upon relative deprivation, he concluded that it was not material suffering which provoked and embittered the working population, but rather "the scandal of corrupted customs," of riches extravagantly and irresponsibly paraded before men "too prone to envy." [117] He argued that if workers were suddenly to earn 10 francs per day for eight hours of work, socialism would lose little of its force because the crisis was produced, rather, by a moral disorder: the envy of the poor rubbing up against the vanity and extravagance of the rich. He accused the rich of having become a caste of parvenus and adventurers, sterile idlers unwilling to put their wealth to social use. "Do you think there would be," he asked, "many socialists in a nation which counted a large number of Peabodys?" The obvious solution was to reawaken the privileged to the "sentiment of responsibility and the spirit of sacrifice" in keeping with the natural functions of wealth so as to re-create social bonds which had been severed by recent economic developments.

By the 1890s, Picot and Cheysson were similarly trying to check the momentum of the socialists while keeping alive the image of a society without class divisions or, at the least, without class antagonism. Cheysson spoke of the need to develop an *esprit de corps* within industry which identified workers and employers as part of a single team — *la famille ouvrière.*[118] In spite of increasing class antagonisms due to advancing industrialization and working-class self-consciousness, Cheysson revived Saint-Simon's dream of a harmony of interests among "the productive classes." In fact, this dream had never really disappeared from public pronouncements. In 1875, Melun reported to the National Assembly that "the patron is not a master in the absolute sense of the word; he is the first member of the great family of workers in which those who direct and those who execute participate equally."[119] Although he acknoweldged that paternalism had lost its legitimacy, rather than abandon it Cheysson urged that it become more discreet:

> Wherever [there are] these ideas of defiance and antagonism, unfortunately so widespread today, the protection of workers, no matter how beneficent it may be, has had its day, because it repels and offends them as a constraint on their liberty. As prudent employers take into account this touchy disposition, they substitute, more and more, a discreet protection for their more apparent or direct actions. . . . Patronage must reclothe itself . . . in a form more appropriate to contemporary customs, and at the same time, to political and social conditions.[120]

In 1909, Cheysson wrote that "what was formerly '*noblesse oblige*' is now '*supériorité oblige*,' that devotion to others was the ransom for privilege."[121] In whatever form, the goal was to connect workers to their patrons with durable bonds. Cheysson rejected state interference, however. He pointed to the unfortunate example of Germany, where all forms of insurance (accident, old age, illness) had become mandatory, allegedly causing both the generosity of the employer and the gratitude of the worker to dry up. According to Cheysson, the enactment of legal obligations "disturbs the tête-à-tête within the industrial family with the intervention of the inspector and the tax collector."[122] Instead, he encouraged the French to remain loyal to their national traditions, thus giving added "richness and flexibility" to their solutions, and to limit the state to conducting investigations and to promoting, in subtler ways, interclass solidarity. Specifically, Cheysson recommended that industrialists and businessmen be decorated for their technical expertise only when it was accompanied by acts of social merit. By awarding such honorific incentives, Cheysson expected employers to turn their efforts toward the welfare of their employees.[123] Picot similarly counseled patrons to interest themselves in the families of their workers. As evidence of concern, he recommended that the employer disperse wages on Thursday morning rather than on Saturday night, thus avoiding "the entrapment of the café."[124]

In a more political vein, Picot reemphasized the need for the conservative forces to control the direction of social change. In order to preempt the appeal of the radicals and the socialists, it was incumbent upon representatives of the classes dirigeantes to address directly a series of issues which had heightened antagonisms. Picot wrote in 1896 that "far from blaming reforms, the conservative party must make them the basis of its program. This should not astonish! With our neighbors to the north, in Brussels as in London, the great organic laws of reform were the product of conservative ministries."[125] The goal was to pursue numerous precise reforms that would indicate that the interests of capital and labor were not, at bottom, contradictory. Acceptable remedies included revision of the criminal code, reform of the press law of 1881, administrative decentralization, and streamlining of the committee system in particular and the legislative process in general. At the same time, reformers might encourage the development of food and construction cooperatives, savings and mutual-aid societies, and retirement plans.[126] Picot suggested that the employer hold back part of the weekly wages to be returned in a lump sum at the end of the year to pay for insurance plans.[127] It seems that Picot had arrived at the same conclusion as had Leroy-Beaulieu—that it was not the material wants or the inadequate income of the worker which triggered his discontent, but rather "a host of small injustices."[128] Although the followers of Le Play rejected the passive role adopted by many economists, bourgeois reformers, both social scientists and political economists, dismissed heroic remedies in the hopes of vindicating private initiative informed by enlightened philanthropy.

In the last decades of the century, then, bourgeois reformers worked to stem the tide of social and political change. Housing reform became, for them, the most promising means to resocialize a working class which appeared ever more menacing in its size, life style, and level of organization. The concept of the worker-proprietor surrounded by family and garden in the unpolluted suburban environment seemed to offer precisely that degree of participation in the existing regime which would transform a potential combattant into a père de famille. The promotion of the Mulhouse-style cité ouvrière thus constituted a strategy based on the use of physical space to redefine social space in more acceptable terms. It was appealing at the same time because it conformed to cherished dogmas of economic liberalism. Free enterprise was to provide the context for the emergence of a morally regenerated, materially secure, and politically docile working class. However, the high price of land and the high cost of construction in Paris, coupled with inadequate suburban transportation, relegated the cité ouvrière to the status of a peripheral remedy, serving the needs of a tiny elite segment of the working class. The voluminous literature on the subject obscures the minimal achievements effected during this period. The classes dirigeantes had produced a solution providing greater ideological than material satisfaction. The proletariat had not disappeared.

CH. 5 Housing and Municipal Politics

PUBLIC health concerns and social anxieties had fueled efforts to improve housing conditions for the working class. But the problem of inadequate housing turned, finally, on political issues, either thrust insistently forward or allowed to slide into the shadows by the specific political context. The continuing efforts of hygienists and reformers to improve conditions remained a mere chipping away at the surface of a chronic, worrisome, but somewhat distant problem unless framed and given focus by more immediate political needs. It was, for example, the upheavals of 1848 which evoked the first regulatory legislation, while Napoleon's desire to tie the working classes to their imperial benefactor elicited a brief interest in public sponsorship of workers' housing during the Second Empire. Napoleon's success in pacifying the population, however, removed housing reform from official agendas, and the issue was to reemerge only with the mounting criticism of Haussmann and Napoleon in the closing years of the empire. The reforms of the Commune, which included a moratorium on rents, were, of course, repudiated, and in the immediate succeeding years, problems of order dwarfed all other concerns, while the sharp decline in the Parisian population provided a temporary reprieve to the housing shortage. In the early 1880s, however, a unique combination of circumstances brought the issue of working-class housing to the fore again with a new and compelling urgency.

The coincidence of rising rents, economic recession, and socialist agitation endowed housing issues, in the opening years of the Third Republic, with a serious claim on public attention. The largest wave of immigration of the century, between 1876 and 1881, produced acute housing shortages. (See above, Chap. 3.) An economic slowdown in 1883 and 1884 and a slump in the building industry followed closely upon this extraor-

dinary spurt of growth. And, most important, a fragile political equilibrium undermined the ability of the city to accommodate concurrent economic and demographic dislocation. Newly organized socialist groups were
demanding higher standards of material well-being and a radical reorien-
tation of social and political priorities. It was, then, the proliferation of
socialist schemes couched in radical rhetoric which encouraged public authorities to undertake a careful review of more moderate reform strategies.

The Municipal Council of the Third Republic was, for the first time,
an elected body chosen by universal male suffrage, although it continued
to share administrative authority for Paris with the prefect of the Seine. The
careful manipulation of the council practiced so assiduously by Haussmann
disappeared with the emergence of a popularly elected body, responsible
directly to its constituents. Councilors were therefore receptive in the 1880s
to projects designed to improve housing conditions in the city and con-
templated a higher level of public responsibility for urban housing than
had been suggested since the half-hearted efforts of Napoleon III in the
1850s. The council considered wide-ranging proposals to increase the supply of inexpensive housing that conformed to both sanitary and construction standards. This activity did not, however, produce results. Its failure
marked a turning point in the movement for housing reform which closed
the issue of government sponsorship and official subsidy for the remainder of the century and opened the way, instead, to the more limited sanitary objectives pursued by hygienists and to the fragmentary efforts of private
enterprise. As the intensity of the political challenge faded, so did the determination to create new, inexpensive housing.

POLITICAL PRESSURES

Although working-class issues remained secondary in the decade following the Commune, the problem of exorbitant rents became volatile once
again by 1879. Reports passing between municipal police officers and the
Prefecture of Police indicate that the prospect of increased traffic and windfall gains presented by the International Exposition of 1878 in Paris caused
a precipitous rise in rents. Until the beginning of 1879, workers apparently
endured the new charges with the expectation that rents would shortly return to more normal levels, but when this failed to happen, worker discontent became more vocal. Spokesmen in the thirteenth and twentieth arrondissements asked the Municipal Council to examine the question, and
a petition drawn by Republican-Communalists of the fourteenth arrondissement voiced the popular complaint that the Municipal Council had been
preoccupied with politics while maintaining a "heart-breaking indifference"
to social issues.[1]

It seems clear that heightened political activity among urban workers during 1879–83 was sufficiently disturbing to authorities to draw public attention to housing problems. Banished Communards who had been granted amnesty in 1879 returned to Paris and joined the score of newly formed socialist organizations. Throughout 1882 and 1883, socialist groups spanning a wide ideological spectrum met regularly. They identified working-class housing as a focus for confrontation with both the national and municipal governments. Not surprisingly, then, official interest in housing conditions was first funneled through those responsible for maintaining public order. All requests to hold public meetings had to be approved by police authorities in order to assure that gatherings of significant size could be closely monitored. Thus, in spite of the fact that socialist meetings on rents and housing were rarely inflammatory and were increasingly poorly attended as the issues dragged on without resolution,[2] the continuous flow of reports between the local police and central authorities for Paris surrounded housing problems with an aura of urgency.

Spokesmen for the working classes were beginning to organize in ways which did, in fact, suggest an immediate challenge, and rumors of organized banditry circulated widely. Throughout this period, activists proposed strikes and petitions, which were designed, in large part, to keep the housing issue before the public consciousness. In March 1881, the municipal chief of police reported that "revolutionary committees" were organizing a new kind of strike, that of tenants against landlords. Tenants were to force their own expulsion by refusing to pay rents, whereupon they would descend into the streets with their children and possessions in sufficient numbers to embarrass the government. Reports of this proposed strike continued throughout June and July of that year.[3] Similarly, in the summer of 1882, Paul Lafargue, Marx's son-in-law and an important activist in Paris, urged the formation of a league of tenants to orchestrate resistance. Should a proprietor attempt to confiscate property in order to cover his losses, league members were to assemble at the specified house to intimidate the landlord.[4] The few attempts at nonpayment which did occur received extensive publicity. According to Le Temps, on July 15, 1883, "The proposition, so often formulated in revolutionary meetings, of not paying landlords in order to resolve the crisis in rents has just received its first application. A proprietor named C____ was not able to prevent the removal of one of his tenants, named Couchot, who, aided by his comrades, carried away his furniture without paying his rent to the cry of 'Long Live the Commune!'"[5] The same story was repeated on July 20 in Le Figaro and in La Patrie, which added that the eight people who participated in the evacuation were part of a roving band operating against landlords.

The fears of the authorities seem to have preceded the actual events.

Police reports indicate that in August 1883 there was an organizational meeting of a group of socialists to establish the League for Urban and Rural Rent Strikes.[6] This was to be a support group for tenants wishing to default on overdue rents. It would propagandize the idea of a general suspension of rent payments while offering moral and material assistance to strikers—assistance which included locking up the concierge until furniture and possessions had been removed to a safe place.[7] The league held several meetings in September and October and then apparently dissolved, as no further reference to it occurs in police records.

During the same summer, a Congress on the Question of Rents began meeting throughout the city. Attendance was usually quite small, and the meetings attracted only scattered coverage in the press. In November, the congress issued a report of its work and a summary of the proposals put forward by a broad array of working-class groups. The report called for an end to the sale of communal lands, the creation of mixed housing in all quarters, a ceiling on rents in proportion to the profits earned by the building, the allocation of Fr 50 million annually for the construction of municipal housing to be built by workers' associations, the suppression of insalubrious buildings, and a progressive tax on rents.

The Marxists, led by Jules Guesde, particularly favored highly visible activities which would dramatize discontent and focus resistance. Guesde took the Irish Land League as a model for protest and urged that a massive petition demanding a tax on rents be presented to the Chamber of Deputies accompanied by at least 5,000 petitioners.[8] He proposed rent reductions of 50 percent for lodgings below Fr 400 annual rent, 40 percent for lodgings with rents of Fr 400–1,000, and 30 percent for lodgings of Fr 1,000–4,000. Guesde claimed that it was fairly easy to clear a 20 percent profit on capital invested in housing. He therefore concluded that "with a reduction of 50 percent, this still leaves to 'paternalistic idleness' an income of 10 percent—a fairly nice tip!" Although Guesde admitted that he had virtually no hopes that his demands would be met, he saw the petition as "a good pretext for revolutionary agitation."[9] During the summer of 1882 there were reports that 4,000 signatures had been obtained, although the project was abandoned in the fall.

Socialists met regularly throughout 1882 and into the spring of 1883 to discuss strategies for reducing rents and for assuring a larger supply of inexpensive lodgings. There was little coordination or cohesiveness among the groups. For example, police archives reveal that in arrondissement XIV, public meetings were held by Revolutionary Collectivists, Radical Socialists, and Communalists, while the Socialist-Republican Alliance met in arrondissements X, XI, and XIII, the Radical Democrats met in VII, and so on. The cast of speakers sharing the podium typically sniped at each other over acceptable tactics and priorities, reflecting an unresolved dilemma between the desire to formulate principles and the need to devise practical solutions. A familiar set of objectives emerged, including the destruction of the ancient and obsolete wall of fortifications which surrounded the city and the construction of workers' housing in the no-man's-land between the fortifications and the octroi wall which marked the city limits, the expulsion of foreign workers from the capital, halting the sale of communal land, limiting the profits of housing speculators, and even the immediate confiscation of all property within the city for public use.[10]

Jules Joffrin was one of the most energetic spokesmen for workers' interests and the first working-class socialist to sit on the Municipal Council after the Commune.[11] An adherent of Paul Brousse's possibilist school of municipal socialism, which represented the largest segment of the Parisian working class, he advocated the gradual takeover of all public services by the city.[12] Joffrin agitated for a two-fold program of housing reform: an immediate tax on lodgings vacant more than a month in order to penalize proprietors who artificially sustained high rentals at no personal expense and the construction of working-class housing (cités ouvrières) on a large scale by the city.[13] Joffrin maintained, correctly, that there were more bourgeois lodgings than there were bourgeois families to fill them—that in the eleventh and seventeenth arrondissements, for example, entire streets remained uninhabited because of greedy proprietors with "exaggerated pretensions" who refused to bow to the dictates of the market and left apartments vacant rather than lower rents.[14] He claimed, further, that the problems of supply could not be solved without extensive construction of municipal housing.

Guesde and the Marxists opposed Joffrin's proposals for a variety of reasons. On a theoretical level, they resisted piecemeal improvements within the existing system which led away from political revolution. The establishment of municipal housing would, according to Guesde, accustom workers to the idea of cooperation with the bourgeoisie, diminishing the appeal of the Marxist Parti ouvrier, and would encourage respect for capitalist property instead of preparing the way for eventual expropriation.[15] In the program of the Workers' Party of 1883, Guesde noted the "organic impotence of the municipality" to solve the social problems of the working class and attacked the "monomaniacs of possibilism" who closed the eyes of the working class and diverted its efforts.[16] Guesde decided, nevertheless, that in order to politicize the recalcitrant proletariat, it would be useful to publicize everyday grievances. Accordingly, he considered the campaign to lower rents as "a veritable factory to forge socialists and revolutionaries."[17] The fact that the resulting petition would be rejected was, therefore, all the more reason to instigate it as a technique to expose public authorities as mere agents of the property-owning classes.

On a more immediate level, Guesde spoke for a sizeable group of so-cialists who opposed the ghettoization of workers in cités ouvrières. He argued that such housing could accommodate only a small fraction of the working class, and these would necessarily be the hand-picked choice of the employers—that is to say, the most docile element. The inevitable out-come would be the creation of a new privileged group. Guesde suggested that the betrayal implicit in Joffrin's plan could be inferred from the fact that representatives of the bourgeoisie favored it.[18] He described the sinis-ter potential of workers' housing set just beyond the fortifications, "under the guns of the oppressors," where insurgency could be violently suppressed without shedding a drop of bourgeois blood:

> This transportation of workers [la chair à travail] out of Paris whom [they] are not for the moment able to send to New Caledonia, appears preferable [to them] than the reduction of the proprietor's tithe which we demand. The ancient ghetto of the Jews will be succeeded by the workers' ghetto, which will be readily flanked by barracks, permitting the machine-gunners of order to fire at the least provocation without risk to a single bourgeois.[19]

With less rhetorical flourish but with equal conviction, Voisin, a socialist municipal councilor, opposed the cité ouvrière, observing that the Parisian working class would never consent to be "penned in like sheep," or sub-jected to the stringent personal regulations which typically characterized workers' housing complexes such as those in London.[20]

The fragmentation of the socialist challenge ultimately defused its impact. But the barrage of propaganda that was spread through public meetings and the persistent threat of strikes and demonstrations combined to suggest that the socialist menace was indeed quite real. This was par-ticularly true because 1883 and 1884 were years of economic dislocation which witnessed numerous bankruptcies, extensive unemployment, and a particularly acute recession in the building industry. In response to the in-dustrial crisis, the government ordered an official investigation of its causes and extent.[21] In a revealing series of reports, local police commissioners tended to attribute the recession to labor's stubbornness—especially to the high wages demanded by Parisian workers and the absence of "bonds of solidarity" between employers and employees—while noting, somewhat sec-ondarily, the impact of competition from German goods and the removal of French entrepreneurs to foreign countries where they had access to less costly raw materials and labor. The building trades were in particular trouble because of overdevelopment during the preceding boom period and over-speculation by entrepreneurs, who had borrowed at high rates of interest.

The police commissioner of the quarter Sainte Marguerite in the eleventh arrondissement estimated that of the 25,000 cabinetmakers and 5,000 joiners in his district, two-thirds were without work in March 1883. A similar report was issued in the twelfth arrondissement, while a report in May 1883 indicated that 26,000 out of 80,000 workers in construction-related jobs were unemployed, including excavators, masons, carpenters, and ironworkers. The situation in the spring of 1883 was especially critical because an unusually mild February had drawn large numbers of provincial workers in the building trades to Paris. A rapid drop in the temperature shut down construction work, adding to the numbers of deserted workshops and unemployed laborers.[22]

It was thus the coincidence of socialist agitation and industrial recession in the early 1880s which triggered an effort by public authorities to devise more realistic strategies for assuring a larger supply of inexpensive housing. Both republicans and conservatives rushed to retrieve the housing problem from the arms of "revolutionary socialism." Although there had been no discussions of housing in the Municipal Council between 1870 and 1879, proposals began to appear throughout 1880–82, and by 1883 and 1884, the council was meeting regularly to consider schemes to improve housing conditions.[23] These discussions are significant because they deal directly with the problem of providing additional housing *within* the city. They focus, for the first time, on the issues of real estate speculation and high rentals and on the creation of new lodgings in the center with controlled rent scales.

THE POSSIBILITY OF MUNICIPAL SPONSORSHIP

Proposals submitted to the Municipal Council incorporated a wide variety of strategies to increase the supply of modest lodgings. The most radical, urged repeatedly by Lucien Manier, called for the appropriation for reasons of public utility of all buildings within the city. Joffrin and the possibilists continued to press for direct construction by the municipality and penalty taxes on vacant lodgings. Neither of these initiatives, so aggressively socialist, attracted serious official attention. Discussion focused, rather, on more moderate projects which involved indirect fiscal incentives and a generally less prominent role for the city. Several projects, for example, recommended that the city lease its holdings to workers' associations for ninety-nine years with favorable amortization schedules, tax exemptions, and reduced rates for water and gas. Another project, preserving the exclusively fiscal role of the administration, suggested that working-class housing be financed by revenues raised from levying taxes on migrants to the city (yielding, hypothetically, an estimated Fr 18.5 million per year).

And retreating even further from direct involvement, one councilor urged that the city require those purchasing municipal lands to build on them within a year, noting that in several arrondissements, especially in the twentieth, a large number of properties previously owned by the commune remained undeveloped as speculators waited for substantial appreciation.[24]

As interest in the housing shortage continued to accelerate, the growing number of individual propositions prompted a report by a special commission of the Municipal Council. In February 1883, Theodore Villard issued a summary of the findings of his commission.[25] In spite of voluminous subsequent debate, the conclusions of this first report laid down the basic outlines—and even more, the basic ambiguities and resistances—which characterized the municipal approach to working-class housing for the remainder of the century.

While refusing to endorse any particular proposal, the Villard report did identify the construction of mixed housing, with bourgeois occupants on the lower floors and working-class tenants above, as the ultimate objective of municipal housing strategies. This commitment to an older pattern of usage which had begun to disappear during the rebuilding of the Second Empire suggested a means to lessen class antagonisms and to promote principles of social solidarity. To further this end, official discussions gradually adopted the phrase "low-rent housing" rather than "working-class housing" in symbolic denial of class divisions. Workers and bourgeois were to be reconciled through the experience of structured proximity. In addition, the commission's sponsorship of mixed housing reflected practical considerations. Although private industry continued to favor the Mulhouse model of small single-family units in the suburbs, the Municipal Council explicitly acknowledged that such schemes were inappropriate to Paris, where land was expensive and where workers typically moved their lodgings so as to be near potential worksites. The model of small suburban villages such as those flanking London could not be transferred to the Parisian context because the workday was longer, the continuity of employment unsure, and the transportation system deficient.

The report remained vague as to how to generate an enlarged stock of mixed housing, but it rejected unequivocally direct construction by the city. The commission concluded that such constructions would inevitably be more costly and that additional expenses assumed by the city would require the raising of compensatory revenues, fueling a vicious, pointless circle. Moreover, municipal housing would involve the city, in its capacity as an ordinary landlord, in a morass of administrative difficulties. Councilors argued throughout this period that public housing raised too many problems regarding eligibility and, further, that Parisian workers would, at any rate, refuse to tolerate the accompanying scrutiny by public officials.[26] The commission also advised against earmarking communal lands for working-class housing, warning that the inevitable consequence would be to draw larger numbers of provincials to the city, thus compounding the original problem. Contemporaries hoped actually to reduce the attractiveness of the capital, as the influx of workers seemed the obvious source, according to councilor Levraud, of "misery, insalubrity, and the corruption of moeurs."[27] So pervasive were these anxieties that one councilor recommended levying a 2 franc tax on every person coming to Paris from a distance of more than twenty-five kilometers, while another suggested that each person presenting himself for tenancy in low-rent housing be required to stay at least two years as a means of insuring that the Paris Municipal Council would be responsible, in practice, only for true Parisians.[28]

Not surprisingly, then, the report objected to such a special use of public funds, mirroring the prevailing official reluctance to become directly involved in the housing market. In a typical statement urging municipal restraint, Bartet, director of lighting, walkways, and concessions, noted that the use of "the money of all" to provide for those who had nothing constituted charity and lay outside legitimate municipal functions.[29] He concluded that any scheme to improve housing conditions had to insure that the city's finances would not be overcommitted and that both the "independence of the worker and the freedom of the proprietor" would be respected. The only way to adhere scrupulously to these principles, according to Bartet, would be to encourage the construction of mixed housing, in which at least one-half of the lodgings were for working-class households, by offering tax advantages.

In keeping with this basic orientation, Villard's commission recommended that the city construct several model homes to demonstrate standards of hygiene and comfort. It urged that an immediate solution be found which would offer new housing to 30,000 persons by the end of 1884 through the use of private capital, and looked to an administrative commission appointed in January by the prefect of the Seine to suggest the means for implementing this goal. In the end, therefore, the Villard report offered no concrete program. It claimed that "it was hopeful that solutions would appear . . . that competition would be fierce among private contractors anxious to participate in this enterprise," and suggested that a metropolitan railway would soon play an important role in offering efficient transportation to the center. The Municipal Council repeatedly found it easier and more comfortable to create models and to offer guidelines than to define a long-term reform strategy.

The activity in the Municipal Council coincided with a parallel investigation undertaken by the blue-ribbon administrative commission appointed by the prefect of the Seine on January 29, 1883.[30] This commission was empowered to study all questions related to the creation of inexpensive lodgings for the working class. It divided into three subcommittees: the first to study hygiene problems and to produce a code of sanitary and construction regulations, the second to examine the suitability for building of undeveloped land belonging to the commune and to consider the relationship between transportation and housing, and the third to evaluate the financial feasibility of various propositions. Octave Du Mesnil, one of the foremost Parisian hygienists and a member of the Paris Commission on Unhealthful Dwellings, was active in drawing up construction standards for the first subcommission.[31] The final report was issued by Emile Muller, a prominent architect and civil engineer. Their concerns focused on establishing preventive regulations which would inhibit the physical deterioration of new constructions. For example, Du Mesnil made recommendations on the composition of materials used to build courtyards in order to avoid stagnating wastes and decomposition. He asked that urinoirs be required in all courtyards of buildings in which the ground floor was occupied by wine merchants or other shops servicing a large public clientele and that all buildings employ a concierge, "the agent of cleanliness," who alone could assure the regular removal of household wastes. Du Mesnil required further that there be at least eight meters between the windows of one building and those facing it, and stipulated that no building permit be issued unless the proposed construction would have an elevation of at least three meters above the underground water level and be simultaneously connected to underground sewers.

The second subcommittee of the administrative commission was empowered to survey municipal lands in order to assess their suitability for low-cost constructions and to evaluate these properties with regard to their access to the center. The committee's report indicated which properties were both unencumbered by rights of preemption and sufficiently cheap to be appropriate for working-class housing. At the same time, Councilor Level issued a report on transportation.[32] He urged that the existing system of transportation—including the belt railway line, tramways, and omnibus services—be reorganized so as to provide easy connections between the major railway lines and the belt line circling Paris (thus forming the beginning of a metropolitan rail system), as well as between the belt line and tramway and omnibus stations. He recommended a uniform rate for all distances within the city regardless of the particular means of transport and proposed special trains for workers early in the morning and late in the evening.[33] Level's report was adopted and sent to the minister of public works, who was then negotiating with the railway lines and with the omnibus company. No specific action ensued because the issue became entangled in long-range plans for a system of metropolitan transportation.[34] It seems clear that while contemporaries did see connections between housing and sanitation and transportation systems, they did not consider these problems within a larger framework of planning for urban development, and saw no alternative but to address these issues in a fragmentary and haphazard fashion. Each committee identified the components of a broader solution, but they did not coordinate their respective perceptions beyond making general recommendations.

The third subcommittee on ways and means began to explore financial schemes ranging from national lotteries to far-reaching tax incentives. These discussions were brought into sharp focus in March 1883 by a government proposition to make money available to contractors through the cooperation of the Crédit foncier,[35] the government, and the city administration. This proposal linked national and municipal housing reform efforts and quickly overshadowed all other strategies, as it seemed to provide a concrete plan by which to realize the objectives outlined by the Paris Council.

The first part of the government's proposal stipulated that the Crédit foncier lend a total of Fr 20,000 for the construction of small single houses, valued between Fr 3,000 and Fr 10,000, the mortgages of which would be paid by the state with the borrower paying only interest on the loan. Clearly, the prospect of creating worker-proprietors seemed a goal worthy of official support. Nevertheless, the special commission created by the Municipal Council to study the proposal once again reaffirmed its commitment to mixed housing. The report, written by Charles Amouroux,[36] stated that the sponsorship of single-family dwellings was inimical to the explicit goals of the municipality. The creation of small homes in the center of Paris would, in fact, serve only a small, privileged group of salaried employees and would be inaccessible to the working class, which had neither the continuity of employment nor the income to realistically undertake regular mortgage payments over a twenty-year period. Amouroux cited the example of the housing built at Auteuil by a philanthropic society which rented for Fr 402 excluding taxes, thus exceeding the budget of the vast majority of workers. The plan of the government therefore became a *mirage trompeur,* an illusion, at best, and at worst a deceit, in light of the Parisian context. Amouroux noted further than it was certainly not appropriate for public authorities to drive workers from the city to the outskirts. He observed that if more extensive and efficient transportation were to become a reality, then the admininstration could talk of suburban construction.[37] In the existing situation, the pattern typical of London, where workers lived in suburbs and traveled to the city to work, was not transferable to Paris, where the workday was considerably longer, extending in some seasons to 10:00 or 12:00 in the evening. Not only would the relocation of the working population be impractical, but it would cost the city a substantial sum in the loss of octroi fees.[38] It seemed clear, therefore, that this aspect of the government's proposition was inapplicable to the immediate problem of low-rent housing in Paris.

More to the point, the second section of the proposal, which referred specifically to Paris, provided that the Crédit foncier lend 65 percent of the funds for the construction of all buildings in which at least half of the inhabitable space was reserved for lodgings of Fr 150–300 annual rent. The total loan of Fr 50 million was to be guaranteed by the city and was reimbursable over a seventy-five-year period. The government agreed to exempt houses constructed under this plan from transfer fees, windows and doors tax, and real estate taxes, while the city would grant exemptions from roadway assessments and octroi fees on construction materials. The proposal constituted an attempt to stimulate the construction of inexpensive lodgings through the easing of credit and the burdens of taxation, which fell more heavily on less expensive buildings.[39] Contractors had discovered that it was more profitable to build for the wealthy. This financial package sought to retilt the balance in favor of mixed housing.

The Amouroux report strongly recommended adoption of this section of the proposal, emphasizing once again the direct links between crowding, disease, and industrial unrest. Amouroux argued that in spite of the physical transformation of Paris in the preceding thirty years—in spite of new boulevards, more extensive sewers, a better water supply, and the demolition of slum quarters—mortality due to epidemic disease remained high in the poorest and most crowded sections of the city, where deaths from diphtheria and scarlet fever doubled between 1870 and 1882.[40] The minister of public works echoed these findings. He pointed out that typhoid fever, believed to be spread through the sewers, had been epidemic in Paris since 1871; however, the incidence of the disease had recently declined without changes having been made in the sewer system, an improvement attributable, rather, to the departure of construction workers, who had left the city because of the recession in the building industry, thus reducing the density of working-class districts.[41] Improved health could emerge only through an enlarged supply of working-class lodgings.

The report further blamed the industrial crisis on the shortage of working-class housing. Amouroux claimed that high demand and rising rents had caused workers to strike for higher wages, which inevitably raised costs and closed workshops, thus benefiting foreign competitors. The construction of working-class housing promised relief on a number of fronts—in one step stimulating the building industry, curbing unemployment, easing class tensions, and lowering rents. In the immediate context, the agreement with the Crédit foncier seemed the most practical approach because it could be made operative at once, and neither compromised the city's freedom of action nor drained its budget. Because the Municipal Council could select the kind of tax exemptions offered, it could further assure, through differential incentives, that construction would be undertaken in each arrondissement rather than only on the edges of the city. The proposal represented, according to its supporters, the only viable compromise between allowing full responsibility to rest either with the municipality or with private enterprise.[42]

Amouroux's confidence was not shared by a significant number of municipal councilors, who found the proposed agreement threatening on both political and economic grounds. In fact, the response of city authorities was shaped in large part by corollary unresolved issues between the city and the state. The most volatile political issue dividing the Municipal Council involved shared authority in Paris between the national legislative chambers and the city's administrative officials. The council had long been split between Opportunists, who supported the prerogatives of the state, and Autonomists, who sought to strengthen communal authority, particularly in budgetary matters. By July 1882, the Autonomists held the majority.[43] In practical terms, this meant that issues such as housing, with overlapping national and municipal implications, became enmeshed in the tug-of-war between the joint jurisdictions. For this reason, Amouroux's commission revised the original wording of the proposal. The final draft specified that municipal tax exemptions *could* be offered to prospective builders "if the city so wished." Amouroux was careful to stipulate that within the terms of the agreement, the city retained the full complement of its financial independence.[44] At the same time, Amouroux noted, exemptions would not be granted to proprietors who converted old buildings into smaller apartments because such a plan would diminish municipal revenues, and while the given proposal failed to add to the budget, it did not produce a loss.[45] In spite of these reassurances, Autonomist councilors remained skeptical.

Critics argued further that by guaranteeing the proposed loan, the city's finances became too vulnerable. Not only was the city obligated for seventy-five years, but it would be dealing with joint stock companies that might fail, leaving the city to administer a large number of poorly constructed buildings. Thus, in times of crisis, the city might be swamped with multiple insolvencies and problems of expropriation.[46] Narcisse Leven, one of the most outspoken opponents, claimed that by guaranteeing the loan, the city assumed the responsibility for evaluating the credit and morality of potential borrowers, absorbing the risk that would normally be borne by the bank. He noted that those particularly drawn to the terms of the agreement would not be independent proprietors, but rather, speculators whose solvency would be difficult to assess. He concluded that the city's initial involvement was thus too risky, while the continuing need to see that the construction code had been followed and that rents remained at the specified level placed a responsibility on the city which could not realistically be met.[47] To implicate municipal funds in a venture so compromised by risk was, according to Leven, both foolhardy and dangerous.[48] Amouroux and his supporters countered with the argument that there was, in fact, no other avenue for obtaining such favorable credit terms. They noted that even if some of the borrowers defaulted, the sums for which the city would be liable fell considerably below the amount spent for expropriations each year, an expenditure which was, in effect, nothing less than one class generously granting indemnities to itself.[49] Critics, however, were adamant in their claim that the financial package was simply not a smart business deal.

Perhaps as formidable an obstacle as the concern with financial risk was an entrenched and well-founded reluctance to implicate the city's finances, even indirectly, in an obligation to the Crédit foncier—a reluctance which was the logical conclusion to the legacy of the Second Empire. The final years of Haussmann's tenure had witnessed an outpouring of criticism of the financial irregularities by which the prefect had financed his schemes, and in fact, municipal finances had been badly overstretched.[50] Haussmann left a debt of Fr 1.7 billion, which was not finally fully reimbursed until 1928. All subsequent development plans, therefore, whether general public works measures or housing proposals, were inevitably subject to an underlying determination not to overextend the city's finances. In 1879, the council had agreed to repay Fr 283 million of back debts to the Crédit foncier.[51] With the proposal to subsidize low-cost housing following so closely upon this commitment, it is not surprising that the council proved unwilling to engage in new dealings with the bank.

Opposition to dealing with the Crédit foncier extended beyond the specific terms of the proposal. A fundamental hostility to large financial societies runs as a leitmotif through these discussions, crossing all other lines of political division. Opponents on both the left and the right pointedly noted that financial journals enthusiastically supported the government's proposal, displaying unprecedented interest in the problem of working-class housing—in striking contrast to their usual commitments to the dogmas of political economy. Joffrin complained that the proposition offered by the government had unfortunately diverted attention from the issue of exorbitant rentals, the crux of the housing problem, while setting up a scheme which, far from being "state socialism," constituted "state protectionism for the Crédit foncier" as well as *l'art de faire des rentiers*—a ploy to benefit speculators, landowners, and financiers.[52] He noted that the newspaper *Le Figaro* was supporting Amouroux's report and under-lining the urgency of finding a solution, a sense of urgency which arose, according to Joffrin, from its desire to close a good business deal for the bank.[53] One councilor reported that, as the discussions of the agreement ensued, societies were forming to buy up undeveloped land, "hovering like vultures around these projects."[54] In part this suspicion was apparently a continuation of the antagonisms created by government subsidies to rail-road companies during the Second Empire and reflected legitimate fears that large-scale construction operations, with the help of government sub-sidies, were easing small businesses out of the market.

Amouroux charged that the press had knowingly contributed to mis-understandings on this issue by exploiting popular hostility to the Crédit foncier, and sought to counter this knee-jerk response by emphasizing that the city would guarantee the loan equally from any institution or individ-ual giving comparable credit terms.[55] Critics could not be so easily pla-cated, and the argument that the self-regulating mechanism of supply and demand would provide its own remedy inevitably reappeared. Levraud, for example, insisted that the natural process whereby a glut of luxury build-ings turned speculators to more modest enterprises had been interrupted by the unforutnate appearance of the government's project. Instead of ac-tivating construction, the proposal allegedly had halted all building while entrepreneurs awaited the announced tax exemptions.[56] Levraud feared that the project with the Crédit foncier could not help but encourage specula-tion and corruption. He claimed that there would be numerous opportu-nities for fraudulent dealings over the price of the land, labor, and building materials, which would enable the least honorable men to reap substantial profits from exaggerated estimates of building costs. An informed observer of these debates concluded, in the end, that the proposal eventually col-lapsed because of "bitter and irrational resentments between a segment of the Municipal Council and large financial societies."[57]

To economic liberals, the government's project represented too radi-cal a departure from long-standing policies of nonintervention—a depar-ture that would launch the administration on an irreversible path of state socialism. From this perspective, tampering with taxes challenged the inviolability of the free market, while the introduction of "artificial" ex-emptions pitted new proprietors against old, generating "iniquitous and disloyal competition" which constituted discriminatory favoritism, "bar-barous treatment" of landlords of already existing buildings. State and mu-nicipal participation in the housing market was seen as inevitably expro-priatory and naively "utopian." *Le Temps* concluded that the issue of rents was the fine edge which separated liberal politics from socialism and that administrators ought to be very sure of the potential consequences of their actions.[58] According to one commentator, a policy of tax incentives represented "the first blow to property, which was but the prelude to an uninterrupted succession of attacks." He concluded: "Former confidence in real property will be sharply restricted, capital will become wary and will avoid investing in construction. The public will cease building, . . . private industry will be paralyzed, and, on the day when the state's subsidies are exhausted, the building industry will be dead in Paris."[59]

Amouroux acknowledged the universal dislike, especially in Paris, of government involvement in private enterprise. But he distinguished carefully between the inappropriateness of state socialism and the legitimate responsibility of the state to "encourage progress." Even Gamard, a conservative royalist, admitted somewhat ruefully that, as the municipality had taken away workers' housing, so it would have to find adequate replacements, and "if this be socialism, it can't be helped!" Gamard, an active member of the right, stated: "People cry that we are hurling ourselves toward socialism. I was, for a moment, disturbed by these comments. I wondered how it was possible that I, notary, proprietor, alleged reactionary member of the Municipal Council, fell into such criminal propositions. . . . If a thing is necessary, I subscribe to it without remorse."[60] He pointed out that tax exemptions were not, in practice, entirely novel, since all new houses were afforded three years' immunity, while the new constructions on the rue de Rivoli profited from a ten-year period of grace. Nevertheless, this issue continued to be emotionally charged and substantively unresolved.

Amouroux remained a voice in the wilderness. He was unable even to convince representatives of the working class that the project was in their interest. The Marxists were, of course, unimpressed, and Joffrin continued to seek redress through a tax on unoccupied lodgings. Concurring this time with his leftist adversaries, he claimed that workers would not benefit from the type of housing proposed. By permitting expensive apartments on the lower floors, the proposal allegedly insured that nearby merchants would charge high prices for their goods, and solidified existing class divisions by forcing workers into the upper stories, where they would "roast in the summer and freeze in the winter."[61] Joffrin repeated again and again that the vast majority of workers' groups formally opposed the plan.[62]

THE FAILURE OF MUNICIPAL SCHEMES

In the end, the Municipal Council rejected the financial package between the bank and the city. Following the first heated round of discussions, the council referred the project back to committee in order to devise a building code to insure sanitary and construction standards. It was not until February 1884 that the issue reemerged for further debate. In the interim, nearly 350 individual projects had been submitted for consideration. Amouroux's second report was an impassioned plea for the creation of new low-rent housing, citing as precedents local projects within France and the municipal experiments of foreign cities. Despite Amouroux's arguments, the major provisions of the proposal were defeated. The most important article, which provided for the city's guarantee of the loan from the Crédit foncier, was defeated by a vote of 35 to 25. The provision for tax exemptions to builders of low-rent lodgings was turned down by a vote of 28 to 6, and Joffrin's proposal for the construction of municipal housing was decisively rejected, 48 to 12.[63]

Clearly, the proposal collapsed because it could not attract enough supporters to counter opposition from several independent sources. The problem of how and where to house the poor had raised a matrix of issues which defied resolution. On the one hand, it required a reexamination of the relationship between private industry and public sponsorship, raising the fearful specter of state socialism. Interestingly, public officials had understood their responsibility for housing in the framework of the crisis in the building industry as much as in terms of the social and health problems produced by overcrowding. These dual priorities emerged quite explicitly in the early 1880s in a report by the director of public works which urged the municipality to act as an economic regulator—to initiate public works projects and expand sources of credit during slump periods, and to withdraw from the scene when private industry prospered.[64] The end of the building recession seemed to argue for a return to a more passive public role. On the other hand, housing issues required a clarification of the joint jurisdictions of state and municipal officials in Paris. Municipal authorities were anxious to preserve their independence in housing as well as in the related issues of urban and suburban transportation. The proposal triggered latent but virulent hostilities toward the financial establishment shared by representatives of the working and middle classes, while workers sought more direct and immediate relief from high rents than that offered by the project at hand. The interlocking antagonisms and conflicting objectives evoked by the problem of working-class housing could not be reconciled within the proposed scheme. As if in testimony to these overriding ambiguities, the debates in the council were interrupted repeatedly by votes affirming the urgency of the matter while rejecting all substantive reform proposals.[65]

As the industrial recession subsided and immigration to Paris ebbed, the motivation to devise a comprehensive housing policy faded as well; the momentum for creating innovative strategies had disappeared, and a new lethargy set in. On August 2, 1884, the Municipal Council appointed a new commission on low-rent housing. This group met nine times during 1885 and only sporadically in succeeding years. Independent attempts to revive credit terms and tax benefits comparable to those of the 1883 proposal came before the council intermittently during the next ten years, essentially without success. Most of the projects were rejected outright, and the rest remained permanently lost in committee or caught in limbo between overlapping authorities. A closer look at a few particular episodes illustrates quite clearly the type of lackluster efforts which effectively stonewalled housing reform.

When the Municipal Council rejected the agreement with the Crédit foncier, it did, at the same time, vote to sponsor the construction of four model houses in different arrondissements to demonstrate the feasibility of building sanitary housing which included modest lodgings.[66] During the following October, Poubelle, prefect of the Seine, sent a memoir to the Municipal Council indicating that four sites had been chosen in arrondissements XII, XIII, XIV, and XV to execute this plan.[67] Each project had been assigned a different architect so as to elicit data based upon multiple experiences. The prefect reported that the average estimated rate of return on the capital investment (Fr 3.75/Fr 100)was below the legal rate of interest (Fr 5/Fr 100). He concluded that, in an enterprise which was essentially risky and subject to potential loss of funds due to vacancies and defaults on rent, it would be necessary to offer incentives in order to attract investors.

In January 1885, the Commission on Low-Rent Housing discussed the prefect's memoir. Several members argued that to construct model houses which afforded such a meager rate of return was to take a step backwards, to demonstrate that the creation of mixed housing was impractical. On the other hand, Lyon-Alemand pointed out that the land selected by the administration was too expensive; for example, in arrondissement XII, the site was valued at 100 francs per meter, while not far away, land was available at 25 francs per meter.[68] Moreover, he argued that rents from the more expensive apartments on the lower floors might produce higher revenues than anticipated. The commission finally voted to adopt the model home project and recommended that the Municipal Council open a credit of Fr 850,000 for their construction.[69] The council, however, never discussed the report and never allocated funds. After a year of discussion and revision, the project simply dissolved.

A parallel sequence ensued regarding a proposal, approved by the council in February 1884, that the city lease land for seventy-five years to builders who would construct inexpensive lodgings in accordance with a construction code prepared by the administration.[70] At the end of the lease, the buildings would revert to municipal ownership. Councilors Michelin and Dreyfus presented a report on behalf of the Commission on Low-Rent Housing in which they approved the leasing of communal lands with specific reference to four lots on the rue de Tolbiac in arrondissement XIII.[71] In December 1885, Michelin and Dreyfus noted that no action had been taken on this project, perhaps because of the excessive rigor of the construction code or because of the particular site chosen.[72] They urged the administration to discover the reasons for this lack of success and to devise a new agreement which would be acceptable to the contracting parties. Following this final admonition, the project lapsed.

Several years later, the issue of stimulating the construction of low-cost housing emerged again in slightly different form. In the 1890s, the Municipal Council entertained the idea of setting aside portions of land acquired through expropriations (usually from public works projects) for the construction, by the city, of mixed housing, or of requiring that a certain amount of mixed housing be constructed on these lands as a condition of resale. In April 1890, Deschamps proposed the construction of mixed housing on a parcel of expropriated land in the fifth arrondissement (intersection of rue Monge and rue de la Bûcherie) with the Fr 211,000 which remained from the street operation.[73] The building would house apartments of two rooms and a kitchen for Fr 450 per year, three rooms and a kitchen for Fr 750, and eleven single rooms renting at Fr 150 each, thus attracting mainly small merchants and salaried employees. Deschamps observed parenthetically that it was not possible to build workers' housing on land worth Fr 300–400 per meter. In the subsequent discussion, opponents of the plan argued that such a construction would discredit the concept of low-rent lodgings, and further, that the money which the city retained ought to be used to build housing in working-class districts and not in the bourgeois quarters of the fifth. Proponents countered with the claim that the project ought to be approved as a test case of whether the city could require buyers of land to reserve portions for inexpensive dwellings. In the end, the council, not wanting to reject the plan and thus appear to oppose the principle it embodied, sent it back instead to the commission for more complete studies. Eight months later, the commission reported that to build mixed housing on the rue Monge was no longer feasible, as the actual value of the land had risen from Fr 300 per meter to Fr 600 per meter in the previous six months.[74]

Similar attempts were equally futile. In March 1890, Councilor Vaillant proposed that the city ensure the construction of low-rent housing on parts of the large parcels acquired through the opening of the avenue de la République in the twentieth arrondissement.[75] The proposal was sent to a standing commission of the Municipal Council. One year later, Vaillant reiterated his request, and it was again referred to commission.[76] Later that year, Berthaut and Faillet proposed that, at the same time that estimates for expropriations were being made, the city compile a census of the working population so that those displaced by expropriations could be rehoused in buildings or on land acquired by the city.[77] The proposal was tabled. In December 1893, Vaillant revived his earlier plan, asking that not fewer than one-half of the new constructions built on land resold by the city in the twentieth arrondissement be reserved for working-class housing.[78] He added that his previous propositions had never been reported on by the special commission and urged an immediate response. The following year, the Municipal Council received a petition from 500 residents of the twentieth arrondissement echoing Vaillant's demands.[79] It was sent to the special commission along with a request for a report on Vaillant's propositions. No report emerged, and there the issue died.[80] By the 1890s, the perception of urban housing as an issue for which public authorities could legitimately assume responsibility had slipped away. The Municipal Council had effectively washed its hands of the housing problem, thrusting it, with considerable relief, back to the private sector.

It is not altogether surprising that the issue of working-class housing eluded efforts to find a solution in the closing decades of the century. On a purely technical level, housing reform encountered staggering material difficulties posed by a rapidly changing urban environment. Public authorities of the period had neither the vision nor the institutions to deal with housing in the context of more comprehensive urban planning. They did acknowledge, for example, that the problem of creating healthful housing for the working classes was connected to the presence of good transportation and sanitation services. But the difficulty of coordinating these components proved too overwhelming. Hygienists pointed out that it was useless to build new housing without proper sanitary safeguards; municipal councilors responded that sanitary requirements entailed excessive and prohibitive costs for the proprietor. Du Mesnil admitted that it was precisely those quarters without sewers where land was cheap enough to encourage new constructions—but that such building was foolish unless canalizations to extend sewer lines were effected at the same time. Opponents argued that massive additional expenses could not be undertaken in the near future and that the two issues need not be considered together. The essential contradiction between the ideal of sanitary housing on the one hand and the need to insure low construction costs on the other remained. Where land was sufficiently inexpensive to encourage construction, it was likely that expensive apartments on the lower floors would rent only with difficulty; conversely, more expensive land closer to the center precluded the creation of low-rent lodgings, as entrepreneurs were understandably reluctant to reserve even sections of buildings erected on expensive land for small rentals. The absence of inexpensive, efficient urban transportation limited options and placed solutions even further out of reach.

The government's proposal met specific resistance because of its challenge to both conventional economic orthodoxies and municipal independence. Ironically, once again socialists and conservatives shared opposition on economic grounds, albeit for different reasons, while negotiations with the Crédit foncier were further sabotaged by an intransigent hostility to large financial societies. Levraud's position as "an adversary of all monopolies conceded to large companies" clearly struck a responsive chord. These resistances were solidified by the determination of a majority of councilors to minimize state interference in Parisian affairs—an issue which framed the whole debate. The personal platforms of the men running for the Municipal Council in 1884 indicate that the most significant political division lay between Autonomists, committed above all to communal independence, and Anti-autonomists.[81] The Autonomist majority refused to commit the city's budget to a scheme which they deemed speculative.

These technical difficulties and economic and political reservations were perhaps insurmountable. But in the final analysis, social attitudes and priorities severely restricted the range of acceptable remedies. Housing issues did, after all, touch dangerously on all aspects of "the social question." Middle-class fears of surrounding Paris with a workers' city, "a formidable belt of suffering humanity hostile to the social order," lay always just below the surface. No less than Le Play's disciples, municipal councilors perceived housing strategies as the manipulation of social space; their commitment to mixed housing may be understood in this context. They had endorsed the construction of mixed housing in order to promote "sympathetic solidarity" among the classes and to prevent the excessive concentration of workers in one location. Although the working classes were becoming increasingly politically articulate and self-conscious during this period, representatives of the traditional classes dirigeantes hoped to quash ideological dialogue in favor of the more comforting, but amorphous, concept of solidarity. Ironically, on a practical level these sentiments were not incompatible with the desires of large segments of the working classes, who resisted ghettoization and preferred lodgings close to sources of work.

Yet councilors worried at the same time about the possibility of "disagreeable contacts" and "jealousies" and "dissension" between working-class and bourgeois tenants of the same building, recommending in one instance separate stairways to serve the lower and upper floors and a loge between them to act as a buffer zone.[82] So pervasive were these attitudes that the architect Muller doubted that the financial incentives offered to stimulate construction would be sufficient to overcome the landlord's resistance to converting upper stories to inexpensive lodgings. In 1853 and 1854, he noted, similar attempts to guide private enterprise failed to produce the desired results, a lesson still applicable because "it will always be difficult to draw

together the different classes of the society."[83] In the initial discussions of
the government's proposal, several councilors expressed concern that the
provision requiring that one-half of the surface area be devoted to inexpensive lodgings might produce too many buildings exclusively inhabited
by workers, and recommended instead that the number of small apartments
per building be strictly limited. Inevitably, discussions of working-class
housing also evoked fears of drawing additional workers to the city and
reinforced a determination to discourage the relocation of transient migrants.
The council could not find a way to reconcile its social objectives with its
perception of social realities.

The combination, then, of specific difficulties with the proposal and
a vaguer but equally instrumental anxiety about the social consequences
of a particular use of physical space led to a kind of paralysis. Municipal
councilor Jobbé-Duval spoke for a substantial group of his colleagues when
he wrote that

> there are insoluble questions, and this is one of them. In preoccupying
> yourselves with this issue, you will have succeeded in demonstrating to the
> working class your concern on its behalf; but this is all that you can do.
> Now, is this demonstration useful? Any reasonable man will see that we
> depart from the municipal domain and instead of occupying ourselves
> with the city's business, we lose time in deluding the working class with
> hopeless dreams.[84]

Councilors shared the hopes of bourgeois reformers that the problems of
the poor would disappear as a result of a "leveling up" of the social classes.
In 1883, Muller concluded that the urgency of the situation had been exaggerated, that proprietors of vacant bourgeois apartments would undoubtedly soon reduce rents to attract a broader clientele. He predicted that as
salaried employees and small merchants moved into better quarters, their
lodgings would become available to members of the working class.[85] The
recurring ritual of voting on the urgency of the issue but not on the merits
of a specific remedy, the implicit, vague hope that the problem would resolve itself, captures the underlying resistance of councilors to addressing
the problem, in all its complexity, directly.

The stalemate in which the council found itself was allowed to continue, in part, because the acute crisis had begun to subside. Although rents
did not decline, neither did they continue to rise. While the period 1876–
81 saw an increase of 280,000 to the city's population, the figures for 1881–
86 and 1886–91 (75,527 and 103,407, respectively) indicate that growth had
stabilized at more normal levels. The demographic character of the city also
began to change, as a growing lower middle class of salaried employees,

small merchants, and workers in the service industries pushed unskilled workers even further into the suburbs, where larger industrial units had been established, and outside the jurisdiction of the municipality.

At the same time, socialists in general abandoned housing as a focus for confrontation, choosing instead to mobilize in pursuit of higher wages and greater employee control of the workplace. Even without this shift, however, the alternatives raised by the socialists had been far too radical to be seriously considered. They had, rather, served as a less-than-gentle prod to force working-class issues temporarily to the foreground of political debate. But in the final decade of the century, the political complexion of the Municipal Council was shifting to the right.[86] It seemed evident that the immediate threat of revolutionary socialism had been side-stepped; the challenge to the political order which appeared so real in the 1880s had failed to materialize. By the 1890s, then, much of the political urgency had gone out of housing issues. The problem had been scrutinized from every angle. The list of strategies, with the various arguments for and against their adoption, had become familiar—a familiarity which bred a certain amount of lethargy, if not resignation, in the face of very real difficulties and irreconcilable goals. The intricacies of housing reform had, in the end, exceeded the capacities of municipal politics.

CH. 6 The Regulation of "Microbe Factories": Politics and Public Health

THE failure of public officials either to enlarge the supply of working-class housing or to reduce its cost threw the issue into the laps of hygienists, who were already mobilizing for more effective action. The architect Cacheux confirmed this shift, noting that, since the housing crisis of the early 1880s had abated and population increases were tapering off, the administration in Paris considered the question of low-cost lodgings resolved.[1] In contrast, growing acceptance of germ theories of disease provided hygienists with a compelling rationale for intensifying their regulatory activities. The final two decades of the century thus witnessed a revitalized public health campaign with housing issues at its center. Whereas politicians and bureaucrats had juggled the competing claims of public and private enterprise and had tried to deal with the elusive problems of profiteering and speculation, hygienists redefined housing issues in the context of their own priorities. The focus shifted from finance to the prevention and control of unsanitary conditions as hygienists pursued more stringent codes, greater executive authority, and more effective enforcement of sanitary measures.

During the second half of the century, expanded epidemiological knowledge, more sophisticated statistical methods, and the emergence of professional organizations all served to make more practical and technical the work of public health activists. To a great extent, hygienists abandoned their earlier romantic aspirations to become a therapeutic clergy administering to a regenerated population.[2] Instead, they were more likely to address problems of sanitary engineering or the control of contagious disease.[3] Most important, hygienists at the end of the century forcefully advocated increased regulation in health matters, even at the expense of traditional rights of privacy.[4] Rather than acting as midwives for a utopian social order, hygienists in the 1880s and 1890s helped to preside over the gradual modification of entrenched concepts of political and economic liberalism in the interests of public health. The protection of the health of the population became, under their direction, one of the primary national objectives that justified a new conception of state responsibilities. The goals of hygienists were therefore underscored by their connection to a larger process of political redefinition. Specifically, hygienists sought to codify scattered pieces of legislation so as to provide a coherent body of sanitary standards for all of France. At the same time, they lobbied for the creation of a network of institutions, staffed by professionals, with authority to guarantee uniform, regular enforcement. The core of their agendas for reform included the routine inspection of lodgings, the reporting of contagious disease, mandatory disinfection and vaccination, the creation and enforcement of building codes, required permits for construction and habitation, wider jurisdiction over landlords, more precise definitions of insalubrity, and clear lines of effective authority in matters of health.

Like their counterparts in other industrialized nations, French hygienists were becoming professionally self-aware in the final decades of the century. They formed several new organizations and participated in a string of international conferences to define their areas of concern and to examine a broad spectrum of technical problems.[5] *Annales d'hygiène publique et de médecine légale* continued to be a major forum for the exposition of public health topics, but in 1875, 1877, and 1879 three new journals emerged (*Journal d'hygiène, Bulletin de la Société de médecine publique et d'hygiène professionnelle,* and *Revue d'hygiène et de police sanitaire,* respectively), attesting to the growing vitality of a revamped public health movement. Many of the hygienists were doctors, affiliated with academies in which they taught legal medicine and public hygiene. But there were also a significant number of architects, civil engineers, and statisticians, whose particular expertise was needed to address the issues raised by unprecedented urban growth. Journals were filled with articles defining the new specialty of public hygiene, which encompassed both traditional medical issues and a broader range of technical topics, including such themes as "the role of the architect in the fight against tuberculosis," "architecture and hygiene," and "studies on the hygienic properties of construction materials." The president's address to the First Congress on Sanitary Improvement and Salubrity in 1895, entitled "The Role of the Sanitary Engineer in the Direction and Operation of Municipal Hygiene Bureaus," was typical in its emphasis on the need to complement the doctor's skills with the mathematical and mechanical knowledge of the engineer.

Hygienists themselves were quite anxious to establish the independence of their profession from the medical profession in general. Dr. Vallin issued a representative statement to this effect in the *Revue de médecine légale* in calling for "a new breed of medical specialists" concentrating on hygiene.[6] He argued that one could not be a medical practitioner and a hygienist at the same time—that "the exercise of medicine was incompatible with the scientific and practical study of public hygiene"—because the practitioner was, by definition, more interested in therapeutics than in prevention and saw hygiene measures as potentially annoying limitations on his professional freedom.[7] In a corollary argument, a French hygienist claimed that French hygienists had had fewer successes than their English colleagues, largely because the French were obliged to make their livings elsewhere, while devoting only spare time to public health. He concluded that real progress in hygiene could be achieved only when hygienists became well-paid, full-time professionals.[8]

The prominent hygienists in Paris were in general from the same social stratum and had the same official and quasi-official connections as did their bourgeois-reformer counterparts. The hygienist Du Mesnil, for example, was an active member of the Paris Commission on Low-Cost Housing along with Cheysson, Picot, and Siegfried; Du Mesnil and Monod wrote the sanitary code which was attached to the incentive proposal involving the Crédit foncier; and Brouardel and Monod were spokesmen for the national government's proposed public health law of 1902. These hygienists were thus bound by many of the same assumptions and values as were other groups of reformers. Their interest in health was no less intertwined with fears of a hostile working class and with anxieties produced by the irregularities of the worker's lifestyle. They do not, therefore, stand apart as an entirely separate group. Nevertheless, in the context of housing reform efforts, the professionalization of public hygiene during these decades provided hygienists with priorities that were instrumental in shaping reform activities.

A NEW FOCUS: IDENTIFYING "MICROBE FACTORIES"

Although hygienists continued to address the variety of problems related to surface sanitation (cesspools, gutters, privies, courtyards), the issue of severe overcrowding was quickly becoming a focal point of their discussions. The studies of the Budapest statistician Korosi were frequently cited to corroborate evidence that mortality significantly increased with overcrowding, as did infant mortality owing to congenital abnormalities.[9] The earlier identification of public health with public works had become obsolete. The hygienist Brouardel wrote in the 1880s: "For twenty years, they have extended the length of the sewer system in the city; they have brought in a water supply of improved quality and enlarged quantity; they have opened up new streets through the congested quarters of Paris; they have enlarged old roads . . . and nevertheless, epidemic and contagious diseases exact an ever-increasing toll each year from the population."[10] Dr. Reuss noted in 1882 that most of the illnesses treated by the physicians connected with the Bureau of Public Assistance were the result of defective hygiene generated by overcrowding, for which therapeutics offered no cure.[11] The Comte d'Haussonville concluded, similarly, that "uncleanliness and congestion . . . are the scourge of the poor."[12] Contemporaries did not question the truth of Dr. Vallin's claim that "without being a seer, a well-informed hygienist is able to say: 'Show me your home and I will tell you which illnesses threaten you.'"[13]

In this context, the condition of the lodging houses of the city and of the shantytowns on the periphery became especially important. Lodging houses were inhabited mainly by transient or seasonal workers, by day laborers without regular employment, or by families with children who had been refused housing elsewhere. As early as 1852, a contemporary spoke of his move to a lodging house as "a fatal crisis in his existence," with dire physical and moral consequences.[14] Similarly, a hygienist at the International Exposition of 1878 in Paris blamed overcrowded lodging houses for the fate of unfortunate provincials who left their villages full of strength and vitality only to become scrofulous and consumptive in the city.[15] By the early 1880s, it seemed apparent that transient housing, which began as a temporary expedient, had become a fixture of urban life.

Between 1877 and 1883 Du Mesnil conducted a series of influential investigations into the condition of Parisian lodging houses for the Commission on Unhealthful Dwellings.[16] His reports revealed a sordid tableau of misery, congestion, and disease. In 1876, a population of 142,671 persons was dispersed in 9,050 lodging houses; however, by 1882, although the number of lodging houses had grown by 2,500, the population which they harbored had increased by more than 100,000.[17] Landlords continued to divide up rooms in order to increase the capacity of their lodgings without making comparable renovations in order to add to the ventilation or water supply. In one building on the rue Sainte Marguerite in the faubourg Saint-Antoine, for example, Du Mesnil found rooms housing four tenants that were a mere 2 meters high, 2.60 meters wide, and 5.25 meters long, as well as single, unventilated cubicles of only 1.10 meters in height.[18] Du Mesnil claimed that no improvements had been made in the building for at least twenty-five years. Not surprisingly, contagious disease spread rapidly under these conditions. Du Mesnil reported that Paris lodging houses were the source of several secondary smallpox epidemics throughout France in 1870–71, as workers carried their contagion into the provinces. Similarly, large numbers of those treated during the typhoid epidemics of 1876–

Tenant of a Parisian lodging house. Collection of Roger-Viollet.

77 and 1881–83 came from lodging houses which had long been labeled as particularly insalubrious.[19]

Du Mesnil's exposés produced a call for more stringent controls. The Commission on Unhealthful Dwellings presented a draft of new regulations in 1877 outlining minimal room dimensions and appropriate construction materials, and requiring the immediate reporting of all contagious illness. As a result, a police ordinance in 1878 required a minimum of 14 cubic meters of air per person in lodging houses, but it was not until 1883 that the minimum room height of 2.5 meters was adopted, thus making illegal those rooms which met the requirements for cubic meters of air but in which an adult could not stand upright. Also in 1883, the prefect of police created an inspection service for lodging houses staffed by five permanent and four temporary inspectors.[20] The reports of the Commission on Unhealthful Dwellings of 1889 indicate, however, that although the formal regulations set a new standard, they were, in practice, difficult to enforce.

During this same period, hygienists energetically sought to raze a group of infamous cités which had grown up haphazardly around the city, particularly in arrondissements XIII, XIX, and XX.[21] For example, the Cité Jeanne d'Arc, constructed between 1869 and 1872 on the rue Jeanne d'Arc in arrondissement XIII, consisted of ten buildings housing 2,000 persons. The unhealthful dwellings commission had been bombarded with complaints about these lodgings in 1877, and public authorities were called upon in 1879 to investigate them as the likely source of a smallpox epidemic. Du Mesnil found filthy walkways filled with stagnating wastes, fecal matter overflowing into the cellars, bathrooms which were open holes, courtyards covered with decaying matter, dark stairways and corridors, and humid, cramped rooms. In a parallel investigation, d'Haussonville, whose concerns were as much moral as hygienic, described a typical scene in which a father, mother, and six children shared a single room furnished only with a single bed and two mattresses. The immediacy of the smallpox epidemic led to two deliberations in May and June of 1880 by the Municipal Council, which ordered that the Cité Jeanne d'Arc be cleaned. But a stubborn proprietor successfully resisted making substantial improvements through dilatory legal appeals until 1884. By 1890, many of the original conditions had reappeared.

The Cité des Kroumirs and the Cité Doré were of a slightly different sort: clusters of single-story, makeshift hovels put together from wood and plaster debris, housing 790 persons. There were no privies, no provision of water; men and animals coexisted indiscriminately among the refuse accumulated by the inhabitants, who were largely ragpickers by trade. Du Mesnil's description became famous—"a sort of sewer in the open air"—and in 1882, the Cité des Kroumirs was demolished. The land which had

Interior of a lodging house in which tenants lived dormitory-style. Collection of Roger-Viollet.

supported the slum had been leased from the Bureau of Public Assistance. Du Mesnil notes that these leases contained the stipulation that the agency could reclaim possession of the land on six-weeks' notice: those who built on the land lived perpetually under the threat of expulsion and built, therefore, as cheaply as possible. Reflecting the antagonism which characterized the relationship between the Commission on Unhealthful Dwellings and the Bureau of Public Assistance, Du Mesnil charged that "if the Public Assistance had tried to create a supply of sick to support its hospital services, it could not have done so more effectively."[22] The Bureau of Public Assistance had been caught before in similar situations. Yet, it does seem likely that the particular tenants of these cités could not have afforded better housing, so that the growth of the slum was as much a function of the acute shortage of inexpensive housing in the early 1880s as it was the responsibility of the Bureau of Public Assistance. In light of the adverse publicity, however, the director of public assistance inserted a clause in the bureau's leases after 1889 which required that all dwellings conform to the sanitary prescriptions of the unhealthful dwellings commission.[23] The hygienists had been successful in eliminating a particularly offensive slum, and they had taken steps to prevent similar abuses. But because there was no way to rehouse those displaced, hygienists were unwittingly reenacting the familiar paradox which had compromised all efforts at housing reform.

In focusing attention on overcrowding, hygienists came closer to admitting that poverty lay at the heart of housing problems than did either politicians or middle-class reformers. For poverty they had no solution. They were successful, however, in convincing the government that new housing regulations ought to be the linchpin of a more aggressive public health policy. Although reformers had for decades identified le foyer as the most fundamental source of all social well-being, the growing acceptance of germ theories of disease in the 1880s and 1890s greatly enhanced the clout wielded by hygienists and gave real authority to their reform campaign. They emphasized repeatedly that they had "scientific confirmation" to justify their cleaning-up activities, that resistance to their intervention flew in the face of science, rationality, progress, and social peace. In the final two decades of the century, hygienists saw themselves as part of a new technocracy of trained experts equipped to tackle and resolve problems which had eluded their predecessors.[24]

Speaking with the added stature conveyed by their connections to science, hygienists promised a society free from major scourges. Henri Monod, director of public assistance and hygiene in Paris, maintained that the discoveries of Pasteur had shown that the transmission of disease depended upon "the seed" and "the milieu." Because, therefore, the incidence of disease was closely related to local sanitary conditions, he concluded that not just pestilential disease, but all contagious illness could disappear with proper regulation.[25] Monod thus defined the function of a public health administration as the destruction of germs and the maintenance of an environment inhospitable to their propagation. Improvement in the condition of workers' dwellings was central to this campaign. As references to "microorganisms" and "pathogenic germs" spread through the literature of the period, the squalid quarters of the poor came to be described specifically as "microbe factories" manufacturing disease. Contemporary accounts indicate that some doctors refused to treat the sick who remained housed in their infested quarters. One hygienist warned, for example, that at the end of a thirty-six-hour period, each gram of stagnant dust contained at least five million potentially lethal bacteria.[26] Hygienists had clearly rejected the earlier assumption that the control of disease involved the defense of the national terrain against exotic illnesses imported from abroad. In specific acknowledgment of this new perspective, public hygiene services

Entrance to the infamous Cité Doré, boulevard de la Gare, arrondissement XIII, by Atget, 1912. Collection of the Bibliothèque historique de la ville de Paris.

Ragpickers' huts, 1900. Collection of Roger-Viollet.

were transferred in 1889 from the Ministry of Agriculture and Commerce to the Department of the Interior.[27]

The virulence of tuberculosis during these decades kept housing issues at the forefront of debate. While mortality from tuberculosis was declining in other European capitals, it remained relatively static in Paris, thus heightening the urgency of the situation.[28] (See Chap. 3.) Brouardel observed that although periodic epidemics such as cholera shook the population from its accustomed inertia and prompted immediate preventive measures, in fact, the number of cholera deaths in the two years 1854–55 was less than the annual tuberculosis mortality.[29] Citing an old Persian proverb which predicted that "where the sun and air do not enter, the doctor comes often," Brouardel pointed to the dark, humid, exiguous lodgings of the poor as the ideal breeding ground for the tuberculosis organism, which became all the more dangerous in congested areas. According to the statistician Jacques Bertillon, more than one-third of the Parisian population (363 per 1,000) lived in seriously overcrowded lodgings in 1891.[30] The somber story of a succession of young men selling books in an unventilated room, each becoming tubercular in turn, each dying of the disease, became a prototype which enjoyed monotonous repetition in the professional journals and monographs of the period.[31] Hygienists confirmed that contagious disease broke out repeatedly in the same houses, and they began to call for a *géographie médicale* to identify potential sites of epidemic illness.[32] Although they did not ignore the connection between poverty and poor health, they tended to focus on the more proximate issue of housing. French hygienists noted that the English had been able to reduce mortality from tuberculosis with an aggressive attack on insalubrious housing and cited recent jurisprudence in which an English landlord had been held responsible for the outbreak of contagious illness because he had wrongly declared his building sanitary.[33] They concluded that, in the absence of major improvements in housing conditions, such precautionary measures as the use of pocket spittoons and the practice of disinfecting could be only marginally effective in controlling tuberculosis, which was, above all, "an illness of obscurity."

The specific focus on housing in the campaign against tuberculosis was further reinforced by the differential mortality of the various quarters of Paris. The "social scandal" revealed in the disparity between the death rates of the rich and the poor remained a volatile issue of concern to politicians as well as to hygienists. Du Mesnil warned that poor housing was an irritant which could degenerate into a social peril: "These germs are the reprisal of misery against the egoism and indifference of the rich."[34] Monod reported, for example, that in the wealthy quarter Champs Elysées, tuberculosis mortality was 10 per 10,000 population, while the working-class quarter Plaisance sustained a mortality rate of 104 per 10,000.[35] The impact of improved housing on mortality figures was equally well documented. In Godin's well-known model community, the Familistère de Guize, mortality declined from 36.61 per 1,000 to 13.73 per 1,000 in the ten years 1882–91, although the nearby city of Guize had an average minimum mortality rate of 22.28 per 1,000 in the same period. Similarly, the mortality rates in the new housing constructed by the Société des habitations ouvrières de Passy-Auteuil in arrondissement XVI of Paris were significantly lower than in the arrondissement at large.[36]

SOLIDARISM AND PUBLIC HEALTH

The hygienists' focus on differential mortality and contagious disease was given added importance at this time by its connection to prevailing political ideologies and social commitments; that is, the reform campaign of hygienists intersected a changing political climate in which authorities were beginning to contemplate an enlarged role for the state as a means to preserve social peace. The growing organization among socialists had underlined the inadequacy of both the rhetoric and program of traditional liberalism in the context of a mass society. Individualism, laissez-faire economics, and the paternalistic philanthropy of the established classes all seemed increasingly inappropriate. Instead, by the 1890s, politicians substituted the concept of solidarism, which gradually became the rallying cry of the Radical party in its effort to occupy a middle ground between the outmoded policies of liberals and social conservatives on the one hand and the threatening posture of socialists on the other.[37]

Solidarism was designed to defuse social conflict by replacing competitive individualism with associationism, mutualism, and cooperation. It stressed social interdependence, claiming in essence that man was born the debtor of society and that this debt to past generations was to be paid to future generations through the mutual guarantee or insurance of each other against life's risks. Specifically, solidarism sought to revise liberal contract theory, which had allegedly failed to take into account the inequality of bargaining positions among the parties. This loophole could be eliminated, according to solidarists, by state intervention in the form of sanctions—both more precise and more obligatory than those dictated by charity—which would compel citizens to perform a wide range of social duties.[38] Accordingly, the individual was to sacrifice a part of his particular self-interest to advance social goals.[39] In political terms, solidarism provided a means to steal the thunder from the socialists while justifying a limited, but legitimate, extension of the powers of the state. Perhaps more important, on a symbolic level it sought to preserve social stability by engineering a belief in the fundamental connections among all members of the society, who were ostensibly to be joined, both morally and legally, in a system of mutual obligations. By emphasizing mutualism, the proponents of solidarism hoped to get beyond the sentimental and condescending connotations of charity, while substituting the concept of cooperation for the less benign dogma of competition.

The agenda of solidarism called for new legislation to limit the workday and to provide old age pensions and accident and unemployment insurance. It sponsored, in addition, the creation of producer and consumer cooperatives and voluntary associations to coordinate the battles against tuberculosis, infant mortality, and poor housing. In pursuing these goals, politicians described the philosophical underpinings of solidarism as both anti-individualist and antistatist in that a combination of public and private institutions would organize different aspects of social solidarity.[40] Proponents of solidarism remained intentionally vague on the limits of state responsibility while emphasizing the role of cooperative and voluntary societies. This was a precarious road to walk. Leroy-Beaulieu and economic liberals objected to the potential for an indiscriminate increase in the realm of state action, while socialists dubbed solidarists "radishes"—red on the outside but white at the center.[41] Nevertheless, solidarism had wide appeal, and the protection of the public health became a quintessential expression of the practical application of solidarism. Significant groups within the classes dirigeantes had come to believe in their ability to legislate social harmony; tighter housing regulations were to be part of this new reform strategy. For two critical decades, hygienists and prominent republican leaders shared a set of legislative priorities.

Léon Bourgeois, who held almost every important political office during the Third Republic and was prime minister of the first solely Radical cabinet of 1895–96, provided the fullest explanation of the concrete meaning of solidarism. He wrote that "the first, the most pressing of the social obligations which emerge from the fact of solidarity is the obligation to protect human life from the risks which arise from insalubrity."[42] Hygienists elaborated these principles, calling for collective responsibility for health in place of the "funereal solidarity" which then prevailed. They spoke of public health as a "work of fraternal solidarity" and of their new knowledge of the genesis of disease as "laws of sanitary solidarity."[43] Hygienists enlarged upon the theme of social interdependence and argued, in turn, that the "sad right to suicide" permitted by the Melun law, which exempted the homeowner living without tenants from public supervision, could no longer be tolerated. They claimed that the same principle which prevented an individual from stockpiling dynamite in his home ought to apply as well to an unsanitary dwelling: the threat to the community superseded individual property rights. They insisted further on the need to devise building codes grounded in sanitary criteria and enforced by paid inspectors, to simplify legal procedures so as to encourage slum clearance, to make disinfections and vaccinations mandatory, to require the reporting of all incidence of contagious disease, and to create a more efficient, modern public hygiene administration which transferred authority from political to professional personnel and which eliminated the confusing fragmentation of authority in matters of health.[44] Monod concluded that public officials had the responsibility to guarantee that the general interest was not compromised by the ignorance, negligence, or avarice of the few.[45]

In the 1890s, then, politicians were particularly receptive to reforms which promised to neutralize the social, political, and health hazards posed by the working classes, while preserving, at the same time, the essential structures of power and authority. As in the early part of the century, hygienists were claiming once again to be able to dictate norms which would guarantee the physical and political health of the nation. While Le Play's followers hoped to moralize the working classes through the rehabilitation of family life, hygienists invoked the authority of science to justify greater public scrutiny and control of working-class behavior.

REWRITING HOUSING LEGISLATION

The central thrust of the public health movement during the final two decades of the century involved the effort of individual hygienists and of professional hygiene organizations to revise the Melun law of 1850. At least eight specific proposals emerged, including those of the Academy of Medicine, the Society of Public Medicine, the Congress on Hygiene of 1878, the Commission on Unhealthful Dwellings, and the Advisory Council on Public Hygiene. The deficiencies of the first housing legislation had been apparent virtually from the day it was written. Because it left the initiative for its application to local governing bodies, the Melun law remained largely a dead letter in France, except in Paris and Lille. At the time of the International Congress on Hygiene in 1878 it was reported that in Marseille, Rouen, Lyons, Bordeaux, and Nantes, unhealthful dwellings commissions either no longer existed or met only sporadically.[46] Further, the attempt to conciliate private property while meeting the needs of public hygiene had produced substantive and procedural ambiguities in the application of the law. Where unhealthful dwellings commissions did function, their activities were carefully circumscribed. Spurred by this sorry record, professional hygienists had reached broad agreement in the 1880s on a list of necessary changes in existing sanitary legislation and on the requisite institutional structures which would guarantee their effectiveness. Martin Nadaud introduced the first bill to reform the law of 1850 into the Chamber of Deputies in 1881. Owing largely to the inertia of the political process and to the recalcitrance of the Senate, a new public health law did not emerge from the legislature until February 1902.[47]

Reformers in the 1880s focused particularly on the need to expedite the improvements recommended by the unhealthful dwellings commission and other public hygiene agencies whose function was, after all, exclusively advisory. Typically, sanitary legislation entrusted mayors with wide responsibilities for protecting the public health of the commune but withheld the necessary means to render their power effective. Although the mayor could determine that a sanitary nuisance required remedial attention, a peculiar twist of legal reticence prevented him from prescribing the specific remedy.[48] So, for example, when the mayor of Caen ordered the removal of a cesspool situated in a courtyard serving several properties, the Supreme Court of Appeal concluded that there might be a less financially onerous way for the proprietor to control the foul emanations created by the cesspool and that the order for its elimination constituted "an excess of administrative authority."[49] Such subtleties of interpretation necessarily produced delays, while mayors were further constrained by their dependence on tight-fisted municipal councils to appropriate funds for desired programs. In the absence of strong popular commitment, or imminent danger from epidemic disease, the funds were not readily forthcoming.

Even without these financial restrictions, it is clear, as well, that elected officials sitting on the Municipal Council were as bound by political considerations as they were by the needs of hygiene, and were subject to a variety of pressures from proprietors, who were, in fact, their natural constituency. They might therefore choose not to exercise the powers they did hold. Moreover, in deference to the rights of property, the Melun legislation had provided for lengthy appeals procedures through the regular court system. This meant, in practice, that the investigatory process was essentially duplicated, as the appeals courts tended to request additional reports from experts before making judgments in sanitary matters. Improvements were again put off while offenders gained extended periods of grace by availing themselves of all possible procedural delays. The seven-year pursuit of the proprietor of the Cité Jeanne d'Arc was but a well-known example of a familiar pattern.

To streamline the process and put teeth into health legislation, hygienists agitated for the transfer of executive authority from political bodies—that is, from the Municipal Council and the regular administrative courts—to competent professional bodies with both the authority and the funds to act. In 1891, Brouardel, president of the Advisory Council on Public Hygiene, and Monod, director of the Office of Hygiene and Public Assistance, addressed the Chamber and the Senate on behalf of the government as advocates of new legislation which embodied these objectives. Brouardel had taught legal medicine and was instrumental in the creation of the Institut de médecine légale. He had been an important adviser on hygiene to the government for thirty years and participated in drafting the administration's proposal of a new public health law. The professional stature of Brouardel and Monod and the scientific authority implicit in their conclusions gave substance and form to the government's commitment to solidarity. In this case, science reinforced ideology; hygienists and bourgeois politicians shared a vision of social order which could be expressed in terms of public health.

Hygienists urged, first, that every department be divided into sanitary wards supervised by a commission which would take over the duties of municipal Commissions on Unhealthful Dwellings as well as supervise general sanitary conditions in its district. These commissions would be assisted by a sanitary inspection service paid by the state to assure that the prescribed improvements were carried out.[50] Hygienists had argued repeatedly that adequate hygiene could not be guaranteed until administrative authority was vested in professionals who held no other jobs. They noted that members of unhealthful dwellings commissions were volunteers who were potentially in conflict with individual proprietors with whom they had daily dealings. What was needed, they claimed, was a core of professionals without local ties who could act without waiting for specific, individual complaints.[51]

These proposals were approved in the Chamber, but the Senate balked. Senators feared conflicts between local communal authorities and agents of the state. They conjured up dramatic images of a sinister pattern of excessive centralization in which an inspection service represented one more step toward the abyss. With cries of approval from the right, Volland prophesied that

> by the law of hygiene that you consider today, you will have armed the representatives of the central power with the right to penetrate when they wish, on an order from Paris, day or night, into the interior of our homes; to bring, in defiance of all the guarantees prescribed by the criminal code, into the interior of our homes their war on microbes, and under the pretext of the search for a germ or the execution of a disinfection, to open our most intimate possessions and our most secret drawers. This, in fact, is what will happen.[52]

A colleague echoed his warning: "Adieu to intimate expressions! At the very moment when two spouses converse more or less tenderly, the sanitary inspector will burst into their home to make a report."[53] In the midst of general hilarity, a senator from the left sardonically observed that "love does not exclude hygiene." Senators dubbed the bill "le triomphe de fonctionnairisme," although Monod indicated that in most cases, inspectors attached to the *enfants assistés* would be given expanded duties in order to hold down the number of new bureaucrats.[54] Fear of functionaries prevailed, however, and the new legislation emerged without inspectors, thus fundamentally undermining the impact of the sanitary commissions.

A similar scenario accompanied the attempts of hygienists to gain some financial independence from municipal councils and to enlarge their jurisdiction in the litigation of sanitary matters. They asked that state and departmental funds augment the communal budget for hygiene services, while the Paris Commission on Unhealthful Dwellings suggested further that funds be earmarked in the municipal budget to provide temporary lodgings for those evicted as a result of demolitions or condemnations. The prefect of the Seine responded to this proposal in a letter to the minister of commerce, May 12, 1882, in which he stated that to give the commune such responsibility "would involve considerable expenses and would be a source of abuses which would be difficult to monitor." He concluded somewhat wishfully that, at any rate, such circumstances were fairly rare. The legislature decided to set aside the issue.[55]

Hygienists pressed further to eliminate delays in the litigation of public health issues by removing intermediary procedures and by granting sanitary commissions full appellate authority. The regular administrative courts (the Council of State and the Council of the Prefecture) which ordinarily heard all appeals on decisions of the Municipal Council had no expertise in hygiene; therefore, in the proposed new legislation, they retained appellate jurisdiction only on technical legal matters separate from the merits of the case. Again, the Senate could not be convinced. Several senators decried the new "tyranny of hygiene" which turned private property over to hygienists.[56] Instead, they insisted upon retaining final authority in ordinary civil tribunals.

It appears, then, that hygienists had mixed success in gaining greater executive authority in questions of public health. Senators, particularly, were reluctant to allow power to escape from the usual political channels. Rather than expand the role of sanitary commissions, they chose, instead, to close some of the most obvious loopholes of the Melun law by strengthening the hand of mayors, who were given, in the law of 1902, enlarged powers to protect the health of the commune: they gained jurisdiction over all houses, even those inhabited solely by the proprietor; they could order that improvements be executed at the landlord's expense; they could act even in the absence of a direct complaint. But hygienists were quick to point out that the excessive timidity of the legislators had emasculated the new law. They argued that to give elected mayors enforcement powers in sanitary matters was to create an essential paradox at the core of health legislation.[57] Mayors would have to be "veritable heroes" to rigorously apply an annoying and potentially costly regulation to the constituency which elected them.[58] It was precisely mayors who could not assume executive responsibility. One commentator wrote that, in this situation, "authority collides with resistance from powerful interests. Placed between the pressing exigencies of public health and the fiercer and more combative financial interests of proprietors, they have everywhere established an unfortunate compromise which only imperfectly satisfies property owners and has the aura of a challenge defiantly flung at hygiene."[59]

Brouardel noted ruefully that of 36,000 mayors in France, certainly no more than 1,000 at best had any competency in hygiene. Yet the legislators could not bring themselves either to give sanitary commissions executive authority or to establish an independent, paid professional inspection service. By leaving the final word with elected local officials, the new legislation preserved the freedom not to act.

In addition to these questions of jurisdiction and power which defined a public health strategy based on regulation, hygienists pursued a strategy based on prevention. From the very beginning of its operations, the Paris Commission on Unhealthful Dwellings noted that new constructions became, within years and even months, as unsanitary as the older buildings of the city. They sought a comprehensive building code prescribing both structural regulations and the control of building materials, as well as an inspection prior to habitation to ensure that proper sanitary safeguards had been followed. In 1880, the unhealthful dwellings commission issued a report on the healthfulness of constructions. It made extensive specific recommendations which were adopted by the prefect of the Seine in order to provide precise guidelines for implementing the prefectural decree of March 26, 1852, requiring that builders conform to "the prescriptions which may be necessary in the interests of public safety and salubrity."[60] But without an inspection procedure, there was no way to enforce these regulations before the building became so unsanitary as to evoke a complaint, and those buildings not aligning the public roadway, particularly those squeezed into the interior of a block or the shacks in the open fields on the outskirts of the city, were not covered by the 1852 decree.

The early drafts of the law of 1902 provided that, in communes of more than 5,000 people, all building plans be submitted for approval to the mayor's office, which would issue permits of occupation following a formal inspection.[61] These provisions applied to the modification of older buildings as well. On the advice of the departmental hygiene council, a mayor could apply them additionally to communes with a population of less than 5,000. The Senate again raised the cry of excessive and inappropriate regulation from the center.[62] The Comte de Maillé quipped: "Will one be able to dress oneself without permission from the government?" Proponents argued that it was indeed less costly and less troublesome to prevent unsanitary conditions than to enforce remedial measures; however, the senators' sense of the priority of private property could not be set aside.

The final draft of the law eliminated the inspection of new constructions, made no reference to the modification of older buildings, and required building permits only in those communes with a population greater than 20,000.[63]

The reluctance of senators to tamper too extensively with existing institutions and conventional processes mirrored a significant strand of conservative opinion which watched with alarm the growth of a professional bureaucracy. The economist Leroy-Beaulieu succinctly summarized this perspective. He noted the progressive increase of sanitary police powers and warned that an excess of neglect involved fewer perils than an excess of intrusion—that doctors and philanthropists were, after all, "by nature proud spirits who at all times experienced an inclination to tyranny and to the sin of pride." From this point of view, "a nation which would deliver itself to a medical academy would suffer in its liberty without sufficient compensation in health or longevity." One of the perils of modern society, according to Leroy-Beaulieu, was the domination of specialists. And, he continued, "specialism and fanaticism usually go together."[64]

These fears could not easily be overridden. A disheartened hygienist observed that "one can truly say that the legislation of 1902 has given hygienists *une satisfaction platonique*" by tranquilizing informed opinion without making substantive gains.[65] But that is to minimize the real achievements of the public health movement in the final third of the century. The barrage of criticism against the Melun law had produced a more specific definition of hygiene which was becoming generally accepted. For example, although the Commission on Unhealthful Dwellings, the International Congress of Hygiene (1878), and the Academy of Medicine had consistently urged that the provision of water be understood as a fundamental obligation of the landlord, actual jurisprudence had produced contradictory positions on this issue. As late as 1885, a Paris judge maintained that the provision of water in a multifamily dwelling was not a measure which concerned public health, but one which referred, rather, "to the convenience and well-being" of the tenants.[66] Du Mesnil noted, however, that by the end of the decade, the idea that water was an indispensable component of salubrity had gained general acceptance and could be required by the appropriate hygiene authorities and upheld by the courts.[67] Similarly, hygienists had argued for a broad definition of the outbuildings for which the unhealthful dwellings commission could assume jurisdiction. Private lanes and alleys off the public thoroughfare were typically in an unacceptable sanitary condition. Authorities could do little but require that the extremities be sealed off at either end. Under pressure from hygienists, however, private ways came to be considered as part of the outbuildings of the contiguous dwellings and therefore within the jurisdiction of the commission.[68]

The law of 1902 did represent a major step in the modernization of the administration of public health. It established uniform standards of external salubrity for all of France, regularized procedures for controlling contagious disease, and extended the jurisdiction of public authorities in the regulation of private dwellings. In contrast to the Melun law, it was mandatory—that is, its provisions did not have to wait for municipal action in order to take effect. The new law extended public jurisdiction over housing to *all* houses in a condition injurious to the health of its inhabitants or to neighbors, due to insalubrity from all causes, not just from those inherent in the building itself. Procedures for appeals were simplified and penalties stiffened. The law further codified and updated regulations for the control of contagious disease, specifically requiring mandatory vaccination and disinfection and the reporting by doctors, midwives, and health officers of all contagious illness. In every commune of at least 2,000 inhabitants it established bureaus of hygiene under the authority of the mayor, who was charged with enforcing the sanitary provisions of the law. If the death rate in a commune exceeded the average nationwide mortality for three years, the prefect was required to conduct an investigation and could order the execution of the necessary improvements. In order to establish guidelines for mayors with little experience in health administration, on May 30, 1903, the minister of the interior issued a circular defining precisely the scope of a mayor's responsibility in such areas as the salubrity of dwellings, the prevention of contagious disease, general sanitation, and enforcement and penalties.

In Paris, the duties of the mayor were to be fulfilled by the prefect of the Seine with the cooperation of an unhealthful dwellings commission of thirty members (fifteen named by the prefect, fifteen by the Municipal Council). The responsibilities of the prefect included the salubrity of private ways, the salubrity of houses and their outbuildings, water catchment and its distribution, the service for disinfection, vaccination, and the transport of the sick. The prefect of police was given authority, with the assistance of the Council of Hygiene and Salubrity of the Seine, to supervise measures taken against contagious illness, to receive declarations of contagious illness, to supervise infringements of the vaccination regulations, and to regulate the sanitary condition of lodging houses. The 1902 law thus retained the division of authority on public health matters in Paris which had existed, with minor revisions, for most of the century.

PUBLIC HEALTH AND NATIONAL PRIORITIES

All of these provisions indicate that a consensus had been reached on necessary minimal safeguards to protect the public health. This consensus reflected, in part, the commitments of hygienists in the preceding decades and the example of comparable foreign legislation and, in part, the particular conjunction of hygiene and politics in the Third Republic. In examining the legislation of 1902, it seems clear that, in the end, the priorities of the legislators determined the parameters within which reform could occur. Where hygienists seemed to challenge long-standing assumptions about private property and political authority, legislators resisted innovation. Conversely, where medical evidence neatly coincided with well-established, well-articulated national objectives, new legislation was forthcoming. It was not fortuitous that public health reformers gained greater access to the government at a time when national anxieties were expressed in the biological imagery of organic degeneration. The government's interest in contagious disease was, in fact, magnified at this time by its increasing preoccupation with issues of national strength. Hygienists' claims to be able to provide more effective control of common diseases coincided with French fears of losing place in the international arena—fears which focused on the might of the military and the size of the population. The first report to the Chamber on the proposed health legislation stated that "the sanitary state of a country is indifferent neither from the point of view of the development of the population nor from the point of view of the security of the country."[69] Brouardel touched a raw nerve when he observed to the Senate that the French had made the epidemiological discoveries but it was the neighboring countries which benefited.[70] Discussions of the proposed legislation repeatedly returned to the theme of military strength. The members of the Senate were told that "germs were more lethal to the army than the bullets of the enemy."[71] Monod, dubbing smallpox "the shame of a civilized society," noted tellingly that during the Franco-Prussian war, the German army lost fewer than 400 soldiers to smallpox while the French army lost 23,000.[72] Reflecting similar anxieties, Jules Simon wrote in 1892 that a member of the German parliament had spoken against increases in the military budget because "we [Germans] do not have to make these sacrifices when the French lose a battle every year."[73] When hygienists argued further that uniform health regulations for all of France were necessary because recruits from rural areas with poor sanitary controls could infect an entire unit, their words fell on receptive ground. Brouardel pointed out that by improving the water supply, deaths in the army from typhoid fever had been reduced from 32 per 10,000 to 12 per 10,000. Because battalions were often housed in private homes rather than in barracks, Brouardel argued that comparable regulation of the sanitary condition of housing was needed.[74] Hygienists were thus able to draw fairly tight connections between worries about national strength on the one hand and the control of contagious disease (including smallpox vaccination, mandatory reporting of illness, and housing conditions) on the other.

Similarly, the falling growth rate of the population added to the urgency of public health reform. Contemporaries viewed the decline of the birthrate as a warning signal pointing to national decadence. Because it was more difficult to engineer a rise in the birthrate, the conservation of lives seemed the necessary corrective. Brouardel noted that France lost 125,000 each year to tuberculosis, 20,000 to typhoid fever, and 15,000 to smallpox. Most important, many of the preventable illnesses struck those under twenty-five, who had not yet formed families, thus reducing both the actual population and the chances for demographic recovery.[75]

By the 1890s, then, it seems that the government had identified the health of the population with its national security concerns and was consequently willing to entertain more active involvement in sanitary regulation. Nevertheless, this involvement stopped short of dealing with the pressing problem of clearing out large pockets of slum dwellings. The law of 1902 sidestepped this crucial issue completely by its failure to revise the outdated compensation procedures established by the law of May 3, 1841, for expropriated buildings in irremediable condition. Because the law set no limits on the amount of compensation, juries (populated largely by the *haute bourgeoisie*) tended to award inflated indemnities which made large-scale removal financially impractical, while proprietors postponed making improvements in the hope of reaping larger profits through expropriation. Hygienists deplored this form of speculation, which turned the lodgings of the poor into "human slaughter-houses," as proprietors sought expropriation as a financial favor.[76] Du Mesnil's investigations produced a prototypical description of a wealthy slum-lord surveying his vacant, deteriorating properties but refusing to make repairs, while cursing "the intervention of hygiene" which had evicted his tenants.[77] The sanitary census indicated that certain houses perpetually had significantly elevated mortality rates, making their demolition all the more imperative. For example, between 1893 and 1904, 38 percent of the deaths of the city came from 5,363 houses, or less than 7 percent of the houses. Similar concentrations of tuberculosis could be pinpointed.[78] Thus, toward the end of the century hygienists increasingly sought the demolition of properties in irremediable condition. Despite their efforts, no legislation emerged to facilitate the acquisition of slum areas cheaply and expeditiously.

In a recent study of the growth of Paris, Anthony Sutcliffe has described this expropriation bottleneck as "a financial and conceptual straightjacket" bequeathed by Haussmann to his successors.[79] Yet, it is apparent that the problem persisted because of a lack of will rather than a failure of imagination. Suggested remedies emerged from nearly every conference on housing reform, giving hygienists cause to hope that the 1902 law would provide a solution. In 1904, Jules Siegfried brought in a bill modeled after an English law of 1890 which, in effect, granted compensation for site value

only. The indemnity was to be calculated on the basis of the building's revenue; however, excess rents beyond the normal capacity of the building, as
well as the costs of repairing the property, would be subtracted from the
final payment.[80] The bill reached the Senate in 1910, but by the outbreak
of World War I no action had been taken. Similarly, a bill introduced by
Rendu in 1911 to facilitate the acquisition of whole areas without requiring
that the unsanitary condition of each individual building be established
had to await action until after the war.

   It is not altogether surprising that at the same time that hygienists
were gaining in stature and influence, their demands met with increasing
resistance. While legislators trod softly on accepted perceptions of the rights
of property, individual proprietors became more aggressive in protecting
their economic self-interest. The early reports of the Commission on Unhealthful Dwellings indicate that landlords offered little opposition to the
recommended repairs, in part because property values were rising so rapidly that expenditures were soon recouped and, in part, because the administration was generous in granting delays. The tone began to change
at the end of the Second Empire, with resistance gaining momentum during the final two decades of the century. The 1866–69 reports refer to "the
ever-growing ardor with which proprietors attack and dispute even the principles of the law of 1850"; similarly, the 1872–76 reports note "a little more
resistance" on the part of proprietors.[81] According to Hudelo, proprietors
and building entrepreneurs voiced "strong resistance" to the regulations for
new constructions proposed by the unhealthful dwellings commission in
1880, claiming that such detailed prescriptions constituted an "infringe-
ment on the free exercise of their property" and made new buildings too
costly.[82] In a formal petition, lodging-house keepers demanded that those
establishments opened before 1883 be released from the strict standards applicable to new lodging houses and asked, instead, that they be held to the
less rigorous requirements applied to an ordinary proprietor.[83] In the reports of 1884–89, the commission attributed the growing number of appeals and refusals to comply not to the fact that tighter controls were being
exercised, but rather, to the emergence of *agents provocateurs* who, "ad-
vertising their services in cleverly worded circulars," promised to obtain an
attenuation or an annulment of the prescriptions or at least to secure delays in their execution. The commission claimed that, in most cases, the
proprietors failed in the end to reverse the judgments but were able to create protracted delays.[84] For example, by a law of July 10, 1894, the municipality required that proprietors of buildings situated on streets with a sewer
provide for the direct, underground evacuation of solid and liquid wastes
to the sewer (tout à l'égout). Homeowners combined to form the Syndicat
des propriétaires to marshall resistance to this law. The final series of appeals from this organization was not heard until March 1900.[85]

Fears of the "tyranny of hygiene" emerged also from the general population concerned with issues of personal privacy and property rights, and were reinforced by a segment of the medical profession. Discussions of the law on the declaration of contagious diseases brought these anxieties to the fore. The original draft of the 1902 legislation had required the reporting of contagious illness by doctors, health officers, and midwives, and, in their absence, by heads of families, hotel and lodging-house-keepers, and those responsible for treating the sick. The Senate limited responsibility to the doctor, health officer, and midwife, claiming that there was something "inhuman" about a father having to declare the illness of his child. It is apparent that the stigma attached to contagious disease evoked considerable anxiety. Monod observed that the new law would be effective only if doctors agreed to comply with it. Previously they had resisted making declarations owing to some sensitivity on their part to the question of professional secrecy, but largely out of fear of alienating their clientele. A head of household resistant to declaration would typically argue: "You will injure my business, my sales, my credit. If you persist, we will find another doctor."[86] The law on the declaration of transmissible illness had no more bitter adversaries than medical practitioners, causing hygienists to complain that the doctor had become the accomplice of his clients, even to the point of making voluntary errors in diagnosis.[87]

Tuberculosis had been omitted from the list of illnesses requiring mandatory declaration because of the heightened emotions which surrounded the disease. Dr. Josias reported to the Academy of Medicine that the consequences of the declaration would be extremely harmful to the patient without producing a compensatory sanitary guarantee:

> It is as if, by the declaration, the patient is put on the Index; the frequent disinfections of his home will brand him as a public danger; he will not be able to find work in common; sometimes, in the face of the fears of his neighbors, he may not be able to lodge himself; misery and moral distress will exacerbate his illness; and, in spite of all this, it is not even possible to protect others from contagion.[88]

In addition to worries about adverse social and economic consequences, families sought to avoid disinfections which might damage their furniture, curtains, and linen. The general population thus joined private physicians and proprietors in resisting hygiene measures which were annoying and costly, destructive of both privacy and property.

In conclusion, it seems clear that in the last quarter of the century, hygienists did orchestrate an aggressive campaign to clean up and clear out unsanitary dwellings. Significantly, the moralizing which characterized hygiene literature between the 1840s and the 1870s had largely disappeared;

instead, hygiene measures were justified in the context of a program to wipe out "microbe factories" and to control the spread of contagious disease. Hygienists sustained an intense lobbying effort, well documented and statistically verified, to enlarge the jurisdiction of public health professionals and to produce effective guidelines, codes, and procedures in matters affecting public hygiene. The comprehensive public health law of 1902 was largely the result of the pressure they had brought to bear beginning as early as 1880.

Hygienists surrounded their reform activities with the authority of the new science of epidemiology, promising a society with greater physical and political security. The words of Dr. Roques capture, quite succinctly, the new sense of mission and self-confidence which characterized the efforts of hygienists in the closing decades of the century. He wrote: "It is absolutely necessary for the state to intervene in combatting infectious disease. . . . The state must take the initiative for the general welfare when the inertia or ill-will of certain persons compromises the health of the collectivity. . . . There is no incompatibility with individual freedom when the issue is public health."[89] Nevertheless, the dictates of science and medicine do not automatically translate into policy, and hygienists met significant resistance to the extension of their authority from bureaucrats, legislators, medical practitioners, and ordinary citizens. The degree to which their campaign succeeded was largely the result of its conjuncture with broader political objectives. The commitment to solidarity in matters of health among powerful political leaders seemed to require some legislative reforms. But solidarism sought essentially to adjust laissez-faire liberalism without implicating the government in the provision of greatly expanded services. The need to protect traditional institutions and to proceed with due caution on issues involving the sanctity of property limited the range of acceptable innovations. In the end, it was the intersection of the demands of hygiene with perceived political interests which shaped the content of the new public health law.

More important to the housing reform campaign as a whole was the fact that better regulation did not guarantee better housing for the poor. With no alternative housing for evicted tenants or subsidies for large-scale sanitary improvements, both rents and overcrowding would continue to increase. In narrowing their focus, hygienists had defined more limited goals. They had staked out new territory but had not solved municipal housing problems. Hygienists were as much at a loss in this arena as the politicians had been.

Conclusion

IN the minds of bourgeois social reformers, urban workers who emerged daily from their infested hovels posed a menace which was, at once, biological, moral, and political, placing the whole of society at risk. Neither the political order nor social stability could be secure in the presence of this chronic and unhealthy poverty which had become so visible in late-nineteenth-century Paris. As public authorities increasingly gained control of common sanitary hazards—slaughterhouses, marshy terrain, cesspits, and household garbage—the working population itself appeared the ultimate source of contamination.[1] Physical pollution had acquired a predominantly social dimension. Not surprisingly, housing reform became a first priority for overlapping groups of reformers because it seemed the most promising way to disinfect and pacify the working classes. Removed from his hovel, the worker became safe—no longer a carrier of disease or a prey to socialist fantasies. Both sponsors of suburban cités ouvrières and proponents of mixed housing in the center city hoped that proximity to a bourgeois lifestyle would imbue the worker with the traditional middle-class attributes of respectability and responsibility. The working classes were expected to "level up" into the mainstream of bourgeois society. Those who did not or could not were dismissed either as personally retrograde—the undisciplined and the unworthy—or as the hard-core poor, the residuum, for whom nothing could be done. The rest, however, were to be resocialized to mimic their middle-class mentors.

This optimistic prospect notwithstanding, the poor remained poor, clustered in overcrowded, unsanitary lodgings. And the threat persisted. While the nineteenth-century scourges of diphtheria, whooping cough, typhoid fever, and smallpox declined in the prosperous western sections of the city, mortality and morbidity rates remained high in the impoverished eastern arrondissements. When asked if the construction of low-cost housing, as well as the fight against tuberculosis and the protection of the public health, were social applications of political solidarity, Charles Gide replied with unusual candor that "it is possible. However, one can say without being too cynical that the fear of being infected ourselves is surely involved here."[2]

Le Play and his followers dominated housing-reform activities because they spoke most directly to these anxieties. With the support of the most prominent political economists of the time, they attempted to generate enthusiasm within the building industry for the construction of complexes of housing units on the Mulhouse model, presenting such projects as lucrative business ventures with acknowledged social utility. With such investments entrepreneurs could increase their profits while discharging social obligations and ensuring, indirectly, their own future. The hopes to create worker-proprietors culminated in the Siegfried law of 1894, which established the mechanisms, through Commissions on Low-Cost Housing, to funnel capital into the construction of inexpensive housing and to favor those contractors who took up the task with fiscal immunities.

In spite of a prolific, almost evangelical, propaganda campaign, cités ouvrières did not become a reality on any significant scale. They were, in fact, unworkable from almost every perspective. Only a tiny fraction of the working class enjoyed sufficiently regular employment to consider long-term mortgage obligations, while construction costs and land values in and around Paris dictated basic amortization rates beyond the means of most workers. Cités ouvrières did not address the needs of workers who sought lodgings near potential sources of work in the center of the city, nor was there, throughout this period, adequate transportation to the periphery where the desired low-rise constructions would have to be built. And perhaps most importantly, builders sought higher rates of return than could be secured from working-class housing. The appeal to social conscience had, in the end, a narrow audience. Rather than providing a practical solution to the problem of working-class housing, the cité ouvrière concept epitomized the effort of the established classes to cling to normative standards of social and economic life. It preserved the integrity of private enterprise, encouraged the development of the bourgeois virtues which were grounded in privacy and thrift, and reinvigorated the conventional paternal charity of the privileged in more modern form. Despite its apparent merits, the solution did not work.

In the closing decades of the century, several factors came together to give more specific shape to the housing reform campaign. The population of Paris continued to grow at alarming rates; most important, this growth occurred primarily in the working-class arrondissements. The sense, shared by the established classes, of festering masses crowded into the eastern half of the city became particularly vivid in the 1880s with the mobilization of socialist organizations to challenge the economic and political order. Focusing the worker's resentments, socialists promised to secure better living and working conditions. Guesde, in fact, acknowledged that he would use grievances about high rents and real estate speculation to forge an army of socialist revolutionaries.

As in earlier periods, instability in politics provided the impetus for a more careful consideration of housing issues. The socialist challenge, arising as it did in the context of a mass democracy, required a response, and the Paris Municipal Council began to examine schemes to improve housing which were both practical and closely attuned to Paris conditions. The most important project to this end involved national and municipal tax incentives, and subsidies from the Crédit foncier, guaranteed by the city, to all contractors who would build mixed housing. Debates on this proposal indicate that public intervention in the housing market generated so much fundamental resistance that the council found itself unable to devise the mechanisms by which such a project could be realized. Although councilors readily voted to affirm the urgency of the problem, they could not reach any agreement on the specific terms by which to extend municipal support to private contractors.

By the 1880s, the conditions of the real estate market in Paris posed serious material difficulties. But ultimately more important than the practical problems were the political and financial reservations of the municipal councilors. The discussions of public-sponsored housing occurred against a backdrop which prejudiced the issue from the outset. Napoleon and Haussmann had so overstretched the city's finances that the politicians and administrators of the Third Republic were arranging repayment schedules for old debts to the Crédit foncier of billions of francs throughout this period. In spite of the fact that the city's finances would be well protected by the proposed credit scheme, and in spite of the absence of better alternatives, the councilors would not, in the end, approve a plan even remotely likely to increase municipal indebtedness. Given the preexisting reluctance of conservatives to extend the role of government, and given their fears that publicly subsidized housing would generate unfair competition with private industry, the additional opposition to dealing with the Crédit foncier effectively eliminated the most creative scheme to emerge in the 1880s. As the rate of population growth tapered off and the socialists turned their attention elsewhere, municipal authorities essentially removed themselves from the fray. Following the intensive activity of 1881–84, the council addressed housing issues only sporadically and without significant results. As the immediate crisis subsided, public officials in Paris were for the most

part relieved to allow private enterprise to resume primary responsibility
for the housing market.

Although the municipal housing reform campaign had essentially col-
lapsed, the national government did not abandon its effort to improve conditions of working class life. By the 1880s, and especially in the 1890s, a
significant group of the traditional political leadership had begun to promote specific legislative reforms to defuse working-class discontent while
preserving the essential structures of power and authority. The state was
to become the agent of social peace. By giving the worker protection against
some of the shocks which threatened his very existence, the state could promote the integration of the working classes into the body politic. The regulation of unsanitary housing was thus representative of a broader reform
strategy designed to make the worker more secure. It included, as well, a
readiness to require social and industrial insurance, to promote producers'
and consumers' cooperatives, and to create new commissions, with working-
class representation, to mediate grievances. The ideology of solidarism
emerged to ease this transition to a more interventionist, albeit limited role
for the central government.

The simultaneous professionalization of public hygiene provided some
direction for politicians seeking social reform through legislative fiat. For
much of the century, hygienists had been influential, perhaps even central,
in setting normative standards of social and physical well-being. Having
addressed pervasive anxieties about the pollution of public spaces, they increasingly turned their attention to the sanitary improvement of domestic
space—particularly to the condition of workers in their most intimate environment. With the enhanced authority conveyed by the discoveries of Pasteur and Koch, hygienists elaborated a set of priorities which matched their
expertise. They campaigned especially for the revision of the Melun law
in order to expand the jurisdiction of public officials in health matters and
to create effective public health institutions staffed by paid professionals
and endowed with executive authority. They insisted upon the need to regulate the sanitary condition of all houses, even those where the proprietor
lived alone, regardless of the causes of the insalubrity. They sought further
to prevent the development of unsanitary conditions by devising construction codes and insisting upon follow-up inspections. In their effort to control the spread of contagious illness, hygienists promoted the mandatory
reporting of disease, to be followed by the disinfection of the patient's home.
With the recognition of tuberculosis as the disease most resistant to control and most closely tied to the dark, humid quarters of the poor, hygienists urged the demolition of buildings in irreparable states of insalubrity.

The concern of hygienists to reduce death rates and to control the
incidence of contagious illness coincided with important objectives pur-

sued by the national government. Politicians were genuinely alarmed by the declining birth rate, a trend which suggested national decadence, and by persistently high mortality in working-class districts, the perennial sources of infection, and implicitly, of sedition. Even more, the poor physical condition of the working population seemed to undermine the industrial and military capabilities of the nation. Without seriously compromising accepted commitments to a limited role for the state, the government could use public health regulations to clear up blighted areas while demonstrating, at the same time, its concern for the working-class population.

It is clear that the preoccupations of hygienists converged with both the symbolic and the material interests of the administration. The public health law of 1902 embodied these shared commitments. Where the goals of the hygienists coincided with broader national objectives, new policies emerged; however, where hygienists sought major innovations in the existing locus of authority in health matters, or further modifications of accepted standards of rights of privacy, legislators, especially in the more conservative Senate, resisted. The new law did provide for better and more efficient regulation of the sanitary condition of urban housing. But it did not make the demolition of slum properties more feasible. It did not create an inspection service to assure the municipality that approved building plans had, in fact, been carried out. Nor did it transfer final authority in health matters from politicians to health professionals. In revamping the administration of public health, the French chose to move forward with caution, respecting whenever possible traditional political channels and rights of property.

It is apparent, then, that the record of housing reform in the half-century spanned by the Melun law and the public health act of 1902 was one of minimal achievement. Although diverse groups of reformers struggled to find solutions to the shortage of decent, inexpensive housing, the strength of their political and economic convictions most often precluded substantive action. Bourgeois reformers were determined to protect private enterprise, but the free market did not provide an adequate supply of working-class housing. The fairly conservative fiscal incentives which were offered failed to make low-rent constructions attractive to contractors; more direct government involvement in construction remained unacceptable, as was any form of control on rents or profits. It was not until 1901 that legislators agreed to require landlords to pay taxes on undeveloped properties, a small attempt to redress the balance in favor of tenants which had been urged for two decades. The success achieved by hygienists was possible because they had, in effect, redefined the housing problem, focusing not on the intransigent problems of supply, but rather on refining regulations accepted in principle since the Melun law. In the end, none of the bourgeois reformers who addressed housing problems at this time could conceive of practical strategies for increasing the supply of working-class lodgings.

The resignation which Leroy-Beaulieu had expressed proved to be warranted. He repeated in 1891 his long-standing conviction that the state could effectively prescribe remedies to inadequate housing when the problem arose from the condition of the buildings: the size of courtyards and rooms could be regulated; ventilation, water, and sewers could be required. But according to Leroy-Beaulieu, it would be much more difficult to assure that all classes could afford to pay for healthful lodgings.[3] The architect Cacheux echoed his sentiments. He wrote that repressive laws would be effective only when there were enough suitable lodgings for all workers. In most cases, he concluded, "public authority is impotent in the presence of men who have nothing."[4] Within the framework of nineteenth-century priorities, the problem of inadequate working-class housing could not be solved. Housing reform had been, above all, an effort to renegotiate class relationships on terms defined by the bourgeoisie. At the close of the century, the goal remained elusive.

Reference Matter

Notes

Preface

1 While the population doubled between 1801 and 1851, the number of houses only increased from 26,801 in 1817 to 30,770 in 1851. Anthony Sutcliffe, *The Autumn of Central Paris: The Defeat of Town Planning, 1850–1970* (London, 1970), 115. Detailed descriptions of Paris may also be found in David H. Pinkney, *Napoleon III and the Rebuilding of Paris* (Princeton, 1958); Pierre Lavedan, *Nouvelle Histoire de Paris: Histoire de l'urbanisme à Paris* (Paris, 1975); idem, "Paris à l'arrivée d'Haussmann," *La Vie urbaine,* nos. 3 & 4 (1953).

2 Erwin H. Ackerknecht, "Hygiene in France, 1815–1848," *Bulletin of the History of Medicine* 22 (1948): 143.

3 Adeline Daumard, *Maisons de Paris et propriétaires parisiens au XIXe siècle, 1809–1880* (Paris, 1965); Gérard Jacquemet, "Belleville aux XIXe et XXe siècles: Une méthode d'analyse de la croissance urbaine à Paris," *Annales: Economies, sociétés, civilisations* 30 (July–August 1975): 819–43.

4 Pinkney, *Napoleon III and the Rebuilding of Paris;* Sutcliffe, *The Autumn of Central Paris;* Norma Evenson, *Paris: A Century of Change, 1878–1978* (New Haven, 1979); and the following by Pierre Lavedan: *Histoire de l'urbanisme: Époque contemporaine* (Paris, 1952); *Nouvelle Histoire de Paris; Les Villes françaises* (Paris, 1960); and "Paris à l'arrivée d'Haussmann."

5 Roger H. Guerrand, *Les Origines du logement social en France* (Paris, 1967); Gareth Stedman Jones, *Outcast London: A Study in the Relationship between Classes in Victorian Society* (Oxford, 1971); Enid Gauldie, *Cruel Habitations: A History of Working-Class Housing, 1780–1918* (London, 1974); Anthony S. Wohl, *The Eternal Slum: Housing and Social Policy in Victorian London* (Montreal, 1977).

6 See, for example, Louis Chevalier, ed., *Le Choléra: La première épidémie du XIXe siècle* (La Roche-Sur-Yon, 1958); Asa Briggs, "Cholera and Society in the Nineteenth Century," in *European Political History, 1815–1870: Aspects of Liberalism,* ed. Eugene C. Black (New York, 1967).

7 By George Rosen: *A History of Public Health* (New York, 1958); *From Medical Police to Social Medicine: Essays on the History of Health Care* (New York, 1974); and "Disease, Debility, and Death," in *The Victorian City: Images and Reality,* ed. H. J. Dyos and Michael Wolff (London, 1973). By Erwin H. Ackerknecht: *Medicine at the Paris Hospital, 1794–1848* (Baltimore, 1967); "Anticontagionism between 1821 and 1867," *Bulletin of the History of Medicine* 22 (1948): 562–93; and "Hygiene in France, 1815–1848," ibid., 117–55. Ann F. La Berge, "Public Health in France and the French Public Health Movement, 1815–1848" (Ph.D. diss., University of Tennessee, 1974). William Coleman, *Death Is a Social Disease: Public Health and Political Economy in Early Industrial France* (Madison, 1982).

CH. 1. PUBLIC HEALTH AND PUBLIC ORDER IN THE FIRST HALF
OF THE NINETEENTH CENTURY

1 Erwin H. Ackerknecht, "Hygiene in France, 1815–1848," *Bulletin of the History of Medicine* 22 (1948): 117–55; George Rosen, *A History of Public Health* (New York, 1958); Ann F. La Berge, "Public Health in France and the French Public Health Movement, 1815–1848" (Ph.D. diss., University of Tennessee, 1974).

2 Rosen, *A History of Public Health,* 175.

3 Ibid., 131.

4 Jean-Pierre Peter, "Malades et maladies à la fin du XVIIIe siècle," *Annales: Economies, sociétés, civilisations* 22 (1967): 711–51.

5 Michel Foucault, *The Birth of the Clinic: An Archaeology of Medical Perception,* trans. A. M. Sheridan Smith (New York, 1973), 31–33.

6 George Rosen, "The Philosophy of Ideology and the Emergence of Modern Medicine in France," *Bulletin of the History of Medicine* 20 (1946): 328–37; Owsei Temkin, "The Philosophical Background of Magendie's Physiology," ibid., 10–35. When the Institut was founded in 1795, the Ideologues formed part of a section for the analysis of sensations and ideas which was part of the class of moral and political sciences. Napoleon suppressed this section in 1803.

7 Ackerknecht, "Hygiene in France," 138.

8 "Prospectus," *Annales d'hygiène publique et de médecine légale* 1 (1829).

9 Erwin H. Ackerknecht, *Medicine at the Paris Hospital, 1794–1848* (Baltimore, 1967), 154–55.

10 Rosen, *A History of Public Health,* 252.

11 Etienne Cabet, *Voyage en Icarie* (Paris, 1842); Charles Fourier, *Théorie de l'unité universelle,* 4 vols. (Paris, 1838).

12 Iago Galdston, "Social Medicine and the Epidemic Constitution," *Bulletin of the History of Medicine* 25 (1951): 10–11.

13 Léonce de Lavergne, "Note sur le dénombrement de la population de 1856," *Séances et travaux de l'Académie des sciences morales et politiques* 39 (1857): 217.

14 Louis Chevalier, *Laboring Classes and Dangerous Classes in Paris during the First Half of the Nineteenth Century,* trans. Frank Jellinek (New York, 1973), 152.

15 Ibid., 155.

16 J. B. Monfalcon and A.P.I. de Polinière, *Traité de la salubrité dans les grandes villes* (Paris, 1846), 39.

17 *Revue générale de l'architecture et des travaux publics* 6 (1845–46): 150.

18 Roger H. Guerrand, *Les Origines du logement social en France* (Paris, 1967), 74.

19 David H. Pinkney, *Napoleon III and the Rebuilding of Paris* (Princeton, 1958), 152.

20 *Revue générale de l'architecture* 9 (1851): 247–49.

21 Chevalier, *Laboring Classes and Dangerous Classes*, 190–92.

22 Descriptions of the arrondissements of Paris may be found in Adeline Daumard, *La Bourgeoisie parisienne de 1815 à 1848* (Paris, 1963), and in Chevalier, *Laboring Classes and Dangerous Classes*.

23 An examination of the percentage of tenants paying a personal property tax in 1846 indicates a sharp division between the arrondissements with the highest proportion of taxpayers (I, II, III) and those with the lowest (VIII, IX, XII). Daumard, *La Bourgeoisie parisienne*, 182.

24 Ibid., 184.

25 Chevalier, *Laboring Classes and Dangerous Classes*, 196–97; Anthony Sutcliffe, *The Autumn of Central Paris: The Defeat of Town Planning, 1850–1970* (London, 1970), 151–52.

26 *Revue générale de l'architecture* 6 (1845–46): 153.

27 Chevalier, *Laboring Classes and Dangerous Classes*, 139.

28 Frégier wrote in response to a competition on the following topic: "Research according to positive observations on the elements which compose in Paris or in any other large city that part of the population which forms a dangerous class because of its vices, its ignorance, and its misery; indicate the means which the administration, rich and affluent men, and intellectual and hard-working workers might use to improve this dangerous and depraved class." La Berge, "Public Health in France," 105.

29 Ibid., 119. Economic liberals tended to point both to the ineffectiveness of this type of public health regulation and to the damage sustained by commerce and industry.

30 S. E. Finer, *The Life and Times of Sir Edwin Chadwick* (London, 1952), 298.

31 *Revue générale de l'architecture* 7 (1847): 252–54.

32 Ibid. 6 (1845–46): 507–9.

33 Dr. Réveillé-Parise, "Conseils hygièniques ou préservatifs contre le choléra-morbus asiatique," *Le Moniteur universel,* April 12, 1849, p. 1330.

34 See, for example, Monfalcon and Polinière, *Traité de la salubrité,* 16; Claude Lachaise, *Topographie médicale de Paris* (Paris, 1822).

35 Réveillé-Parise, "Conseils hygièniques ou préservatifs," *Le Moniteur universel,* April 16, 1849. The keynote sounded in advice on how to prevent cholera was moderation—"*la vie doit être reglée, uniforme, et exempte de tout excès.*" Food and drink were to be taken in small quantities; some exercise was salutory but it should not be excessive; and overwork was to be avoided. Doctors cautioned the population to guard against changes in temperature and recommended avoiding night breezes and wearing a flannel belt to keep the skin temperature even. One's usual regime was to be observed without variation.

36 Erwin H. Ackerknecht, "Villermé and Quetelet," *Bulletin of the History of Medicine* 26 (1952): 317–29.

37 L. R. Villermé, "De la mortalité dans les divers quartiers de la ville de Paris, et des causes qui la rendent très différente dans plusieurs d'entre eux, ainsi que dans les divers quartiers de beaucoup de grandes villes," *Annales d'hygiène publique et de médecine légale* 3 (1830): 294–341.

38 *Recherches statistiques sur la ville de Paris et le département de la Seine* 6 (1860). The death rates per 1,000 population in 1846 by arrondissement were: II, 13; III, 15; IX, 53; XII, 58. In 1849, the death rates per 1,000 for cholera were: II, 8.2; III, 8.7; IX, 39.4; XII, 50.1.

39 J. A. Blanqui, *Des classes ouvrières en France pendant l'année 1848* (Paris, 1849).

40 Monfalcon and Polinière, *Traité de la salubrité,* 49, 88–89.

41 Paul Taillefer, *Des cités ouvrières et de leur nécessité comme hygiène et tranquillité publiques* (Paris, 1852).

42 Armand de Melun, *De l'intervention de la société pour prévenir et soulager la misère* (Paris, 1849).

43 Chevalier, *Laboring Classes and Dangerous Classes,* 155.

44 See Louis Chevalier, "Le Choléra à Paris," *Le Choléra: La première épidémie du XIXe siècle,* ed. Louis Chevalier (La Roche-Sur-Yon, 1958); Asa Briggs, "Cholera and Society in the Nineteenth Century," in *European Political History, 1815–1870: Aspects of Liberalism,* ed. Eugene C. Black (New York, 1967).

45 Monfalcon and Polinière, *Traité de la salubrité,* 92.

46 Guerrand, *Les Origines du logement social en France,* 66.

47 Ibid., 149.

48 La Berge, "Public Health in France," 304.

49 A. Grun, *Le Moniteur universel,* August 26, 1849.

50 Rosen, *A History of Public Health*; La Berge, "Public Health in France," p. 208.

51 For example, on August 11, 1850, Dumas, the minister of agriculture and commerce, sent a ministerial circular to departmental prefects urging them to establish hygiene councils in their departments.

52 During the Second Empire, the Municipal Council was nominated by the prefect of the Seine and had little independent authority.

53 La Berge, "Public Health in France," 170–72; Ordonnance de police concernant la salubrité des habitations, November 20, 1848, revised and updated November 23, 1853.
    On October 10, 1859, many of the health functions directed by the prefect of police were transferred to the prefect of the Seine. These included responsibilities for maintenance of roadways; the sweeping and washing of streets; the removal of dirt, snow, and ice; and the cleaning of sewers and cesspits. Nevertheless, the unfortunate division of authority remained.

54 *Le Moniteur universel,* August 27, 1849; René Baehrel, "La Haine de classe en temps d'épidémie," *Annales: Economies, sociétés, civilisations* 3 (July–September 1952): 351–60.

55 Guy Thuillier, "Hygiène et salubrité en Nivernais au XIXe siècle," *Revue d'histoire économique et sociale* 3 (1967): 317.

56 The commission visited those homes reported as unsanitary and filed recom-

mendations with the mayor, who transmitted the report to the proprietor. If landlords resisted making the prescribed repairs, the Municipal Council acted as the court of appeals. The law further established a procedure for appeals to the Prefectural Council, the Council of State, and the Court of Summary Jurisdiction, and fines for noncompliance, which were, in practice, little more than token penalties.

57 Michel Chevalier, "Les Questions politiques et sociales; L'Assistance et la prévoyance politiques: Rapport de la Commission," *Revue des deux mondes,* 1850: 976.

58 *Rapport fait par M. Henri de Riancey, au nom de la commission d'assistance et de prévoyance sur la proposition de M. de Melun (Nord), relative à l'assainissement des logements insalubres,* December 8, 1849. The reports on and discussions of Melun's bill may be found in the *Moniteur universel* and are reprinted in full in Gustave Jourdan, *Législation sur les logements insalubres: Traité pratique* (Paris, 1879).

59 See J. B. Duroselle, *Les Débuts du catholicisme social en France, 1822–1870* (Paris, 1951). Napoleon III publicly took credit for the law on several occasions. In fact, the government did support the version of the bill which finally passed, but was not responsible for its conception.

60 *Rapport fait de M. Riancey,* December 8, 1849.

61 Anatole de Melun, second deliberation on the proposition of M. de Melun, March 6, 1850. The first deliberation was passed over with no debate.

62 *Rapport fait de M. Riancey,* December 8, 1849.

63 Théophile Roussel, second deliberation on the Melun bill, March 6, 1850. Interestingly, even Roussel was reluctant to apply the restrictive aspect of the law to proprietors living in their own homes and chose, rather, to include them in the tax benefits offered. Apparently proprietors could be coaxed but not badgered.

64 Anatole de Melun, *Proposition du citoyen de Melun (Nord) relative à l'assainissement et à l'interdiction des logements insalubres,* July 25, 1849.

65 *Rapport fait de M. Riancey,* December 8, 1849.

66 Wolowski, second deliberation on the Melun bill, March 6, 1850.

67 Raudot, ibid.

CH. 2. WORKING-CLASS HOUSING IN THE SECOND EMPIRE

1 In practice, this law was ineffective in clearing out slum areas. Juries tended to offer high indemnities for expropriations, so that large-scale demolitions in depressed areas were impractical. At the end of the century, hygienists and housing reform activists fought to rectify the problem by compensating slumlords for site value only, but by World War I, legislation to this effect was still stuck in committee. See below, Chapter 6.

2 *Rapport général sur les travaux de la Commission des logements insalubres,* 1851.

3 The French used below-ground apartments in imitation of a practice established earlier in England. The unhealthful dwellings commission pointed out, however, that while English cellar lodgings had windows at ground level for light

and ventilation, these were not present in the Parisian apartments. Water and stagnating sewage frequently seeped into these cellar lodgings. In 1856 Daumier issued a lithograph in which one proprietor says to another: "I have made two below-ground apartments . . . and when by chance one of these lodgings is vacant, I will cultivate mushrooms."

4 Until a prefectural ordinance in 1883, household garbage was dumped into the gutters, where it was gone through by ragpickers. Thereafter, each house had to collect its garbage in lidded bins. Ragpickers protested en masse to the assembly that their livelihood was lost. The most successful ones frequently tipped the concierge for the privilege of exclusive rights to examine the lidded bins in the interior courtyards. See A. Faure, "Classe malpropre, classe dangereuse? Quelques remarques à propos des chiffonniers parisiens au XIXe siècle et de leurs cités," *Recherches. L'Haleine des faubourgs: Ville, habitat, et santé au XIXe siècle* (December 1977)79–103.

5 Excess humidity was such a problem that hygienists frequently recommended dry-sweeping rather than washing. At the end of the century, as attention focused on the control of tuberculosis, hygienists saw that it was essential to break the long-standing habit of dry-sweeping and urged women to dust with a wet cloth so as to get up all contaminated particles.

6 *Rapport général de la Commission des logements insalubres,* 1860–61.

7 Ibid., 1866–69.

8 Ibid.

9 Alfred Des Cilleuls, *L'Administration parisienne sous la 3e République* (Paris, 1910), 195. Des Cilleuls commented further that the nature of politics during the Third Republic produced, by contrast, a commission which operated "with excessive zeal."

10 *Rapport général de la Commission des logements insalubres,* 1862–65.

11 Ibid., 1866–69.

12 Ibid., 1852–56, 1857–59.

13 Ibid., 1857–59.

14 Ibid., 1860–61.

15 Ibid., 1866–69. In his interpretation of the Melun law, Gustave Jourdan suggests that if domestics and other employees share the same apartment with their employer, they may be considered as part of the family. If, however, they have separate lodgings in the same building, they are, in fact, tenants and fall within the jurisdiction of the unhealthful dwellings commission. Jourdan, *Législation sur les logements insalubres: Traité pratique* (Paris, 1879), 48.

16 For example, the first commission named by the Municipal Council in 1850 included: MM. Boutron, former member of the Municipal Council, member of the Council of Public Hygiene and Salubrity; Bareswil, professor of chemistry at l'Ecole Turgot; Beau, former member of the Municipal Council; Bruyere, architect-surveyor; Dumez, chief clerk of the Commercial Court; Georges, judge of the Commercial Court; Jahan (de), master of requests at the Council of State; Letellier-Lafosse, member of the Chamber of Commerce; Melier, president of the Académie de médecine; Mort, member of the Conciliation Board; Richaud, master of requests at the Council of State; Seguier, member of the Académie des sci-

ences; Thoyot, engineer-in-chief of bridges and roads; Trébuchet, head of the Sanitary Bureau in the Prefecture of Police, member of the Council of Public Hygiene and Salubrity. With the annexation of the suburban communes in 1860, the commission was enlarged to include a representative from each arrondissement as well as representatives from seven official bureaus, including the inspector-general of bridges and roads, the engineer-in-chief of the public thoroughfare (central division), the engineer-in-chief of the public thoroughfare (suburban division), the engineer-in-chief of water and sewers, the director of the Highway Department of Paris, the head of the Division of Public Works, and the head of the Bureau of Roadways. The prominence of the membership remained unchanged.

17 There was, for example, considerable discussion of whether a particular passageway was a private way and therefore the responsibility of the commission or, rather, a public thoroughfare falling within the jurisdiction of regular municipal authorities. Usually a road was viewed as public if there was unlimited, unimpeded access to it.

18 For example, a decision from the Prefectural Council on June 13, 1866, held that the landlord was responsible for the insalubrious condition of a water closet built by the tenant. Jourdan, *Législation sur les logements insalubres,* 326–27.

19 Ibid., 327 (affaire Cailleux).

20 Ibid., 331.

21 Typical cases involved the conversion of a dwelling into a kennel and hen-house (Tourseiller, April 22, 1874), and the transformation of a dwelling into a blacksmith's shop (Veuve d'Estournelles, June 30, 1869). In both situations, the law of 1850 could not be invoked.

22 In the case of M. Brunot, January 11, 1870, the court held that the proprietor could not be required to install a *urinoir* because the clients of the subtenant, a wine merchant, were fouling the courtyard, although police ordinances could be invoked.

23 *Rapport général de la Commission des logements insalubres,* 1866–69. The commission was further hindered by court delays that often rendered its activities meaningless; thus a new dwelling might be excessively humid during its first year of occupancy, but the condition no longer existed by the time the case was completed. Nevertheless, tenants usually were not evicted in the interim and had to endure the unhealthy environment. See Emile Laurent, "Les Logements insalubres et la loi de 1850," *Séances et travaux de l'Académie des sciences morales et politiques* 117 (1882): 680.

24 Laurent, "Les Logements insalubres et la loi de 1850," 681.

25 *Congrès international d'hygiène et de démographie à Paris en 1889: Comptes-rendus* (Paris, 1890), 376–78.

26 This is in sharp contrast to the situation in the 1880s and 1890s, when the profits were not as high and the prescribed repairs were so stringent that landlords formed organizations to oppose the intrusion of the unhealthful dwellings commission. See below, Chapter 6.

27 Archives Nationales (hereafter, AN), F⁸ 210, *Circulaire à MM les Préfets, 27 décembre 1858, Son Exc. le Ministre de l'Agriculture, du Commerce, et des Travaux publics.*

28 A. J. Martin, "Réforme de la législation sanitaire française," in *Congrès international d'hygiène et de démographie, 1889*, 873.

29 For example, the Commission on Unhealthful Dwellings of Amiens initially condemned a large number of buildings as unfit for habitation. It subsequently acknowledged the need to proceed with greater caution, as its actions had inadvertently increased crowding and raised rents in the remaining properties. *Rapport général de la Commission des logements insalubres*, 1852–56.

30 Ibid.

31 See David H. Pinkney, *Napoleon III and the Rebuilding of Paris* (Princeton, 1958), for a complete discussion of the transformation of Paris during the Second Empire.

32 Ibid., 94.

33 *Rapport général de la Commission des logements insalubres*, 1851.

34 Pinkney, *The Rebuilding of Paris*, 37.

35 Anthony Sutcliffe, *The Autumn of Central Paris: The Defeat of Town Planning, 1850–1970* (London, 1970), 17–20.

36 Ibid., 13.

37 Pinkney, *The Rebuilding of Paris*, 25–29.

38 Sutcliffe, *The Autumn of Central Paris*, 20–22.

39 The First Network involved roads which lay largely within the inner boulevards of Old Paris and were financed by subsidies from the state. The streets of the Second Network lay between the inner boulevards and the octroi wall and were funded jointly by the state and the city. The Third Network included miscellaneous roads built entirely by the city. Pinkney, *The Rebuilding of Paris*, 59. For a further discussion of the public works policies of the Second Empire, see also Pierre Lavedan, *Histoire de l'urbanisme: Époque contemporaine* (Paris, 1952); Louis Girard, *La Politique des travaux publics du Second Empire* (Paris, 1952); Sutcliffe, *The Autumn of Central Paris*.

40 *Résultats statistiques du dénombrement de 1896 de la Ville de Paris* (Paris, 1896), xx.

41 Georges Haussmann, *Mémoires du Baron Haussmann*, 3 vols. (Paris, 1890), 2: 454–57.

42 Ibid., 458.

43 Lavedan, *Histoire de l'urbanisme*, 93.

44 Haussmann, *Mémoires*, 2: 460–61. Haussmann's figures are calculated according to the *valeur matricielle*, the taxable base, which represented four-fifths of the actual value. The numbers reported, therefore, would be the number of rentals below Fr 312.50, which had a *valeur matricielle* of Fr 250.00.

45 *Recherches statistiques sur la ville de Paris et le département de la Seine*, vol. 6 (Paris, 1860). The arrondissements with fewer than forty inhabitants per house were I and II — the two wealthiest arrondissements — and IV and XI.

46 Charles Gourlier, *Des voies publiques et des habitations particulières à Paris* (Paris, 1852), 6.

47 Adeline Daumard, *Maisons de Paris et propriétaires parisiens au XIXe siècle, 1809–1880* (Paris, 1965), 203.

48 Daumard, *Maisons de Paris*, 200, presents the following statistics on the average property tax paid per house in Paris:

Year	Average for all Paris	Average for demolished houses	Average for new constructions[a]
1855	120.00	108.00	122.00
1856	121.00	116.00	155.00
1857	122.00	112.00	138.00
1858	124.00	107.00	144.00
b	—	—	—
1861	84.50	79.50	75.56
1862	84.12	77.00	74.76
1863	83.65	83.62	88.77
1864	83.99	82.21	104.98
1865	85.62	83.92	102.83
1866	86.64	80.58	96.71
1867	87.11	85.01	144.50
1868	89.33	85.37	127.91
1869	90.87	85.51	121.11
1870	92.25	75.44	123.12
1871	93.73	50.79	130.86
1872	95.98	82.80	196.62

[a]New constructions were tax-exempt for three years after completion. Thus, a house first taxed in 1855 had been finished in 1852.

[b]Note that the annexation of the suburban communes in 1860 produced a drop in the average property tax paid per house.

49 Haussmann, *Mémoires,* 2: 454.

50 Françoise Marnata, *Les Loyers des bourgeois de Paris, 1860–1958* (Paris, 1961). Marnata gives the following figures on the average selling price of a square meter of undeveloped land, figured with the 1913 value of 100 as the basis:

1860	26.0	1865	46.8
1861	31.2	1866	49.1
1862	32.9	1867	53.1
1863	39.3	1868	50.2
1864	43.3	1869	54.3

51 Louis Lazare, *Les Quartiers pauvres de Paris* (Paris, 1869), 71.

52 A. Cochin, "Paris, sa population, son industrie," *Séances et travaux de l'Académie des sciences morales et politiques* 69 (1864): 275.

53 For example, Sutcliffe, *The Autumn of Central Paris,* 123, estimates that rents increased 42 percent in the decade 1852–62 and 9 percent in the period 1862–76. Georges Duveau, *La Vie ouvrière en France sous le Second Empire* (Paris, 1946), 359, cites figures showing a 50 percent increase between 1850 and 1860 and a further 50 percent increase in the following decade.

54 Denis Poulot, *Question sociale: Le sublime ou le travailleur comme il est en 1870 et ce qu'il peut être* (Paris, 1872), 47.

55 AN, F^8 239, Préfecture de Police, *Note sur la situation actuelle des classes ouvrières dans Paris et dans la banlieue, 25 juin 1855.*

56 Lazare, *Les Quartiers pauvres,* 55. Lazare further charged that Haussmann's claim to have raised the level of rents exempted from property taxes from Fr 250 to Fr 400 was, in fact, specious, as the Fr 400 rentals were the same ones which cost Fr 200 before Haussmann's public works activities.

57 Roger H. Guerrand, *Les Origines du logement social en France* (Paris, 1967), 95.

58 AN, F^8 239, Chambre de Commerce de Paris, *Rapport addressé à Messieurs les membres de la Chambre de Commerce de Paris sur la question relative aux salaires des ouvriers et à l'augmentation de loyers et de denrées alimentaires,* by Horace Say, June 15, 1855.

59 Duveau, *La Vie ouvrière,* 379, concluded that between 1855 and 1869 wages increased on the average of 30 percent but prices sustained an increase of more than 45 percent, leaving the worker with a diminished standard of material well-being.

60 Haussmann, *Mémoires,* 2: 448, 461.

61 Préfecture de Police, *Note sur la situation actuelle des classes ouvrières.*

62 *Paris désert: Lamentations d'un Jérémie Haussmannisé,* n.d.

63 Guerrand, *Les Origines du logement social,* 84.

64 J. J. Danduran, *Les Propriétaires en 1863: Études physiologiques* (Paris, 1863). See also *Pourquoi des propriétaires à Paris: Dédié aux locataires* (Paris, 1857); Louis Veuillot, *Les Odeurs de Paris* (Paris, 1867); Alexandre Weill, *Qu'est-ce que le propriétaire d'une maison à Paris: Suite de Paris inhabitable* (Paris, 1860).

65 Victor Bellet, *Les Propriétaires et les loyers à Paris* (Paris, 1857), 6, 57.

66 Daumard, *Les Maisons de Paris,* 23, 37.

67 Danduran, *Les Propriétaires en 1863.*

68 Alexandre Weill, *Paris inhabitable: Des loyers de Paris ce que tout le monde pense et que personne ne dit* (Paris, 1860), and *Qu-est-ce que le propriétaire d'une maison à Paris: Suite de Paris inhabitable.*

69 Weill, *Paris inhabitable,* 40. Daumard, in *Les Maisons de Paris,* 38, has recently reaffirmed this judgment, calling the Second Empire "the blessed epoch of the proprietor."

70 Maxime Du Camp, *Paris: Ses organes, ses fonctions, et sa vie dans la seconde moitié du XIXe siècle,* 6 vols. (Paris, 1884), 6: 255.

71 Lazare, *Les Quartiers pauvres.* Halbwachs has found that expropriations constituted a higher percentage of total demolitions during the Second Empire than at any other time in the century. In 1852–58, expropriations represented 52 percent of demolitions; in 1862–68, 29 percent; in 1875–81, 11.7 percent; in 1882–89, 6.8 percent. Maurice Halbwachs, *La Population et les tracés de voies à Paris dupuis un siècle (Paris,* 1928), 184–85.

72 Daumard, *Les Maisons de Paris,* 266.

73 Ibid., 220; Gérard Jacquemet, "Belleville aux XIXe et XXe siècles: Une méthode d'analyse de la croissance urbaine à Paris," *Annales: Economies, sociétés, civilisations* 30 (July–August, 1975): 826.

74 A. Corbon, *Le Secret du peuple de Paris* (Paris, 1863), 200.

75 Pinkney, *The Rebuilding of Paris,* 165.

76 Comte d'Haussonville, *Misère et remèdes* (Paris, 1886), 36.

77 Lazare, *Les Quartiers pauvres,* 54; Eugène Cramouzaud, *Etudes sur la transformation du XIIe arrondissement et des quartiers anciens de la rive gauche* (Paris, 1855), 74.

78 Lazare, *Les Quartiers pauvres,* 86–89. Not only were expenses greater in the eastern communes, but competition for jobs from foreign workers who accepted lower wages was intense. Duveau, *La Vie ouvrière,* 208, estimates that 70,000 Germans and Belgians came to Paris during the Second Empire. Many of the Germans were employed as street sweepers, while the Belgians worked in the manufacture of furniture.

79 Lazare, *Les Quartiers pauvres,* 119.

80 Ibid., 69; Jules Simon, *Paris aux parisiens* (Paris, 1869). Simon made these comments on the neglect of eastern Paris in the larger context of a Republican demand for an elected, representative municipal council, independent of the prefect and emperor.

81 Ferdinand de Lasteyrie, *Les Travaux de Paris: Examen critique* (Paris, 1861), 178.

82 Simon, *Paris aux parisiens*; du Camp, *Paris: Ses organes, ses fonctions,* 5: 6.

83 *Rapport général de la Commission des logements insalubres, 1852–56, 1860–61.* The commission stated, "It would be unfair to ask more from a law which often imposes heavy expenses on proprietors, because in most cases they fall on properties of modest value."

84 The focus on the destructive aspect of public works was not confined to authorities in Paris. It was, rather, somewhat of a contemporary orthodoxy. For example, the medical officer of health in Glascow stated: "The destructive part of the duty of the authorities is of more importance, if possible, than the constructive; the first and more essential step is to get rid of the existing haunts of moral and physical degradation and the next is to watch carefully over constructing and reconstructing, leaving, however, the initiative of these usually to the law of supply and demand." Quoted in Gareth Stedman Jones, *Outcast London: A Study in the Relationship between Classes in Victorian Society* (London, 1971), 198.

85 Haussmann, quoted in Sutcliffe, *The Autumn of Central Paris,* 117.

86 "Mémoire présenté par le Sénateur Préfet de la Seine au Conseil général du département," *Le Moniteur universel,* December 24, 1861, pp. 1795–98.

87 Guerrand, *Les Origines du logement social,* 78.

88 Paul Taillefer, *Des cités ouvrières et de leur nécessité comme hygiène et tranquillité publiques* (Paris, 1852), 12. Taillefer recounted an incident during the coup d'état of December 2, 1852, in which a crowd appeared at the Cité Napoleon to pull the emperor's name off the signpost and entrance gates and call upon the residents to raise barricades. The working-class residents of this government-subsidized housing allegedly refused to join the opposition.

89 Jules Simon, "Sociétés coopératives de construction de logements," *Séances et travaux de l'Académie des sciences morales et politiques* 75 (1866).

90 Duveau, *La Vie ouvrière,* 359.

91 Lavedan, *Histoire de l'urbanisme,* 341.

92 These buildings, like the Cité Napoleon, did not attract working-class tenants

and were let to speculation. V. Du Claux, "Petits Logements parisiens," *Annales d'hygiène publique et de médecine légale*, 3rd ser. 9 (1883): 475.

93 Emile Muller and Emile Cacheux, *Les Habitations ouvrières en tous pays* (Paris, 1879), 64–65. Parisian recipients of subsidies included the builders Puteaux, Camille, Rozière, and Pereire, who constructed houses on the boulevard St. Jacques, boulevard Montparnasse, boulevard de Grenelle, boulevard Mazas, and rue de Belleville. The average annual rental for two rooms and a kitchen was Fr 250. Fr 5,870,000 were distributed to the asylums of Vesinet and Vincennes for convalescing workers, and another Fr 300,000 went to the cités of Mulhouse.

94 AN, F¹² 6824, *Cité ouvrière à Paris: Faubourg Saint-Antoine. Maisons isolées avec jardins. Projet soumis au Ministre de l'Intérieur, Emile Muller Ingénieur*, December 10, 1853.

95 Muller and Cacheux, *Les Habitations ouvriéres*, 145–63. To counteract this problem, a group of workers formed a cooperative building society in Paris in August 1867. They received a gift from Napoleon of forty-one houses on the avenue Daumesnil, and with capital raised through shares and loans, built the villa des Rigoles in arrondissement XII. This society failed, according to a contemporary, because it was directed by men poorly acquainted with the problem of workers' housing and with the special conditions of Paris.

96 Lazare, *Les Quartiers pauvres*, 82.

97 Chambre de Commerce de Paris, *Rapport sur la question relative aux salaires des ouvriers*, by Say.

98 Louis René Villermé, *Cités ouvrières* (Paris, 1850).

99 Lynn Lees, "Metropolitan Types: London and Paris Compared," in *The Victorian City: Images and Reality*, ed. H. J. Dyos and Michael Wolff (London, 1973), 416. The literature of the period was filled with comparisons between the educated, refined, and intelligent Parisian worker and the ignorant, boorish, and immoral provincial. For good examples see Lazare, *Les Quartiers pauvres*, 65, and Villermé, *Cités ouvrières*.

100 Villermé, *Cités ouvrières*. In fact, in 1867, only two industrialists in the department of the Seine made special provisions for lodging their personnel. Guerrand, *Les Origines du logement social*, 119.

101 AN, F⁸ 210, Minister of the Interior to Minister of Agriculture, Commerce, and Public Works, October 1, 1861.

102 Comte Ad. de Madre, *Des ouvriers et des moyens d'améliorer leur condition dans les villes* (Paris, 1863), 19–23.

103 *Rapport général sur les travaux du Conseil d'hygiène publique et de salubrité du département de la Seine, 1848–1858*.

104 Guerrand, *Les Origines du logement social*, 75.

105 Villermé, *Cités ouvrières*.

106 Guerrand, *Les Origines du logement social*, 114.

107 See, for example, AN, F¹² 6824, *Règlement à l'usage des locataires. Cités de Marcq-en-Baroeul*.

108 Emile Muller, *Cité ouvrière à Paris: Faubourg Saint-Antoine . . . Projet soumis au Ministre de l'Intérieur*, Emile Muller.

109 Muller and Cacheux, *Les Habitations ouvrières*, 64.

110 Duveau, *La Vie ouvrière,* 348.

111 Auguste Blanqui, "Des cités ouvrières," *Séances et travaux de l'Académie des sciences morales et politiques* 17 (1850): 240.

112 Henry Fougère, *Les Délégations ouvrières aux Expositions universelles sous le Second Empire* (Montluçon, 1905), 20–21.

113 Villermé, *Cités ouvrières.*

114 Pinkney, *The Rebuilding of Paris,* 126. Although Haussmann provided Paris with a larger and better water supply, he failed to set adequate standards for its distribution. Individual proprietors retained control of the decision whether or not to subscribe to city water, so that the landlord's willingness to pay water rates ultimately determined the quality of the available water supply.

115 See, for example, Weill, *Paris inhabitable;* de Madre, *Des ouvriers et des moyens d'améliorer leur condition dans les villes;* Simon, *Paris aux parisiens.*

116 Weill, *Qu'est-ce que le propriétaire d'une maison à Paris,* 9.

117 See especially Duveau, *La Vie ouvrière;* Pierre Lavedan, *Histoire de l'urbanisme;* and idem, *Nouvelle histoire de Paris: Histoire de l'urbanisme à Paris* (Paris, 1975).

CH. 3. HEALTH AND HOUSING ISSUES REDEFINED

1 Georges Duveau, *La Vie ouvrière,* 202–18.

2 Arthur Raffalovich, *Le Logement de l'ouvrier et du pauvre* (Paris, 1887), 261.

3 *Annuaire statistique de la ville de Paris et du département de la Seine,* 1886.

4 Georges Picot, *Séances et travaux de l'Académie des sciences morales et politiques* 121 (1884): 442. From 1861 to 1901 the population increased by the following percentages:

1861–1866	7.6%	1881–1886	3.3%
1866–1872	1.4%	1886–1891	9.1%
1872–1876	7.4%	1891–1896	3.6%
1876–1881	14.1%	1896–1901	7.0%

5 The population of Paris for the years graphed in Figure 3.1 was as follows:

1861	1,696,141	1886	2,344,550
1866	1,825,274	1891	2,447,957
1872	1,851,792	1896	2,536,834
1876	1,988,806	1901	2,714,068
1881	2,269,023		

6 *Résultats statistiques du dénombrement de 1896 pour la ville de Paris et le département de la Seine.* Between 1861 and 1896, the population in arrondissements I–X increased from 946,125 to 1,013,001; the population in arrondissements XI–XX increased from 750,016 to 1,523,833.

7 Lucien Flaus, "Les Fluctuations de la construction d'habitations urbaines," *Journal de la Société de statistique de Paris,* nos. 5–6 (May–June 1949): 185–221; Françoise Marnata, *Les Loyers des bourgeois de Paris, 1860–1958* (Paris, 1961); Préfecture du Département de la Seine, *Documents statistiques recueillés et coordinés par le Service de la Commission des contributions directes de la ville de Paris* (Paris, 1884).

8 In the two better-off quarters of arrondissement XVII, the number of lodgings increased by 65.3 percent between 1878 and 1889, while the population increased only by 46.4 percent. In the two less comfortable quarters, the percentage increase in lodgings (33.4%) exceeded the percentage increase in population (23.5%), but by a considerably smaller amount.

9 *Annuaire statistique de la ville de Paris et du département de la Seine,* 1881.

10 See especially Flaus, "Les Fluctuations de la construction," 194, 214; Gérard Jacquement, "Belleville aux XIXe et XXe siècles: Une méthode d'analyse de la croissance urbaine à Paris," *Annales: Economies, sociétés, civilisations* (July–August 1975): 824–31.

11 Jacquemet's data is derived from his examination of the subdivision of parcels of land between 1843 and 1860. These documents included the profession of the purchaser.

12 The number of employees in transportation grew from 130,000 in 1870 to 360,000 in 1910 for the country as a whole, while those employed in banking and commerce increased by 50 percent in the same time period.

13 By 1900, the working-class population was concentrated in the communes surrounding Paris and had largely evacuated the city itself.

14 Jacquemet, "Belleville aux XIXe et XXe siècles," 829–31.

15 Fernand Pelloutier and Maurice Pelloutier, *La Vie ouvrière en France* (Paris, 1900), 228.

16 Ibid., 197.

17 Emile Cacheux, *L'Economiste pratique* (Paris, 1885), 59. Cacheux recommended that more flexible standards be maintained, e.g., that the city accept roadways sufficiently wide to allow two vehicles to pass on the condition that the buildings not be too high and that they be built so as to leave 12 meters width between constructions.

18 Marnata, *Les Loyers,* 28. Using a base of Fr 100 per square meter of undeveloped land in 1913, Marnata found the following average prices:

1870	Fr 48.50	1880	Fr 51.40	1890	Fr 60.60
1871	42.10	1881	47.90	1891	69.30
1872	42.70	1882	46.80	1892	65.80
1873	39.80	1883	49.10	1893	68.20
1874	36.40	1884	46.20	1894	71.00
1875	38.70	1885	45.00	1895	78.60
1876	45.00	1886	45.00	1896	77.40
1877	45.60	1887	53.70	1897	78.00
1878	49.10	1888	53.10	1898	79.70
1879	51.40	1889	54.90	1899	81.50

19 Ville de Paris, Monographies municipales, *Les Logements à bon marché: Recueil annoté des discussions, délibérations et rapports du Conseil municipal de Paris,* by Lucien Lambeau (Paris, 1897), 375.

20 Emile Muller and Emile Cacheux, *Les Habitations ouvrières en tous pays* (Paris, 1879), 67.

21 Cacheux, *L'Economiste pratique,* 8–12.

22 R. Laborderie, *Les Habitations à bon marché en France* (Bordeaux, 1902), 130. The first building, of seven stories on the rue Jeanne d'Arc, contained 35 lodgings. The second, built in 1889 on the boulevard de Grenelle, contained 45 lodgings. The third and fourth were built in 1890 on the avenue de Saint-Mande (55 lodgings) and in the rue d'Hautpoul (54 lodgings), respectively.

23 It seems clear that considerably higher profits could be reaped from building more expensive housing. Nevertheless, there is evidence that workers distrusted the motives of builders who constructed cités ouvrières and suggested that substantial gains were being made. In a police report of public meetings about rents, the reporter indicates that there is popular distrust of the alleged "philanthropic sentiments" of the builders Cacheux and Minder, as it is believed that they speculate in lands and dwellings. In his work at Mulhouse, Cacheux had reportedly used a German labor force. See Archives de la Préfecture de Police, BA 486, Report of November 11, 1882. Similarly, a police reporter noted in May 1884 that Olivier and Fouquiau, architects who had planned to build low-cost housing with the cooperation of *sociétés coopératives ouvrières,* had broken relations with the workers' groups because the workers did not trust the architects and believed that they were being exploited for the profit of the builders. The well-known investigations of the Pelloutier brothers in 1900 also suggested that builders were more self-interested than public-spirited. Pelloutier and Pelloutier, *La Vie ouvrière en France,* 197. The architects and sponsors of working-class housing would not have denied these charges as, in fact, they promoted such enterprises as good investments. Nevertheless, these insinuations indicate that the projects were surrounded with a haze of suspicion.

24 Le Comte d'Haussonville, *Misère et remèdes* (Paris, 1886), 80.

25 Emile Cacheux, *Etat en l'an 1885 des habitations ouvrières parisiennes* (Paris, 1885).

26 Lambeau, *Les Logements à bon marché,* 106.

27 Paul Leroy-Beaulieu as quoted in Benoît Malon, *Le Socialisme intégral, 2e partie: Des réformes possibles et des moyens pratiques* (Paris, 1894), 374.

28 Raffalovich, *Le Logement de l'ouvrier,* 278–79. Raffalovich noted that annual earnings based upon daily wages had to be corrected so as to account for seasonal unemployment and other irregularities of employment.

29 Jacques Bertillon, *Huitième Congrès international d'hygiène et de démographie: Comptes-rendus et mémoires, Budapest, 1–9 septembre 1894* (Budapest, 1896), 423.

30 Jeanne Singer-Kerel, *Le Coût de la vie à Paris de 1840–1954* (Paris, 1961), 233.

31 Archives de la Préfecture de Police, BA 486, *Enquête sur les loyers à Paris, 1871–1891.*

32 Cacheux, *L'Economiste pratique,* 78.

33 Octave Du Mesnil, *L'Habitation du pauvre* (Paris, 1890), 159. Du Mesnil had had an illustrious career as an hygienist. He served on the Paris Commission on Unhealthful Dwellings, the national Advisory Council on Hygiene, and as a consultant to the Prefecture of Police and to scores of committees dealing with industrial health, personal hygiene, and working-class housing. He practiced medicine at the Asile national de Vincennes and published widely.

34 Georges Piart, *Locataires et propriétaires: Etude sociale sur les abus de la propriété à l'égard de la location* (Paris, 1882), 9–10. The proprietor did have the right to insert into the lease restrictive clauses prohibiting children; however, if the lease did not specifically state that the contract would be void if children were produced, then the birth of a child was not legal cause for eviction. Victor Emion and Charles Bardies, *Dictionnaire des usages et règlements de Paris et du département de la Seine en matière de locations, constructions, voirie, etc.* (Paris, 1893), 172.

35 Piart, *Locataires et propriétaires*, 16.

36 Emion and Bardies, *Dictionnaire des usages*, 229; Louis Pabon, *Manuel pratique des propriétaires et locataires* (Paris, 1906).

37 Emion and Bardies, *Dictionnaire des usages*, 231.

38 Piart, *Locataires et propriétaires*, 39.

39 *L'Intransigeant*, July 22, 1882.

40 Piart, *Locataires et propriétaires*, 39. The building contained thirty-two small rooms, each of which rented for Fr 150 per year.

41 Ibid., 21; Emion and Bardies, *Dictionnaire des usages*, 174; Archives de la Préfecture de Police, BA 486.

42 It became customary to require advance payment although it was not sanctioned by law.

43 Piart, *Locataires et propriétaires*, 49.

44 *L'Economiste français*, May 24, 1879.

45 Lambeau, *Les Logements à bon marché*, 45–53. It was not until January 1901 that a tax was imposed on undeveloped property in Paris.

46 Préfecture du Département de la Seine, *Documents statistiques*, graph 6.

47 In the *Enquête sur les loyers* (Archives de la Préfecture de Police, BA 486) the police commissioners report extensively on the evictions of workers on rent days.

48 Préfecture du Département de la Seine, Direction municipale des travaux du cadastre de Paris, Commission des contributions directes, *Le Livre foncier de Paris*, pt. 1, *Valeur locative des propriétés bâties en 1900*, graph 10, "Nombre des locaux d'habitation dans chacun des 80 quartiers de Paris en 1878, 1889, et 1900." Although the center became somewhat less overcrowded, pockets of decaying buildings on narrow, filthy streets off the main boulevards remained. One observer of the fifth arrondissement dubbed them "Hell at the gates of Paradise."

49 Du Mesnil, *L'Habitation du pauvre*, 22.

50 Haussonville, *Misère et remèdes*, 63; Raffalovich, *Le Logement de l'ouvrier*, 269.

51 Georges Picot, quoted in R. Laborderie, *Les Habitations à bon marché en France* 25.

52 Piart, *Locataires et propriétaires*, 40.

53 Du Mesnil, *L'Habitation du pauvre*, 14–24 and passim.

54 Pelloutier and Pelloutier, *La Vie ouvrière*, 228–32.

55 Du Mesnil, *L'Habitation du pauvre*, pp. 34, 190.

56 Octave Du Mesnil and Dr. Mangenot, *Enquête sur les logements, professions, salaires, et budgets (loyers inférieurs à 400 francs)* (Paris, 1899).

57 Ibid., 34.

58 Ibid., 8–11. Investigators typically drew a tight connection between loose morals, alcoholism, and poor living conditions.

59 Préfecture du Département de la Seine, Direction municipale des travaux du cadastre de Paris, Commission des contributions directes, *Le Livre foncier de Paris: Valeur en capital des propriétés bâties et non bâties en 1901* (Paris, 1902), table 5, "Le régime des eaux, des vidanges, de l'éclairage, du chauffage et le degré de salubrité des immeubles de chacun des 20 arrondissements de Paris en 1902."

60 Dr. Depoully, "L'eau dan les logements ouvriers," *Bulletin de la Société de médecine publique et d'hygiène professionnelle* (1900): 130.

61 *Le livre foncier de Paris: Valeur en capital . . . 1901*, table 5.

62 Ibid.

63 Jacques Bertillon, *Essai de statistique comparée du surpeuplement des habitations à Paris et dans les grandes capitales européennes* (Paris, 1894), 3–4. According to Bertillon, these statistics have some inaccuracies because 22,268 households (including 10,412 single-person households) did not indicate the number of rooms in their lodgings.

64 *Résultats statistiques du dénombrement de 1896 pour la ville de Paris et le département de la Seine.* The editors of this survey claimed that it was more accurate than that taken in 1891. The census-takers exercised more precise control on the responses, and only 4,490 respondents failed to indicate the number of rooms in their lodgings.

65 In contrast, 26.6 percent of the population inhabited sufficient space (one room per person); 13.8 percent inhabited fairly large space (more than one room and less than two per person); 7.8 percent inhabited very large space (two rooms or more per person); 1 percent lived in boats and other irregular vehicles; and 5 percent remained unknown. *Résultats statistiques,* xxviii.

66 *Résultats statistiques.*

67 *Le Livre foncier de Paris,* pt. 1, *Valeur locatitive . . . 1900,* graph 11, "Prix moyen des loyers d'habitation dans chacun des 80 quartiers de Paris en 1900."

68 *Résultats statistiques du dénombrement de 1886 pour la ville de Paris et le département de la Seine.*

69 Pelloutier and Pelloutier, *La Vie ouvrière,* 297.

70 Of these, 42 percent had lived in Paris for less than six months, and 68 percent came to the refuge for the first time. The night refuges typically required baths and disinfected clothing. In 1891, the Asile Benoît-Malon distributed 988 articles of clothing and gave work to 471 men. *Annuaire statistique de la ville de Paris et du département de la Seine,* 1891, p. 626.

71 The workshops repaired shoes and manufactured clothing for the municipal charitable institutions for a salary of Fr 4.25 per day plus food. In addition, workers were paid Fr 1.25 per hundred for bundles of firewood (*margotins*); Fr 1.65 per cubic meter of wood sawed; and Fr 1.00 per hundred for *briquettes*.

72 In addition, private charitable organizations founded seven shelters: The Société philanthropique set up three for women, and the Oeuvre de l'hospitalité
   de nuit established four more for men.

73 François Roques, *Les Logements insalubres: La loi de 1902, le casier sanitaire
   des maisons* (Toulouse, 1906), 45.

74 Jacques Bertillon, *De la fréquence des principales maladies à Paris pendant la
   période 1865–1891* (Paris, 1894), 320–21.

75 Average rents (in francs) in the arrondissements in 1900 were as follows:

Very poor		Poor		Comfortable		Wealthy	
XX	215.50	XII	324.59	IV	481.31	I	916.71
XIII	254.49	XI	327.75	X	502.18	IX	1114.95
XIX	259.31	XIV	335.83	VI	717.58	VII	1178.09
XV	281.58	III	446.25	II	742.58	XVI	1440.80
XVIII	296.87	V	451.61	XVII	753.51	VIII	2643.46

76 Jacques Bertillon, "Mouvements de population et causes de décès selon le degré
   d'aisance à Paris, Berlin, Vienne," *Dixième Congrès international d'hygiène et
   de démographie à Paris en 1900: Comptes-rendus* (Paris, 1901), 961.

77 Bertillon, *De la fréquence des principales maladies,* 114.

78 Henri Turot and Henri Bellamy, *Le Surpeuplement et les habitations à bon marché* (Paris, 1907), 9.

79 Juillerat as quoted in François Roques, *Les Logements insalubres: La loi de 1902,
   le casier sanitaire des maisons,* 81.

80 Henri Monod, "La Législation sanitaire en France," in *Les Applications sociales
   de la solidarité: Leçons professées à l'Ecole des hautes études sociales,* by
   P. Budin et al., with a preface by Léon Bourgeois (Paris, 1904), 152.

81 Du Mesnil, *L'Habitation du pauvre,* 189.

CH. 4. WORKING-CLASS HOUSING AND *les Classes Dirigeantes*

1 Georges Picot, *Séances et travaux de l'Académie des sciences morales et politiques* 121 (1884): 445.

2 Emile Cheysson, "Le Taudis: Ses dangers, ses remèdes" (paper presented at the
   Congrès de l'Alliance d'hygiène sociale à Nancy, June 23, 1906), reprinted in
   Oeuvres choisies (Paris, 1911), 337.

3 Report No. 8, 1883, by M. Villard in Ville de Paris, Monographies municipales,
   *Les Logements à bon marché: Recueil annoté des discussions, délibérations,
   et rapports du Conseil municipal de Paris,* by Lucien Lambeau (Paris, 1897), 69.

4 Paul Leroy-Beaulieu, *Essai sur la répartition des richesses et sur la tendance à
   une moindre inégalité des conditions* (Paris, 1883), 30.

5 Emile Trélat, "Cités ouvrières, maisons ouvrières," *Exposition universelle internationale de 1878 à Paris: Comptes-rendus sténographiques,* no. 10, Congrès international d'hygiène tenu à Paris 1–10 août 1878 (Paris, 1880), 538–52.

6 Jules Simon, *L'Ouvrière* (Paris, 1861), 334–35.

7 Georges Picot, *Conférence sur l'amélioration des petits logements* (Paris, 1894), 4.

8 Le Comte d'Haussonville, *Misère et remèdes* (Paris, 1886), 84.

9 Jules Simon, "Sociétés coopératives de constructions de logements," *Séances et travaux de l'Académie des sciences morales et politiques* 75 (1866): 247.

10 *Rapport général sur les travaux de la Commission des logements insalubres*, 1851.

11 Simon, *L'Ouvrière*, 176.

12 See the movement's own definition of itself in the first issue of its main organ, *La Réforme sociale* 1 (1882): 302. Le Play's followers were infused with an evangelical fervor which they brought to a wide array of overlapping social issues. They typically held multiple memberships in philanthropic organizations. For example, Georges Picot belonged to the Société philanthropique, the Société d'économie sociale, the Musée social, and the Office central des oeuvres de bienfaisance. Emile Cheysson also belonged to the Musée social and the Société d'économic sociale as well as to the Ligue antialcoolique, the Alliance d'hygiène sociale, the Société générale des prisons, the Comité central des oeuvres d'assistance par le travail, and others.

13 Emile Cheysson, "Notice biographique," in *Oeuvres choisies.*

14 For example, Jules Siegfried served as minister of commerce in 1893 and was prominent in the National Assembly. For a detailed discussion of the network of bourgeois reformers, see Sanford Elwitt, "Social Reform and Social Order in Late-Nineteenth-Century France: The Musée Social and Its Friends," *French Historical Studies* 11 (Spring 1980): 431–51.

15 A. de Foville, *Notice historique sur la vie et les oeuvres de M. Georges Picot* (Paris, 1910).

16 Frédéric Le Play, *Le Programme des Unions de la paix sociale* (Tours, 1876), 93.

17 Ibid., 99.

18 Ibid., 105, n. 3.

19 Ibid., 123.

20 Ibid., 136.

21 Cheysson, "Le Taudis," 337.

22 Simon, "Sociétés coopératives de constructions de logements," 247.

23 Edmond Demolins, "Les Habitations ouvrières," *La Réforme sociale* 1 (1881): 301–6.

24 Simon, "Sociétés coopératives de construction de logements," 260–63.

25 In his study of working-class housing at Mulhouse, A. Penot wrote that the formidable problem posed for social economy is "to cause the disappearance of the proletariat from modern society." See Jules Siegfried, *Les Cités ouvrières* (Havre, 1877).

26 Simon, *L'Ouvrière*, 167–68.

27 Jules Siegfried, *Quelques Mots sur la misère: Son histoire, ses causes, ses remèdes* (Havre, 1877), 205; Joseph Lefort, "Les Logements ouvriers" (paper presented at the Association française pour l'avancement des sciences, Congrès de Clermont-Ferrand, August 24, 1876), Georges Picot, *La Lutte contre le socialisme révolutionnaire* (Paris, 1896), 11; Trélat, "Cités ouvrières, maisons ouvrières," 542.

28 Ernest Passez, "La Désorganisation de la famille et ses conséquences sociales," *La Réforme sociale* 34 (1897): 311.

29 Simon, "Sociétés coopératives de construction de logements," 256.

30 Paul Leroy-Beaulieu, *De l'état moral et intellectuel des populations ouvrières et de son influence sur le taux des salaires* (Paris, 1868), 128–29.

31 Trélat, "Cités ouvrières, maisons ouvrières," 542. A worker could rent lodgings at Mulhouse (including two rooms, a kitchen, a garret, a cellar, and a garden) on the condition that the worker cultivate the garden himself, send his children to school, make a deposit each week at a savings bank, and pay 15 centimes to the fund for health insurance.

32 Emile Cacheux, *L'Economiste pratique* (Paris, 1885), 5.

33 E. Brelay, "Le Logement et l'alimentation populaires," *La Réforme sociale* 34 (1897): 484.

34 Georges Picot, *Conférence sur l'amélioration des petits logements,* 7.

35 Jacques Bertillon, *Essai de statistique comparée du surpeuplement des habitations à Paris et dans les grandes capitales européennes* (Paris, 1894), 4.

36 Siegfried, *Quelques Mots sur la misère,* 214.

37 Emile Cheysson, "Le Confort du logement populaire," *Bulletin de la Société française des habitations à bon marché* (1905), reprinted in *Oeuvres choisies,* 373–76.

38 Siegfried, *Quelques Mots sur la misère,* 215. According to Siegfried, the list of acceptable remedies for misery available through the private sector included instruction, insurance, association, and leisure activities.

39 Paul Leroy-Beaulieu, *La Question ouvrière au XIXe siècle* (Paris, 1899), 335.

40 Georges Picot, "Self-Help for Labor: Some French Solutions to Working-Class Problems" (address delivered to the Liberty and Property Defense League, December 8, 1891).

41 Picot, *Conférence sur l'amélioration des petits logements,* 7–8.

42 Georges Picot, "Les Moyens d'améliorer la condition de l'ouvrier," *La Réforme sociale* 21 (1891): 42.

43 Picot, *Self-Help for Labor;* and "Les Moyens d'améliorer la condition de l'ouvrier," 45.

44 Picot, "Les Moyens d'améliorer la condition de l'ouvrier," 43.

45 Picot, *Conférence sur l'amélioration des petits logements,* 7–8.

46 Léon Say, *Séances et travaux de l'Académie des sciences morales et politiques* 121 (1884): 446.

47 Georges Picot, *Un Devoir social et les logements d'ouvriers* (Paris, 1885), 42. This was especially true at that time because of a harsh winter with large industrial unemployment and declines in agricultural production.

48 Picot, *Conférence sur l'amélioration des petits logements,* 9.

49 Picot, *La République: Ses veritables adversaires* (Gien, 1892), 5.

50 D. Leprince, *Les Logements à bon marché: La propriété immobilière rendue accessible aux travailleurs* (Paris, 1888), 3.

51 Picot, "Les Moyens d'améliorer la condition de l'ouvrier," 40.

52 Picot, *Conférence sur l'amélioration des petits logements,* 8–9.

53 Georges Picot, "Les Logements d'ouvriers à Londres," *Séances et travaux de l'Académie des sciences morales et politiques* 124 (1885): 693.

54 Arthur Raffalovich, in "Dans quelle mesure l'état doit-il intervenir dans la ques-

tion des logements insalubres?" (report of meeting of the Société d'économie politique), *Journal des économistes* 28 (1884): 505.

55 Biographical information on Leroy-Beaulieu is from G. Vapereau, *Dictionnaire universel des contemporains,* 6th ed. (Paris, 1893–95).

56 G. de Molinari, in "De l'intervention de l'état et des municipalités dans la question des loyers," *Journal des économistes* 25 (1884): 443.

57 Ibid., 446.

58 Henri Baudrillart, "L'Amélioration des logements d'ouvriers dans ses rapports avec l'esprit de famille," *Séances et travaux de l'Académie des sciences morales et politiques* 131 (1889): 220.

59 Leroy-Beaulieu, *Essai sur la répartition des richesses,* 189.

60 Paul Leroy-Beaulieu, "Liberty and Property: The Two Main Factors of Human Progress" (paper presented at the fourteenth annual meeting of the Liberty and Property Defense League, March 2, 1897). According to Leroy-Beaulieu, in 1879 M. Rampol, a philanthropist, died, leaving £60,000 to the municipality to distribute to workingmen's associations and cooperative societies. The municipal council apparently lost £8,000, and all but a third of the total remained undispersed.

61 Leroy-Beaulieu, *Essai sur la répartition des richesses,* 190.

62 Paul Leroy-Beaulieu, *L'Etat moderne et ses fonctions* (Paris, 1891), 206–8.

63 Arthur Raffalovich, in "Dans quelle mesure l'état doit-il intervenir dans la question des logements insalubres?" Also his *Le Logement de l'ouvrier et du pauvre* (Paris, 1887), 289.

64 Leroy-Beaulieu, *Essai sur la répartition des richesses,* 226.

65 Baudrillart, "L'Amélioration des logements d'ouvriers," 220.

66 Leroy-Beaulieu, *Essai sur la répartition des richesses,* 192; idem, *L'Etat moderne et ses fonctions,* 391.

67 F. Passy, "De l'intervention de l'état et des municipalités dans la question des loyers," 453.

68 Leroy-Beaulieu, "Liberty and Property." The motto of the Liberty and Property Defense League, before whom this address was delivered (see n. 60, above), emblazoned on each publication, read: "To uphold the principle of Liberty, and guard the rights of Labour and Property of all kinds against undue interference by the State; and to encourage Self-Help versus State-Help." In France, the analogous society was the Société pour la défense et le progrès social.

69 Leroy-Beaulieu, *L'Etat moderne,* 243, 292, 391. He warned that the state is always menaced by the possibility of becoming the prey of fanatics—"fanatics of religion, fanatics of rapid and unlimited progress, fanatics of the natural sciences and their transposition in the social order, fanatics of temperance, of morality, of equality." Accordingly, state power ought to be kept to a minimum.

70 Antony Roulliet, *Les Habitations ouvrières à l'Exposition universelle de 1889 à Paris* (Nancy, 1889); Picot, *Séances et travaux de l'Académie des sciences morales et politiques* 121 (1884): 445; Demolins, "Les Habitations ouvrières," 306. These constructions were located on impasse Boileau near the avenue de Versailles.

71 It was suggested that the tenant make a down payment of Fr 1,000, which would lower rent payments by Fr 80 or shorten the amortization period by five years.

Demolins, "Les Habitations ouvrières," 306. By 1883, the price of these houses had risen to Fr 9,500. See Lambeau, *Recueil annoté des discussions . . . du Conseil Municipal de Paris,* 351.

72 Cacheux, cited in d'Haussonville, *Misère et remèdes,* 404.

73 Of the 4,434,314 savings books in France as of December 31, 1882, 1,002,256 contained less than Fr 20, and 1,604,010 contained Fr 100 or less. The average deposit in Paris (Fr 98) was considerably less than the average for all of France (Fr 217) because living expenses were higher in the city. D'Haussonville observed that not only were prices high in Paris, but the Parisian worker had come to expect to live "comme un monsieur." D'Haussonville, *Misère et remèdes,* 386, 405–6.

74 Picot, *Séances et travaux de l'Académie des sciences morales et politiques* 121 (1884): 445.

75 Roulliet, *Les Habitations ouvrières à l'Exposition universelle de 1889 à Paris,* 85.

76 L. Reuss, "Les Maisons ouvrières de la rue de Mouzaia," *Annales d'hygiène publique et de médecine légale,* 3rd ser. 26 (1891): 113–21. These houses included a kitchen and storeroom on the ground floor, two bedrooms and a privy on the second floor, and a garret. Household wastes flowed directly to an underground sewer (*tout à l'égout*).

77 Cacheux, *L'Economiste pratique,* 10–11.

78 It seems that the image of the worker-proprietor had penetrated official circles as well. In a parliamentary investigation in 1872 of conditions of work and the relationship between employers and employees, a series of questions solicited information about the emergence of societies designed to assist the worker in becoming his own landlord. The commissioner of police in the thirteenth arrondissement replied that no such societies existed and that nearly all the employers of the quarter had begun as workers and had become proprietors without assistance: "These new rich indicate that there is but one way to arrive at this goal—unceasing work, economy, and temperance." A later questionnaire in 1884 on the situation of workers in industry and agriculture asked about the difficulty in finding lodgings, the scale of rents, and whether the rent had been replaced by an annuity which ultimately translated into ownership. Archives de la Préfecture de Police, BA 400, Enquête parlementaire sur les conditions du travail en France, October 1872; Archives de la Préfecture de Police, BA 399, Enquête parlementaire sur la situation des ouvriers de l'industrie et de l'agriculture en France, 1883–1884.

79 See especially Siegfried, *Les Cités ouvrières.*

80 Jules Siegfried, "Les Habitations à bon marché," in *Les Applications sociales de la solidarité: Leçons professées à l'Ecole des hautes études sociales,* by P. Budin et al., 221, 232.

81 *Journal officiel: Documents parlementaires,* annexe no. 2059, sess. of April 7, 1892, *Rapport sommaire fait au nom du 21ᵉ commission d'initiative parlementaire chargée d'examiner la proposition de loi de M. Jules Siegfried . . . relative aux habitations ouvrières.*

82 Henri Turot and Henri Bellamy, *Le Surpeuplement et les habitations à bon marché* (Paris, 1907), 75.

83 In the original law, it was left to the conseil général to determine if a committee was necessary. Not surprisingly, the Senate argued in 1906 that to require departmental financial support limited local autonomy too severely. See Turot and Bellamy, *Le Surpeuplement,* 76.

84 Roulliet, *Les Habitations ouvrières à l'Exposition de 1889,* 98. The Congress on Low-Cost Housing resolved that "low-cost houses ought to enjoy, either permanently or in the period following their construction, special exemptions from the taxes which weigh on property."

85 Turot and Bellamy, *Le Surpeuplement,* 85, 87.

86 Ibid., 89. It was not until 1904 that the Assistance publique loaned Fr 150,000 to the Société anonyme des logements hygièniques à bon marché.

87 Siegfried, "Les Habitations à bon marché," 221.

88 See Cacheux, *L'Economiste pratique,* 18; Alfred Fillassier, *De la détermination des pouvoirs publics en matière d'hygiène* (Paris, 1902), 373; Fernand Pelloutier and Maurice Pelloutier, *La Vie ouvrière en France* (Paris, 1900), 197.

89 E. Muller and O. Du Mesnil, "Des habitations à bon marché: Au point de vue de la construction et de la salubrité," *Annales d'hygiène publique et de médecine légale,* 3rd ser. 22 (1889): 153.

90 Turot and Bellamy, *Le Surpeuplement,* 24–26. A half-century earlier, Corbon wrote in *Le Secret du peuple de Paris:* "[The worker] does not want to build his house as he is directed on the land which he is advised to buy. He prefers to pitch his tent as if he glimpses in the distance the object of his ardent hopes—the radiant city where his ideal of justice reigns." Quoted in d'Haussonville, *Misère et remèdes,* 80.

91 Turot and Bellamy, *Le Surpeuplement,* 27–28.

92 B. Malon, *Le Socialisme intégral,* part 2, *Des réformes possibles et des moyens pratiques* (Paris, 1894), 388.

93 Archives de la Préfecture de Police, BA 486.

94 Brelay, "Le Logement et l'alimentation populaires," 481.

95 d'Haussonville, *Misère et remèdes,* 80.

96 Emile Cacheux, *Etat des habitations ouvrières à la fin du XIXᵉ siècle* (Paris, 1891), 6.

97 Leroy-Beaulieu, *Essai sur la répartition des richesses,* 64, 186. According to Leroy-Beaulieu, if certain proprietors abused their rights, this was not significant because in most cases the regime of private real property was so beneficent that one should not contemplate restraining it.

98 Baudrillart, "L'Amélioration des logements d'ouvriers," 228.

99 Raffalovich, *Le Logement de l'ouvrier,* 290.

100 *Séances et travaux de l'Académie des sciences morales et politiques* 121 (1884): 447.

101 Leroy-Beaulieu, *L'Etat moderne,* 390.

102 An exception to this general pattern appeared in Raffalovich, *Le Logement de l'ouvrier,* 287, in which he stated that "the crux of the problem of unhealthful housing is the poverty of those who live packed into foul slums." This perception produced only resignation, however.

103 Leroy-Beaulieu, *L'Etat moderne,* 391; Brelay, "Dans quelle mesure l'état doit-il

intervenir dans la question des logements insalubres?" 510; Brelay, "Le Logement et l'alimentation populaires," 483.

104 *Séances et travaux de l'Académie des sciences morales et politiques* 121 (1884): 447.

105 Ibid.

106 Brelay, "Le Logement et l'alimentation populaires," 483.

107 Baudrillart, "L'Amélioration des logements d'ouvriers," 229.

108 Raffalovich, *Le Logement de l'ouvrier,* 280.

109 Leroy-Beaulieu, *Essai sur la répartition des richesses,* xi, 183–86.

110 Passy, "De l'intervention de l'état et des municipalités dans la question des loyers," 453.

111 By the 1880s, many observers had become disillusioned with the kinds of building projects which had increased prosperity during the Second Empire. Economists blamed current problems on the "unconsidered actions" of the state and municipalities, which had contributed to abnormal and erratic spurts of growth, industrial instability, demographic imbalances, and the escalation of rents. It seemed important in the 1880s to inhibit rather than encourage urban growth. In a discussion of rents in Paris in December 1882, Demolins argued that the only remedy was to reverse the migration from rural areas. He urged the wealthy to revitalize the countryside by buying estates outside the city and asked the government to promote administrative decentralization. At the same time, Demolins supported the deportation of certain categories of habitual criminals and encouraged Frenchmen to cultivate "habits of colonization" as did the English. *La Réforme sociale* 1 (1883): 99.

   It is interesting to note that Parisian workers, especially the elite artisans, themselves saw the need to contain migration. In a pamphlet of April 10, 1883, "La Question de Paris," addressed to M. Jules Ferry, minister of public instruction, they attacked Haussmann's policies and called for an end to demolitions and constructions and for the repatriation of foreign and provincial workers at the expense of the municipality and the state. The pamphlet was signed by six mechanics, two chefs, a cook, a civil engineer, three employees (not specified), a painter, a restauranteur, a servant, a joiner, a doctor, a bookkeeper, a publicist, a bronze-fitter, a piano-builder, and a printer. Archives de la Préfecture de Police, BA 486.

112 Leroy-Beaulieu, *Essai sur la répartition des richesses,* 225.

113 Ibid., 193–96, 221; *L'Etat moderne,* 393.

114 Each hackney-carriage (*voiture de place*) paid 1 franc per day and each omnibus Fr 1,500 per year. The yearly sum for taxes on public vehicles totaled Fr 4.5 million in 1883. Leroy-Beaulieu estimated that a worker living outside the city could expect to pay an extra Fr 100–200 annually for transportation, an expense which would be considerably smaller if licensing taxes were reduced. He concluded that the number of public conveyances would double if there were lighter licensing fees. *Essai sur la répartition des richesses,* 219.

115 Leroy-Beaulieu, *Séances et travaux de l'Académie des sciences morales et politiques* 121 (1884): 448; Raffalovich, *Le Logement de l'ouvrier,* 301.

116 Leroy-Beaulieu, *La Question ouvrière au XIXᵉ siècle,* 298–99, 333. Although he no longer considered education of the working class a panacea, Leroy-Beaulieu saw its continued importance in teaching the tenets of political economy: the legitimate origins of property, the beneficial role of capital, the necessity of inheritance, and the real causes of inequality among men.

117 Ibid., 308–9.

118 Emile Cheysson, "Le Rôle social de l'ingénieur" (paper presented to the Société des ingénieurs civils, May 20, 1897), reprinted in *Oeuvres choisies,* 22.

119 *Exposition universelle internationale de 1878: Comptes-rendus sténographiques,* no. 10, *Congrès international d'hygiène,* 549. The conservative classes tended to move back and forth between this image of society as an organic unity and Le Play's concept of an harmonious, well-integrated hierarchy.

120 Cheysson, "La Lutte des classes," 112.

121 Cheysson, "Mon Testament social" (paper presented at the Ligue nationale contre l'alcoolisme, March 23, 1909), reprinted in *Oeuvres choisies,* 5.

122 Cheysson, "Le Rôle social de l'ingénieur," 22.

123 Ibid., 30. Cheysson's experiences with the International Exposition of 1867 suggested to him the importance of establishing a new category of award which recognized social usefulness.

124 Picot, "Les Moyens d'améliorer la condition de l'ouvrier," 45.

125 Picot, *La Lutte contre le socialisme révolutionnaire,* 38.

126 Ibid., 41, 56.

127 Picot, "Les Moyens d'améliorer la condition de l'ouvrier," 45.

128 Leroy-Beaulieu, *La Question ouvrière au XIXᵉ siècle,* 319.

CH. 5. HOUSING AND MUNICIPAL POLITICS

1 Report from the municipal police to the Prefecture of Police, March 6, 1879, Archives de la Préfecture de Police, BA 486, Enquête sur les loyers à Paris 1871–91. (Hereinafter cited as Archives PP.) In his discussion of the operations of the Municipal Council, Cochin suggests that although the council was interested in social issues, the need at this time to replace clerical personnel in education and in public assistance jobs drained the budget and precluded the development of new programs. D. Cochin, *Paris: Quatre Années au Conseil Municipal* (Paris, 1885).

2 On April 8, 1883, a speaker addressing a group of twenty persons in arrondissement XIV commented: "It is said that people are becoming bored with this series of conferences on rents which produce nothing." The Congress on Rents, which began meeting in May and scheduled four meetings per month, was forced to cancel meetings several times during July because no one appeared. During the summer, in addition, Guesde and Lafargue, Marxist agitators, were imprisoned (until November 1883), and this, too, produced a decline in activity.

3 See reports in Archives PP, BA 486, of March 18, 1881; June 4, 1881; July 11, 1881.

4 Archives PP, BA 486, report of July 4, 1882.

5 *Le Temps,* July 15, 1883.

6 Archives PP, BA 486, report of August 22, 1883.

7 *La Bataille*, September 11, 1883. According to law, the rights of the landlord preempted those of all other creditors. He was entitled to confiscate all property, except the bed, in lieu of rent payments.

8 Archives PP, BA 486, reports of June 13, 1882, and August 7, 1882.

9 Guesde, in *Le Citoyen*, June 19, 1882; Jules Guesde, *Ça et là* (Paris, 1914), 229.

10 Archives PP, BA 486: Congrès sur les loyers, July 1883; resolutions of November 1, 1883; and reports of January 14, 1883, and June 9, 1883. Lucien Manier, the spokesman for immediate confiscation, appeared regularly at public meetings throughout the city. Although he probably spoke more often than any other individual, his influence was limited by the fact that he continued, single-mindedly, to propose a plan which enjoyed the least chance for serious consideration. Even the Marxists opposed Manier's approach. Lafargue maintained that the houses belonged to the workers, not to the proprietors, because of the labor they had invested in building them and their contributions in rents. He rejected Manier's proposal, stating that the "houses have been paid for twenty times by the tenants; their repurchase would be a colossal theft."

11 Joffrin, a mechanic, is listed in the *Dictionnaire biographique du mouvement ouvrier français* as "one of the authors of the rebirth of the workers' movement after the Commune." He returned to Paris in 1880 and in 1882 was elected to the Municipal Council from the quarter Grandes-Carrières in the eighteenth arrondissement. In his program, he called for a code obligating proprietors regarding maintenance and rent, and requiring that landlords rent to workers in any trade, having any number of children, without demanding payment in advance.

12 The electoral program of the Possibilists included (1) the transformation of large monopolies (such as those providing bus and tramway service, water, and gas) into public services to be sold at cost price or delivered free; (2) the establishment of municipal industries to provide work; (3) the opening of municipal granaries, bakeries, and butcher shops; (4) the construction of municipal housing and the imposition of a 20 percent tax on unrented lodgings and undeveloped property; (5) the creation of a free medical service; and (6) the establishment of a Labor Exchange. In contrast to the political focus of the Marxists, the Possibilists emphasized the issues of everyday life, concentrating on a "social revolution." See Sylvain Humbert, *Les Possibilistes* (Paris, 1911).

13 Joffrin presented propositions to this effect to the Municipal Council on August 7, 1882, and June 14, 1883. Ville de Paris, Monographies municipales, *Les Logements à bon marché: Recueil annoté des discussions, délibérations, et rapports du Conseil Municipal de Paris,* by Lucien Lambeau (Paris, 1897), 580–82. (Hereinafter cited as Lambeau.)

14 During this period of acute shortage of working-class lodgings, the number of vacancies in the city as a whole was growing. See above, Chapter 4.

15 Jules Guesde, *Ça et là.*

16 Jules Guesde and Paul Lafargue, *Le Programme du Parti ouvrier: Son histoire, ses considérants, ses articles* (Lille, 1890), 49–52.

17 Guesde, *Ça et là,* 229.

18 Ibid., 244, 247.

19 Guesde, *Le Citoyen,* June 19, 1882.

20 Archives PP, BA 486, report of May 5, 1883.

21 Archives PP, BA 399, Enquête parlementaire sur la crise économique et industrielle, 1883–1884.

22 Ibid.

23 See Lambeau, passim.

24 Lambeau, 10, 120, 36.

25 Report no. 8 of 1883 by M. Villard, February 9, 1883, Lambeau, 54–76.

26 Report no. 1 of 1884 by M. L.-C. Cernesson, Lambeau, 790 ff.

27 June 11, 1883, Lambeau, 538. Concern about the growth of the city was similarly reflected in a proposal by Orion on February 26, 1883 (Lambeau, 164) which noted that poorly paid agricultural workers were drawn to Paris by the promise of higher salaries. He claimed that it was necessary to attack the problem at its source and reorganize agriculture. There is little doubt that Orion was voicing the common fear of making Paris more appealing to provincials.

28 November 27, 1883, Lambeau, 678.

29 January 24, 1883, Lambeau, 106–7.

30 Lambeau, 95 ff.

31 Lambeau, 215–18, 220–36, 251, 268.

32 Report no. 41 of 1883 by M. Level, Lambeau, 477 ff.

33 Lambeau, 293, 315–28, 477, 518.

34 The situation in Paris was atypical in that the omnibus company escaped the municipal regulation common in most European cities. The issue of urban mass transportation was further complicated by city versus state conflicts which significantly retarded the development of a metropolitan railway. The first debates opened in 1871, but the first lines of the Metro were not operating until 1900. Disagreements arose on technical matters (steam versus electricity, above versus below ground) as well as on questions of administrative authority. In the end, the state conceded jurisdiction to city authorities, who sought to protect city revenues by keeping the railway exclusively urban. Lines were not extended into the suburbs until 1920. See Pierre Lavedan, *Nouvelle Histoire de Paris: Histoire de l'urbanisme à Paris* (Paris, 1975); John P. McKay, *Tramways and Trolleys: The Rise of Urban Mass Transport in Europe* (Princeton, 1976).

35 The Crédit foncier was a private bank, founded in part by government subsidy during the Second Empire, and controlled by a small group of oligarchs.

36 Report no. 40 of 1883, in Lambeau, 488 ff. In the last years of the Second Empire, Amouroux had been affiliated with the International and active in agitation against the government. He fled France but returned to be part of the Commune. Once again, he was forced to leave France, but returned with the amnesty and became a founding editor of *Le Radical.* He was elected to the Municipal Council in 1881 from arrondissement XX (La Charonne) and served until 1885.

37 In fact, the Municipal Council had been negotiating with the bus companies for a year for twelve new lines without obtaining any. February 20, 1884, Lambeau, 858.

38 Opponents of a suburban transportation system argued in 1895 that the Metro

would encourage emigration from the center, costing the city Fr 30 million out of the Fr 150 million collected annually on commodities entering the city.

39 The Crédit foncier did not ordinarily lend directly to entrepreneurs who possessed only land and would provide funds only when the construction was at least half completed. Those who wished to borrow in order to build were sent to an intermediary bank which charged a commission each time installment payments were made on the loan, adding approximately 9.5 to 11 percent to the total costs.

40 Lambeau, 487, 593. According to the statistics of Dr. P. Brouardel, for every 100,000 inhabitants, mortality between 1870 and 1882 increased as follows: typhoid fever, from 48 to 96; diphtheria, 53 to 101; smallpox, 11 to 74; measles, 30 to 43; scarlet fever, 7 to 18.

41 Lambeau, 724–25, 842. Amouroux cited statistics to show that during the typhoid epidemic of 1882, mortality in the dense working-class quarters ranged from 15.06 per 10,000 inhabitants to 32.63 per 10,000. In contrast, eight of the least dense sections of the city sustained a mortality rate of less than 6 per 10,000 inhabitants.

42 February 15, 1884, Lambeau, 841–43.

43 Cochin, *Paris: Quatre Années au Conseil Municipal*; Jacques Ultor, *La Question des loyers, du pain, du travail et le Conseil Municipal de Paris* (Paris, 1884); Ernest Gay, *Nos Ediles* (Paris, 1895); C. de la Barrière and L. Moquant, *Le Nouveau Conseil Municipal de Paris: Biographies et programmes des 80 conseillers municipaux élus en mai 1884* (Paris, 1884).

44 April 28, 1883, Lambeau, 436, 457.

45 May 16, 1883, Lambeau, 507.

46 June 20, 1883, and February 20, 1884, Lambeau, 594, 918.

47 February 13, 1884, Lambeau, 830 ff. The director of public works maintained, on the other hand, that the administration of the terms of the agreement would not, in practice, be too taxing. Requests for loans would be addressed to the prefect, who would determine whether the plan conformed to the regulations, evaluate the credit of the potential borrower, and make a recommendation to the Municipal Council. A special committee of the council would study the entire proposal and issue a final recommendation. Supervision of construction could be assumed by the forty practicing *commissaires voyeurs*.

48 June 20, 1883, Lambeau, 594. In his statement to his constituency in 1884, Leven commented that he was opposed to all unnecessary charges on the budget. He specifically attacked the project with the Crédit foncier, stating that "it is not by favors extended to speculation, to the detriment of the whole body of taxpayers, but by the spontaneous efforts of industry, by the development of inexpensive transportation between the center and the periphery, that we can expect to lower rents."

49 February 20, 1884, Lambeau, 924.

50 Jean Bastié, *La Croissance de la banlieu parisienne* (Paris, 1964), 196.

51 Anthony Sutcliffe, *The Autumn of Central Paris: The Defeat of Town Planning, 1850–1970* (London, 1970), 56–58.

52 June 13, 1883, and February 15, 1884, Lambeau, 574–77 and 870–72.

53 June 13, 1883, Lambeau, 575.

54 February 13, 1884, Lambeau, 814–19.

55 May 16 and June 20, 1883, Lambeau, 502, 606.

56 February 13, 1884, Lambeau, 814–19.

57 Report from meeting of the Société d'économie politique, "De l'intervention de l'état et des municipalités dans la question des loyers," *Journal des économistes* 25 (1884): 452.

58 *Le Temps,* June 18, 1883.

59 A. Fougerousse, "Pour la construction des petits logements," *La Réforme sociale* 1 (1883): 401–7. Similarly, *Le Soleil* warned that Joffrin's plans to tax unoccupied lodgings and to build municipal housing "would gradually lead to the confiscation of workers' housing and then, of all inhabited buildings, by the City of Paris." *Le Soleil,* June 15, 1883.

60 June 13, 1883, Lambeau, 568.

61 February 15, 1884, Lambeau, 872.

62 These groups included the Congrès régional du centre, representing forty-seven trade organizations, thirty-seven socialist groups, and two cooperative societies; the Congrès sur les loyers; and a group of workers in the building industry. June 13 and June 20, 1883, Lambeau, 574–82, 605–8.

63 February 20, 1884, Lambeau, 931–58.

64 March 20, 1883, Lambeau, 277–79.

65 For example, in the summer of 1883, Manier proposed the opening of three construction sites by July 14 in symbolic affirmation of democratic commitments while the council was formulating long-term policy. He urged the appropriation of Fr 10 million for low-rent housing, which would be built according to plans approved by the government and supervised by the Municipal Council. After some discussion, Manier asked for a vote on the urgency of the question. The vote on the urgency of the matter passed (21 to 19), while a vote on the merits of the proposal produced a defeat. Amouroux noted, further, that most critics of specific proposals wished to table the issue so as not to have to commit themselves publicly to any specific stand before the next elections. Lambeau, 642–45, 632.

66 Joffrin attempted to amend the proposal to include the stipulations that the work would be done exclusively by trade unions according to the city's wage scale and that the work day would not exceed eight hours. The council agreed that the construction project would be put to bid and that only workers' unions would be eligible. It rejected the eight-hour work day.

67 Memoir of Poubelle, Prefect of the Seine, to the Municipal Council, October 15, 1884, Lambeau, 1005–8.

68 January 27 and 31, 1885, Lambeau, 1016–18 and 1034–37.

69 Report no. 14 of 1885 by M. Dreyfus, February 25, 1885, Lambeau, 1060.

70 This proposal was passed by a vote of 37 to 15, and a construction code was adopted in January 1885.

71 Report no. 126 of 1885 by M. M. Michelin and Dreyfus, February 4, 1885, Lambeau, 1041–44.

72 There is some indication that the rate of return on buildings constructed on the rue de Tolbiac would not have exceeded 2 to 3 percent.

73 April 17, 1890, Lambeau, 1198.

74 December 31, 1890, Lambeau, 1214.

75 March 5, 1890, Lambeau, 1190. Edouard Vaillant sat on the Municipal Council between 1884 and 1893, and was a former member of the Commune.

76 March 25, 1891, Lambeau, 1217.

77 July 17, 1891, Lambeau, 1221. The year before, Paul Brousse had made a similar proposition, in which he asked the council to anticipate housing shortages caused by public works projects and make provision for rehousing those displaced.

78 December 1, 1893, Lambeau, 1223–25.

79 December 5, 1894, Lambeau, 1239.

80 Gérard Jacquemet has recently studied patterns of habitation in Belleville and has found that the new housing built at the end of the century was largely for employees in the growing tertiary sector of the economy and not for the working classes. See above, Chapter 3. Gérard Jacquemet, "Belleville aux XIXᵉ et XXᵉ siècles: Une méthode d'analyse de la croissance urbaine à Paris," *Annales: Economies, sociétés, civilisations* 30 (July–August 1975): 819–43.

81 de la Barrière and Moquant, *Le Nouveau Conseil Municipal de Paris*.

82 Lambeau, 95 ff.

83 May 1, 1883, Lambeau, 275.

84 June 22, 1883, Lambeau, 625.

85 Lambeau, 225.

86 In his recent book, *France, 1870–1914: Politics and Society* (London, 1977), R. D. Anderson writes that "Paris was, of course, the traditional headquarters of the Left, but it lost that position at the end of the century. In the 1890s, Radicals and Socialists still dominated its politics," but Radicalism was "'the state of mind of the petty bourgeoisie.'" He continues: "The problem for the Radicals was that while it was desirable to offer reforms in order to retain the working class vote, the larger part of their support came from peasants, shopkeepers, and middle class people who were content with things as they were, suspicious of the State, and devoted to the values of individualism. Why risk losing their essential votes by trying to put ambitious programmes into practice?" Pp. 59 and 99.

Ch. 6. The regulation of "microbe factories"

1 Emile Cacheux, *Etat en l'an 1885 des habitations ouvrières parisiennes* (Paris, 1885), 5.

2 See Chapter 1 for typical examples of the rhetoric of the public health movement in the first half of the century.

3 This general pattern in America has been described by Barbara Gutman Rosenkrantz in her book *Public Health and the State: Changing Views in Massachusetts, 1842–1936* (Cambridge, Mass., 1972).

4 See Ann F. La Berge, "Public Health in France and the French Public Health

Movement, 1815–1848" (Ph.D. diss., University of Tennessee, 1974), and especially William Coleman, *Death Is a Social Disease: Public Health and Political Economy in Early Industrial France* (Madison, Wis., 1982), for a complete discussion of Villermé's reluctance to promote greater government intervention. Except in his campaign to outlaw child labor, he hoped to rely on the enlightened self-interest of private parties and the gradual advance of civilization to ameliorate health conditions.

5 Some of the most important conferences were the Congrès international d'hygiène, Paris, 1878; Congrès international d'hygiène et de démographie, Paris, 1889; Huitième Congrès international d'hygiène et de démographie, Budapest, 1894; Premier Congrès d'assainissement et de salubrité, Paris, 1895; Dixième Congrès international d'hygiène et de démographie, Paris, 1900.

6 E. Vallin, "Hygiènistes et médecins," *Revue de médecine légale* (1902): 222.

7 For example, doctors were among the most bitter adversaries of the effort to require the declaration of all cases of contagious disease to public authorities. See the text of this chapter at notes 86 and 87.

8 *Premier Congrès d'assainissement et de salubrité à Paris, 1895: Comptes-rendus des travaux* (Paris, 1897).

9 François Roques, *Les Logements insalubres: La loi de 1902, le casier sanitaire des maisons* (Toulouse, 1906), 26.

10 Brouardel quoted in Roques, *Les Logements insalubres,* 28–29.

11 L. M. Reuss, "Des logements insalubres et de leur influence sur certaines maladies," *Journal de thérapeutique* 9 (1882): 611.

12 Le Comte d'Haussonville, *Misère et remèdes* (Paris, 1886), 76.

13 E. Vallin, "La Surveillance sanitaire des maisons," *Revue d'hygiène* 5 (1883): 627–39. In his article "L'Influence du logement sur la santé des habitants d'une grande ville" (see n. 31, below), Cacheux attributed a long list of illnesses to unsanitary dwellings. He stated that humidity engenders rheumatism, fevers, bronchitis, pneumonia, consumption, laryngitis, heart disease, rickets, and flu, and aggravates chronic illness. Further, throat ailments, diarrheas, and migraines resulted from the faulty drainage of household wastes, while headaches and stomach problems allegedly pushed the tenant toward alcoholism.

14 André Cochut, "Paris industriel," *Revue des deux mondes* 88 (1852): 660.

15 Emile Trélat, "Cités ouvrières, maisons ouvrières," *Exposition universelle internationale de 1878 à Paris: Comptes-rendus sténographiques,* no. 10, *Congrès international d'hygiène,* 557.

16 Dr. O. Du Mesnil and Dr. Mangenot, *Enquête sur les logements, professions, salaires, et budgets (loyers inférieurs à 400 francs)* (Paris, 1899); and by Du Mesnil: "Les Garnis insalubres de la ville de Paris," *Annales d'hygiène publique et de médecine légale,* 2nd ser. 49 (1878): 193–232; "Une Rue du faubourg St. Antoine en 1883," ibid., 3rd ser. 10 (1883): 327–37. "Les Logements garnis à Paris," ibid. 23 (1890): 315–26; *L'Habitation du pauvre* (Paris, 1890).

17 Du Mesnil's findings were reported in *Rapport général sur les travaux de la Commission des logements insalubres, 1877–83.* The situation was particularly acute in arrondissement XVIII, where the population had increased from 8,933 to 20, 816 although the number of lodging-houses only increased from 601 to

833. Similarly in arrondissement XIX, the number of lodging-house inhabitants increased from 9,074 to 17,662 while the number of lodging houses went from 517 to 752. Intense overcrowding occurred as well in arrondissements XI, IV, and V.

18 Such rooms usually rented for between 45 centimes and 1 franc per night. Du Mesnil, "Une Rue du faubourg St. Antoine," 329.

19 Du Mesnil, "Les Garnis insalubres de la ville de Paris"; *Rapport général de la Commission des logements insalubres, 1877–83.*

20 E. Vallin, "La Surveillance sanitaire des maisons," *Revue d'hygiène* 5 (1883): 691. In 1884, the Conseil général de la Seine added four inspectors for the suburban communes, and in 1889, four more places were added to the Paris service and one more for the suburban communes.

21 See especially *Rapport général de la Commission des logements insalubres, 1877–83, Annexe V,* "Rapport sur la Cité des Kroumirs"; Du Mesnil, *L'Habitation du pauvre;* H. Marjolin, *Etude sur les causes et les effets des logements insalubres* (Paris, 1881); D'Haussonville, *Misère et remèdes;* Arthur Raffalovich, *Le Logement de l'ouvrier et du pauvre* (Paris, 1887); Préfecture de Police, Conseil d'hygiène publique et de salubrité, *Rapport sur l'insalubrité de la Cité Doré et de la Cité des Kroumirs (13e arrondissement),* 1882.

22 Préfecture de Police, *Rapport sur l'insalubrité de la Cité Doré et de la Cité des Kroumirs.*

23 Du Mesnil, *L'Habitation du pauvre,* 137; *Rapport général de la Commission des logements insalubres, 1884–89.*

24 For an interesting discussion of the orientation of late-nineteenth-century reform, see Jacques Donzelot, *The Policing of Families* (New York, 1979). Donzelot argues that a new stratum of professionals emerged in the late nineteenth century to implement social reform. Their efforts were characterized by an assistance pole, which was advice-oriented, and a medical/hygienic pole, which was seeking to set and enforce norms that would essentially preserve the liberal definition of the state.

25 *Rapport général de la Commission des logements insalubres, 1884–89.*

26 Roques, *Les Logements insalubres,* 16.

27 Henri Monod, "La Législation sanitaire en France," in *Les Applications sociales de la solidarité: Leçons professées à l'Ecole des hautes études sociales,* by P. Budin et al. (Paris, 1904), 122.

28 Anthony Sutcliffe, *The Autumn of Central Paris: The Defeat of Town Planning, 1850–1970* (London, 1970), 110; Monod, "La Législation sanitaire," 152. According to the statistician Jacques Bertillon, the deaths from pulmonary consumption per 100,000 population were 402 in 1872–75; 401 in 1876–80; 460 in 1881–85; and 453 in 1886–90. Jacques Bertillon, *De la fréquence des principales maladies à Paris pendant la période 1865–1891* (Paris, 1894), 133.

29 P. Brouardel, "Le Logement insalubre," *Annales d'hygiène publique et de médecine légale,* 3rd ser. 39 (1898): 101.

30 Jacques Bertillon, *Essai de statistique comparée du surpeuplement des habitations à Paris et dans les grandes capitales européennes* (Paris, 1894), 4.

31 See, for example, E. Vallin, "La Location des maisons insalubres et la respon-

sabilité des propriétaires," *Revue d'hygiène* 13 (1891): 901–7; P. Bouloumié, "La Déclaration des maladies contagieuses-épidémiques et le secret médical," *Bulletin de la Société de médecine publique et d'hygiène professionnelle* 13 (1890): 382–90; E. Cacheux, "L'Influence du logement sur la santé des habitants d'une grande ville," *Huitième Congrès international d'hygiène et de démographie, Budapest, 1894: Comptes-rendus et mémoires* (Budapest, 1896), 4: 526–31; idem, "Influence exercée sur la santé et sur la mortalité par les conditions spéciales des logements dans les grandes villes," ibid., 7:418–23.

32 The first complete survey of the sanitary conditions of the houses of Paris (*le casier sanitaire*) was conducted in 1900. See P. Juillerat, "Sur le casier sanitaire des maisons de Paris," *Dixième Congrès international d'hygiène et de démographie à Paris en 1900: Comptes-rendus* (Paris, 1901), 360–66. The dossier for each building included an extensive physical description of the construction materials of both building and courtyards; a listing of the methods for the evacuation of waste products and a survey of their condition; an analysis of the water supply, including a chemical and micrographic analysis; an analysis of the air and soil; a listing of the number of inhabitants and the number of commercial enterprises; a description of methods of ventilation; and an indication of additional possible proximate causes of insalubrity.

33 See, for example, Monod, "La Législation sanitaire," 152; Vallin, "La Location des maisons insalubres," 906.

34 Du Mesnil, quoted in "Dans quelle mesure l'état doit-il intervenir dans la question des logements insalubres?" (report of meeting of the Société d'économie politique), *Journal des économistes* 28 (1884): 507.

35 Monod, "La Législation sanitaire," 158.

36 Cacheux, "Influence exercée sur la santé et sur la mortalité," 418.

37 Léon Bourgeois, *Solidarité* (Paris, 1896); Bourgeois, "Vues politiques," *Revue de Paris,* April 1, 1898; Budin et al., *Les Applications sociales de la solidarité*; J.E.S. Hayward, "The Official Social Philosophy of the French Third Republic: Léon Bourgeois and Solidarism," *International Review of Social History* 6 (1961): 19–48; Theodore Zeldin, *France, 1848–1945: Ambition, Love and Politics* (Oxford, 1973), 640–82.

38 Hayward, "The Official Social Philosophy of the French Third Republic," 26–29.

39 Charles Gide, "La Coopération," in Budin et al., *Les Applications sociales de la solidarité,* 49, n. 1.

40 Hayward, "The Official Social Philosophy of the French Third Republic," 31.

41 Ibid., 32.

42 Léon Bourgeois, Preface to Budin et al., *Les Applications sociales de la solidarité,* vii.

43 Roques, *Les Logements insalubres.*

44 Prior to the public health law of 1902, health regulations, in the form of prefectural decrees and police ordinances, were frequently more impressive on paper than in practice. Enforcement was irregular and arbitrary, in part a result of overlapping jurisdictions and professional jealousies. For example, in Paris, the Health Council of the Seine supervised external sanitary conditions while the Commission on Unhealthful Dwellings regulated the interior hygiene of lodg-

ings. The reports of the commission noted "this annoying antagonism between the two branches of the sanitary administration of the city of Paris, an antagonism which is as much administrative as scientific and which has often retarded the solution to public health questions." These reports indicate as well that the Bureau of Public Assistance had consistently refused to send referrals to the commission, which was bound by the stipulation that it investigate only those houses *reported* as insalubrious. The ongoing tensions between the commission and the bureau had cost the commission one of its best-informed sources. Hygienists further deplored the parallel authority shared by the prefect of the Seine and the prefect of police, not only because it fed bureaucratic inefficiency, but also because the presence of the police allegedly aroused suspicion and hostility which inhibited the popularization of hygiene matters. *Rapport général de la Commission des logements insalubres, 1877–83.* This problem is also discussed in Raffalovich, *Le Logement de l'ouvrier*; Gustave Jourdan, "De la réforme de la loi du 13 avril 1850 concernant les logements insalubres," *Congrès international d'hygiène et de démographie à Paris en 1889: Comptes-rendus* (Paris, 1890), 385; and Alfred Fillassier, *De la détermination des pouvoirs publics en matière d'hygiène* (Paris, 1902).

45 *Journal officiel: Débats parlementaires, Sénat,* February 9, 1897.

46 Trélat, "Cités ouvrières, maisons ouvrières,"555.

47 Nadaud's bill was reported out of committee in 1883 but was not discussed, and it lapsed by default in the legislative session of 1885. In 1887, the issue emerged again in a bill presented by Lockroy and in one by Jules Siegfried which proposed, as well, a reorganization of hygiene services. Chamberland reported on these two bills to the Chamber of Deputies, but no action was taken. The government then introduced a bill in December 1891 which had been prepared with the assistance of the Advisory Council on Public Hygiene. In 1892, Langlet presented a report on this bill to the Chamber. Discussions ensued, and the Chamber voted in 1893 to approve most of the major articles of the bill. This draft was not discussed in the Senate until 1897. In the midst of prolonged and heated discussions, it was repeatedly returned to committee, where it underwent serious modifications until its final reading in Feburary 1902.

48 Pierre Gayot, *La Question des logements insalubres et la loi du 15 février 1902 relative à la protection de la santé publique* (Lyon, 1905); Monod, "La Législation sanitaire en France"; A. J. Martin, "Réforme de la législation sanitaire française," *Congrès international d'hygiène et de démographie à Paris en 1889: Comptes-rendus,* 868–85.

49 Martin, "Réforme de la législation sanitaire française," 871.

50 *Journal officiel: Débats parlementaires, Chambre des Députés,* June 27, 1893.

51 *Journal officiel: Documents parlementaires,* annexe no. 12, January 14, 1890 (séance du 19 novembre 1889, session extraordinaire).

52 *Journal officiel, Débats parlementaires, Sénat,* 12 février 1897.

53 M. Treille, ibid.

54 *Journal officiel: Débats parlementaires, Chambre des Députés,* June 27, 1893.

55 *Journal officiel: Documents parlementaires, Chambre des Députés,* annexe no.

1842. In an article in the *Revue de médecine légale,* the hygienist Alfred Fillassier cited the example of English legislation of 1890 which stipulated that "every project involving a group of houses located in the county or City of London must provide as many working-class lodgings as those demolished within the neighborhood or the perimeter of the expropriated buildings." He suggested, in addition, that a bank be established to make home improvement funds available to proprietors, who could repay the loan by annuities. Fillassier, "De la législation française en matière de logements insalubres: Etat actuel, réformes nécessaires," *Revue de médecine légale* 13 (1906): 265–68.

56 *Journal officiel: Débats parlementaires, Sénat,* February 4, 1897.

57 Henri Turot and Henri Bellamy, *Le Surpeuplement et les habitations à bon marché* (Paris, 1907), 63.

58 Paul Brousse, *Bulletin municipal de la Ville de Paris,* no. 5 (March 1903): 935.

59 Turot and Bellamy, *Le Surpeuplement,* 63. After 1884, the Paris Commission on Unhealthful Dwellings noted a significant increase in the resistance of proprietors to making sanitary improvements. The reports of 1884–89 refer to a new organization of businessmen who offered their services to proprietors in order to reverse the prescriptions of the Municipal Council or, at least, to effect delays in their execution. In 1890, the reports indicate that an association of proprietors had been formed to oppose application of the 1850 law. See the text below at nn. 81–85.

60 The standards established covered the size and layout of rooms, the control of humidity and odors, ventilation, painting (the use of nonpoisonous materials), maintenance, heating, cooking, lighting, household water and drinking water, courtyards, and systems for the evacuation of wastes. AN, F^8 213, Commission des logements insalubres, Rapport sur la salubrité des constructions, 1880.

61 In Paris, building plans were subject to prior approval under the 1852 decree, but there was no inspection procedure.

62 *Journal officiel: Débats parlementaires, Sénat,* February 2 and 5, 1897.

63 There is considerable evidence throughout this period that hygienists were more zealous than their contemporaries in political office, so that the needs of hygiene were first filtered through a more conservative arena before becoming law. It is useful to examine, for example, the parallel efforts in the early 1880s of an administrative commission on the one hand, and the Commission on Unhealthful Dwellings on the other, to revise the regulations governing the salubrity of buildings and outbuildings in the city of Paris. On almost all fronts, the desiderata issued by the administrative commission were more reserved than those of the unhealthful dwellings commission. Whereas the administrative commission permitted permanent habitation in below-ground quarters with "sufficient light and ventilation," the unhealthful dwellings commission allowed underground lodgings only when specific standards regarding humidity, light, and ventilation were met. The administrative commission proposed that every habitation be provided with water where piping existed. Hygienists argued that this requirement actually condoned the absence of water when piping was not nearby, and insisted that such a loophole could not be allowed. Ultimately, hygienists

could move only as fast as the political process permitted. A. Hudelo, "Le Nouveau Règlement sur les constructions neuves de Paris," *Annales d'hygiène publique et de médecine légale,* 3rd ser. 7 (1882): 305–14.

64 Paul Leroy-Beaulieu, *L'Etat moderne et ses fonctions* (Paris, 1891), 97, 387.

65 Turot and Bellamy, *Le Surpeuplement,* 69.

66 Raffalovich, *Le Logement de l'ouvrier,* 243.

67 O. Du Mesnil, "De l'obligation de l'eau dans les maisons," *Annales d'hygiène publique et de médecine légale,* 3rd ser. 24 (1890): 516–21. Emile Cheysson wrote in 1905 that most municipalities had by that time come to the aid of the landlord by subsidizing the provision of water. For example, in Paris, the city made available to apartments of modest rentals a flow of water at a price of 6 centimes per cubic meter for approximately 54 liters per day per person, instead of payment at the normal rate of 35 centimes per cubic meter. Cheysson, "Le Confort du logement populaire," extract from *Bulletin de la Société française des habitations à bon marché,* 1905, reprinted in *Oeuvres choisies* (Paris, 1911), 359–81.

68 The *Rapport général de la Commission des logements insalubres,* 1884–89, indicates that an expanded definition of outbuildings emerged from a series of lawsuits in the Council of the Prefecture of the Seine between 1885 and 1889. Further, a decree of December 22, 1888, permitted the formation of an association of proprietors to maintain private ways, and a regulation of March 9, 1894, stipulated that this association could compel the compliance of resisting proprietors with contiguous property. Préfecture du Département de la Seine, Direction des affaires municipales, *Note sur l'organisation et le fonctionnement du Bureau de l'assainissement de l'habitation: Logements insalubres, assainissement de l'habitation, casier sanitaire des maisons de Paris,* by P. Juillerat and A. Levy-Dorville (Paris, 1900), 48.

69 *Journal officiel: Débats parlementaires, Chambre des Députés,* June 26, 1893.

70 *Journal officiel: Débats parlementaires, Sénat,* February 12, 1897.

71 Ibid.

72 Ibid., February 9, 1897; Monod, "La Législation sanitaire," 140. Altogether in France, there were more than 58,000 deaths from smallpox in 1870–71 and 221,000 reported cases. In 1901, there were 1,031 smallpox deaths from a population of 14,109,520 living in cities of more than 5,000. By contrast, in a British population of 32,261,003 living in cities of comparable size, only 85 smallpox deaths occurred, while in the entire German Empire in 1897, there were only 5 deaths from smallpox.

73 Jules Simon, *De l'initiative privée et de l'état en matière de réformes sociales* (Paris, 1892).

74 *Journal officiel: Débats parlementaires, Sénat,* February 9, 1897.

75 *Journal officiel: Débats parlementaires, Chambre des Députés,* June 26, 1893; *Débats parlementaires, Sénat,* February 9, 1897.

76 See especially the *Rapport général de la Commission des logements insalubres,* 1877–83 and 1884–89; *Congrès international d'hygiène et de démographie à Paris en 1889: Comptes-rendus; Huitième Congrès international d'hygiène et de démographie, 1894: Comptes-rendus et mémoires.*

77 Du Mesnil, *L'Habitation du pauvre*, 160.

78 Turot and Bellamy, *Le Surpeuplement*, 9.

79 Sutcliffe, *The Autumn of Central Paris*, 112.

80 Jules Siegfried, "Les Habitations à bon marché," in Budin et al., *Les Applications sociales de la solidarité*, 223–24.

81 *Rapport général de la Commission des logements insalubres*, 1866–69 and 1872–76.

82 Hudelo, "Le Nouveau Règlement sur les constructions neuves de Paris," 306–7.

83 Du Mesnil, "Les Logements garnis à Paris," 318.

84 *Rapport général de la Commission des logements insalubres*, 1884–89.

85 Préfecture du Département de la Seine, *Note sur l'organisation et le fonctionnement du Bureau de l'assainissement de l'habitation*, 36.

86 Monod, "La Législation sanitaire," 130–31.

87 Vallin, "Hygiènistes et médecins," 222. The most energetic doctor-hygienists were those with academic and/or bureaucratic connections and therefore more independent of the financial pressures of private practice.

88 Monod, "La Législation sanitaire," 126. In 1903 the Advisory Council on Public Hygiene and the Academy of Medicine agreed on thirteen illnesses which required mandatory declaration (including plague, yellow fever, cholera, typhoid fever, smallpox, scarlet fever, measles, and diphtheria) and on nine illnesses (including pulmonary tuberculosis) for which declaration was optional.

89 Roques, *Les Logements insalubres*.

CONCLUSION

1 Alain Corbin's new monograph, *Le Miasme et la jonquille: L'odorat et l'imaginaire social, 18ᵉ–19ᵉ siècles* (Paris, 1982), appeared too late to be part of this study, but provides a fascinating discussion of the sociomedical and cultural background which promoted the nineteenth-century preoccupation with "deodorizing" social space. Corbin traces the expansion of hygienic concerns that began at the end of the eighteenth century as reformers shifted their attention from the stench of the terrain, stagnating water, and organic decay to a new focus on the "sécretions de la misère."

2 Charles Gide, "La Coopération," in *Les Applications sociales de la solidarité: Leçons professées à l'Ecole des hautes études sociales*, by P. Budin et al. (Paris, 1904), 48.

3 Paul Leroy-Beaulieu, *L'Etat moderne et ses fonctions* (Paris, 1891), 389.

4 Emile Cacheux, *L'Economiste pratique* (Paris, 1885), 52.

Works Cited

ARCHIVAL SOURCES

Archives Nationales

F⁸ 208	Commission de l'assainissement de Paris, September 28, 1880.
F⁸ 210	Logements insalubres.
F⁸ 211	Distribution des rapports de la Commission des logements insalubres, 1851–84.
F⁸ 212	Logements insalubres. Projets de révision de la loi du 13 avril 1850.
F⁸ 213	Logements insalubres et habitations ouvrières. Seine. 1862–98.
F⁸ 239	Situation des ouvriers à Paris, 1855.
F⁸ 241	Residus divers.
F¹² 6824	Divers.

Archives de la Préfecture de Police

BA 399   Enquête sur la crise économique et industrielle, 1883–84.
BA 400   Enquête parlementaire sur les conditions du travail en France. Octobre 1872.
BA 486   Enquête sur les loyers à Paris, 1871–91.
Reconstituted dossiers: BA   886   V. Gelez
                          BA 1126   J. Joffrin
                          BA 1135   P. Lafargue
                          BA 1171   L. Manier
                          BA 1197   M. Nadaud

Archives de la Seine

VD⁴ 3137   Concernant la salubrité des habitations.

VD⁴ 3141–3147   Logements insalubres.
DM⁵ 26–27   Commissions d'hygiène. Logements insalubres, 1852–79.

OFFICIAL SOURCES

Annuaire statistique de la ville de Paris et du département de la Seine. 1881, 1886, 1891, 1896, 1901.

Chambre de Commerce de Paris. *Rapport addressé à Messieurs les membres de la Chambre de Commerce de Paris sur la question relative aux salaires des ouvriers et à l'augmentation de loyers et des denrées alimentaires*. By Horace Say. June 15, 1855.

Empire française. Département de la Seine. Ville de Paris. Mairie du douzième arrondissement. *Commission d'hygiène et de salubrité: Procès verbal de la séance extraordinaire du jeudi, 8 décembre 1853*.

Journal Officiel: Débats parlementaires. Chambre des Députés.

Journal Officiel: Débats parlementaires. Sénat.

Journal Officiel: Documents parlementaires.

Préfecture de la Seine. Commission du règlement sanitaire. *Rapport de M. Paul Strauss, Sénateur, au nom de la sous-commission: Projet de règlement sanitaire*. Paris, 1902.

Préfecture de police. *Note sur la situation actuelle des classes ouvrières dans Paris et dans la banlieue*. June 25, 1855.

Préfecture du Département de la Seine. Direction des affaires municipales. *Note sur l'organisation et le fonctionnement du Bureau de l'assainissement de l'habitation: Logements insalubres, assainissement de l'habitation, casier sanitaire des maisons de Paris*. By P. Juillerat and A. Levy-Dorville. Paris, 1900.

Préfecture du Département de la Seine. Direction des finances. Commission des contributions directes de la ville de Paris. *Les Propriétés bâties de la ville de Paris en 1889 et en 1890*. Paris, 1890.

Préfecture du Département de la Seine. Direction municipale des travaux du cadastre de Paris. Commission des contributions directes. *Le Livre foncier de Paris: Valeur en capital des propriétés bâties et non bâties en 1901*. Paris, 1902.

Préfecture du Département de la Seine. Direction municipale des travaux du cadastre de Paris. Commission des contributions directes. *Le Livre foncier de Paris*. Part 1, *Valeur locative des propriétés bâties en 1900*. Paris, 1900.

Préfecture du Département de la Seine. *Documents statistiques recueillés et coordinés par le service de la Commission des contributions directes de la ville de Paris, 1884*. Paris, 1884.

Recherches statistiques sur la ville de Paris et le département de la Seine. Vol. 6. Paris, 1860.

Recueil de règlements concernant le service des alignements et des logements insalubres dans la ville de Paris. Prepared under the direction of M. Alphand by M. G. Jourdan. Paris, 1887.

République française. Ministère de commerce, de l'industrie, des postes et des télégraphes. *Résultats statistiques du recensement des industries et professions: Dénombrement général de la population du 29 mars 1896*. Vol. 1. Paris, 1899.

*Résultats statistiques du dénombrement de 1896 de la ville de Paris et du départe-
ment de la Seine.* Paris, 1896.
Ville de Paris. Monographies municipales. *Les Logements à bon marché: Recueil
annoté des discussions, délibérations et rapports du Conseil municipal de
Paris.* By Lucien Lambeau. Paris, 1897.

REPORTS AND CONFERENCES

Congrès international d'hygiène et de démographie à Paris en 1889: Comptes-rendus.
Paris, 1890.
*Dixième Congrès international d'hygiène et de démographie à Paris en 1900:
Comptes-rendus.* Paris, 1901.
*Exposition universelle internationale de 1878 à Paris: Comptes-rendus sténogra-
phiques,* no. 10, *Congrès international d'hygiène tenu à Paris 1–10 août 1878.*
Paris, 1880.
*Huitième Congrès international d'hygiène et de démographie: Comptes-rendus et
mémoires (Budapest 1–9 septembre 1894).* Budapest, 1896.
*Premier Congrès d'assainissement et de salubrité, Paris, 1895: Comptes-rendus des
travaux.* Paris, 1897.
*Rapport au nom de la Commission des habitations à bon marché sur la crise du
logement et la création d'habitations à bon marché.* By Henri Rousselle,
Frédéric Brunet, Emile Desvaux, and Dherbecourt. Paris, 1912.
Rapport général sur les travaux de la Commission des logements insalubres. 1851–92.
*Rapport général sur les travaux du Conseil d'hygiène publique et de salubrité du
département de la Seine, 1849–1858.*
Société centrale des architectes. *Rapport fait au Conseil, au nom de la commission
nommée sur la proposition de M. Haron-Romain pour étudier les moyens
propres à assurer l'assainissement des habitations insalubres.* By Adolphe
Lance. 1850.

PRIMARY SOURCES

Allard, E. "Etude sur la salubrité des habitations." *Exposition universelle internationale de 1878 à Paris: Comptes-rendus sténographiques,* no. 10, *Congrès
international d'hygiène tenu à Paris 1–10 août 1878,* 2:289–95. Paris, 1880.
————. "Salubrité des constructions neuves; Modifications aux constructions exis-
tantes, et entretien général des propriétés dans les parties destinées à l'habitation; projet de règlement adopté par la Commission des logements insalubres." *Annales d'hygiène publique et de médecine légale,* 3rd ser. 4 (1880):
545–56.
Barrière, Ch. de la, and Moquant, L. *Le Nouveau Conseil municipal de Paris:
Biographies et programmes des 80 conseillers municipaux élus en mai 1884.*
Paris, 1884.
Baudrillart, Henri. "L'Amélioration des logements d'ouvriers dans ses rapports avec
l'esprit de famille." *Séances et travaux de l'Académie des sciences morales et
politiques* 131 (1889).

————. *Manuel d'économie politique.* Paris, 1857.

Bellet, Victor. *Les Propriétaires et les loyers à Paris.* Paris, 1857.

Bertillon, Jacques. *De la fréquence des principales causes de décès à Paris.* Paris, 1906.

————. *De la fréquence des principales maladies à Paris pendant la période 1865–91.* Paris, 1894.

————. "Des logements surpeuplés à Paris en 1896." *Bulletin de la Société de médecine publique et d'hygiène professionnelle* (1899):111–26.

————. *Essai de statistique comparée du surpeuplement des habitations à Paris et dans les grandes capitales européennes.* Paris, 1894.

————. "Mouvements de population et causes de décès selon le degré d'aisance à Paris, Berlin, Vienne." *Dixième Congrès international d'hygiène et de démographie à Paris en 1900: Comptes-rendus,* 961–80. Paris, 1901.

Blanqui, J. A. *Des classes ouvrières en France pendant l'année 1848.* Paris, 1849.

Boulanger, Alex. "Sur les habitations ouvrières dans Paris: Considérations sur la salubrité du quartier St. Gervais." *Exposition universelle internationale de 1878 à Paris: Comptes-rendus sténographiques,* no. 10, *Congrès international d'hygiène tenu à Paris 1–10 août 1878,* 2:336–47. Paris, 1880.

Bouloumié, P. "La Déclaration des maladies contagieuses-épidémiques et le secret médical." *Bulletin de la Société de médecine publique et d'hygiène professionnelle* (1890): 383–91.

Bourgeois, Léon. *Essai d'une philosophie de la solidarité: Conférences et discussions.* Paris, 1902.

Brelay, E. "Le Logement et l'alimentation populaires." *La Réforme sociale* 34 (1897): 481–509.

Brouardel, P. "Le Logement insalubre." *Annales d'hygiène publique et de médecine légale,* 3rd ser. 39 (1898): 97–106.

————. "La Propreté et l'hygiène." In *Les Applications sociales de la solidarité: Leçons professées à l'Ecole des hautes études sociales,* ed. P. Budin et al., 237–61. Paris, 1904.

Budin, P.; Gide, Ch.; Monod, H.; Paulet, G.; Robin, A.; Siegfried, J.; and Brouardel, P. *Les Applications sociales de la solidarité: Leçons professées à l'Ecole des hautes études sociales.* Paris, 1904.

Cacheux, Emile. *L'Economiste pratique: Construction et organisation des crèches, salles d'asile, écoles, habitations ouvrières et maisons d'employés, hôtels pour célibataires, cuisines économiques, bains, lavoirs, cercles populaires, nourriceries, maternités, dispensaires, hôpitaux, hospices, asiles de nuit, postes de secours.* Paris, 1885.

————. *Etat des habitations ouvrières à la fin du XIXe siècle.* Paris, 1891.

————. *Etat en l'an 1885 des habitations ouvrières parisiennes.* Paris, 1885.

————. "Les Habitations ouvrières exposées en 1889." *Congrès international d'hygiène et de démographie à Paris en 1889: Comptes-rendus,* 428–36. Paris, 1890.

————. "L'Influence du logement sur la santé des habitants d'une grande ville." *Huitième Congrès international d'hygiène et de démographie, Budapest, 1894: Comptes-rendus et mémoires,* 4:526–31. Budapest, 1896.

————. "Influence exercée sur la santé et sur la mortalité par les conditions spéciales des logements dans les grandes villes." Ibid., 7:418–23.

Calland, V. *Suppression des loyers par l'élévation de tous les locataires au droit de propriété.* Paris, 1857.

Challamel, M. J. "Logements insalubres." *Dixième Congrès international d'hygiène et de démographie à Paris en 1900: Comptes-rendus,* 536–48. Paris, 1901.

Chevalier, Michel. "Les Questions politiques et sociales: L'assistance et la prévoyance publiques: Rapport de la commission." *Revue des deux mondes,* 1850: 961–94.

Cheysson, Emile. "Le Confort du logement populaire." *Bulletin de la Société française des habitations à bon marché* (1905). Reprinted in *Oeuvres choisies,* 359–81.

———. "Frédéric Le Play: Sa méthode, sa doctrine, son école." Communication faite à l'Académie des sciences morales et politiques, July 15, 1905. Reprinted in *Oeuvres choisies,* 163–81.

———. "Les Habitations à bon marché depuis la loi du 30 novembre 1894." *Revue d'hygiène* 19 (1897): 422–33.

———. "La Lutte des classes." *La Revue internationale de Sociologie,* November–December 1893. Reprinted in *Oeuvres choisies,* 89–115.

———. "Mon Testament social." Discours à la Ligue Nationale contre l'alcoolisme, March 23, 1909. Reprinted in *Oeuvres choisies,* 1–19.

———. *Oeuvres choisies.* Paris, 1911.

———. "Le Patron: Son Rôle économique et social." Communication faite à la Société de sociologie de Paris, April 17, 1906. Reprinted in *Oeuvres choisies,* 115–45.

———. *La Question des habitations ouvrières en France et à l'étranger: La situation actuelle, ses dangers, ses remèdes.* Paris, 1886.

———. "Le Rôle social de l'ingénieur." Conférence faite devant la Société des ingénieurs civils (May 20, 1897). Reprinted in *Oeuvres choisies,* 19–37.

———. "Le Taudis: Ses dangers, ses remèdes." Paper presented at the Congrès de l'Alliance d'hygiène sociale à Nancy (June 23, 1906). Reprinted in *Oeuvres choisies,* 233–57.

———. *Commentaire de la loi du 13 avril 1850 sur les logements insalubres.* Paris, 1869.

Cochin, A. "Paris, sa population, son industrie." *Séances et travaux de l'Académie des sciences morales et politiques* 69 (1864).

Cochin, D. *Paris: Quatre Années au Conseil Municipal.* Paris, 1885.

Cochut, André. "Paris industriel." *Revue des deux mondes* 88 (1852): 638–70.

Cramouzaud, Eugène. *Etudes sur la transformation du XIIe arrondissement et des quartiers anciens de la rive gauche.* Paris, 1855.

Danduran, J. J. *Les Propriétaires en 1863: Etudes physiologiques.* Paris, 1863.

"Dans quelle mesure l'état doit-il intervenir dans la question des logements insalubres?" *Journal des économistes* 28 (1884).

Delaire, A. *Les Logements ouvriers et le devoir des classes dirigeantes.* Lyon, 1886.

"De la revision de la loi du 13 avril 1850 sur les logements insalubres." Rapport fait au nom de la Commission des logements insalubres de la Ville de Paris par une délégation composée de MM. le Dr. E.-R. Perrin, Allard, le Dr. Brenond, Buisset et Hudelo. *Congrès international d'hygiène et de démographie à Paris en 1889: Comptes-rendus,* 373–402. Paris 1890.

"De l'intervention de l'état et des municipalités dans la question des loyers." *Journal des économistes* 25 (1884): 442–55.

Demolins, Edmond. "Les Habitations ouvrières." *La Réforme sociale* 1 (1882): 301–6.

Des Cilleuls, Alfred. *L'Administration parisienne sous la 3ᵉ République.* Paris, 1910.

d'Haussonville, Le Comte. *Misère et remèdes.* Paris, 1886.

Drouineau, G. "Nos Institutions d'hygiène publique." *Revue d'hygiène et de police médicale* 1 (1879).

Du Camp, Maxime. *Paris: Ses organes, ses fonctions, et sa vie dans la seconde moitié du XIXᵉ siècle.* 6 vols. Paris, 1883.

Du Claux, V. "Petits Logements parisiens." *Annales d'hygiène publique et de médecine légale,* 3rd ser. 9 (1883): 465–76.

Du Mesnil, Octave. "La Cité des Kroumirs." *Annales d'hygiène publique et de médecine légale,* 3rd ser. 7 (1882): 209–19.

———. "De l'obligation de l'eau dans les maisons." Ibid. 24 (1890): 516–21.

———. "Les Garnis insalubres de la ville de Paris." Ibid., 2nd ser. 49 (1878): 193–232.

———. *L'Habitation du pauvre.* Preface by Jules Simon. Paris, 1890.

———. "Les Logements garnis à Paris." *Annales d'hygiène publique et de médecine légale,* 3rd ser. 23 (1890): 315–26.

———. "Projet de règlement sur la salubrité intérieure des maisons de Paris." Ibid. 20 (1888): 28–37.

———. "La Question des courettes de Paris." Ibid. 25 (1891): 367–73.

———. "Une Rue du Faubourg St.-Antoine en 1883." Ibid. 10 (1883): 327–37.

Du Mesnil, Octave, and Dr. Mangenot. *Enquête sur les logements, professions, salaires et budgets (loyers inférieurs à 400 francs).* Paris, 1899.

Ely, Dr. *Paris: Etude démographique et médicale.* Paris, 1872.

Emion, Victor, and Bardies, Charles. *Dictionnaire des usages et règlements de Paris et du département de la Seine en matière de locations, constructions, voirie, etc.* Paris, 1893.

Fillassier, Alfred. *De la détermination des pouvoirs publics en matière d'hygiène.* Paris, 1902.

———. "De la législation française en matière des logements insalubres: Etat actuel, réformes nécessaires." *Revue de médecine légale* 8 (1906): 259–70.

Fougère, Henry. *Les Délégations ouvrières aux expositions universelles sous le Second Empire.* Montluçon, 1905.

Fougerousse, A. "Pour la construction des petits logements." *La Réforme sociale* 1 (1883): 401–7.

———. "La Question des loyers." Ibid. 2 (1882).

Foville, Alfred de. *Notice historique sur la vie et les oeuvres de M. Georges Picot.* Paris, 1910.

Frégier, H.-A. *Des classes dangereuses de la population dans les grandes villes et des moyens de les rendre meilleures.* Paris, 1840.

Gay, Ernest. *Nos Ediles.* Paris, 1895.

Gayot, Pierre. *La Question des logements insalubres et la loi du 15 février 1902 relative à la protection de la santé publique.* Lyon, 1905.

Gide, Charles. "La Coopération." In *Les Applications sociales de la solidarité: Leçons professées à l'Ecole des hautes études sociales,* ed. P. Budin et al. Paris, 1904.

Gourlier, Charles. *Des voies publiques et des habitations particulières à Paris.* Paris, 1852.

Goyard, Dr. *Le Plan de Paris: Considérations d'hygiène et d'économie sociale sur la transformation graduelle de Paris.* Paris, 1885.

Grison, Georges. *Paris horrible et Paris original.* Paris, 1882.

Guesde, Jules. *Ça et là.* Paris, 1914.

————. *Textes choisis, 1867–1882.* Preface and commentary by Claude Willard. Paris, 1959.

Guesde, Jules, and Lafargue, Paul. *Le Programme du Parti ouvrier: Son histoire, ses considérants, ses articles.* Lille, 1890.

"Les Habitations à bon marché: Loi du 30 novembre 1894." *La Réforme sociale* 28 (1894).

Haussmann, Georges. *Mémoires du Baron Haussmann.* 3 vols. Paris, 1890.

Hudelo, A. "Le Nouveau Règlement sur les constructions neuves de Paris." *Annales d'hygiène publique et de médecine légale,* 3rd ser. 7 (1882): 305–14.

Jourdan, Gustave. "De la réforme de la loi du 13 avril 1850 concernant les logements insalubres." *Congrès international d'hygiène et de démographie à Paris en 1889: Comptes-rendus,* 384–402. Paris, 1890.

————. "De l'assainissement des habitations dans la ville de Paris." Ibid., 353–73.

————. *Etude sur le projet de revision de la loi concernant les logements insalubres.* Paris, 1883.

————. *Législation sur les logements insalubres: Traité pratique.* Paris, 1879.

————. *Pouvoirs des maires en matières de salubrité des habitations.* Paris, 1890.

Juillerat, P. "Sur le Casier sanitaire des maisons de Paris." *Dixième Congrès international d'hygiène et de démographie à Paris en 1900: Comptes-rendus,* 360–66. Paris, 1901.

Korosi, J. "Influence des habitations sur les causes de décès et sur la durée de la vie." *Annales de démographie internationale* 1 (1877): 369–81.

Laborderie, R. *Les Habitations à bon marché en France.* Bordeaux, 1902.

Lasteyrie, Ferdinand de. *Les Travaux de Paris: Examen critique.* Paris, 1861.

Laurent, Emile. "Les Logements insalubres et la loi de 1850." *Séances et travaux de l'Académie des sciences morales et politiques* 117 (1882): 666–97.

————. *Les Logements insalubres: La loi de 1850, son application, ses lacunes.* Paris, 1882.

Lavergne, Léonce de. "Note sur le dénombrement de la population de 1856." *Séances et travaux de l'Académie des sciences morales et politiques* 39 (1857).

————. "Note sur le dénombrement de la population en 1866." Ibid. 80 (1867).

Lavallée, Ch. *Société d'encouragement pour l'industrie nationale: Rapport sur diverses communications relative aux habitations ouvrières.* Paris, 1882.

Lazare, Louis. *Les Quartiers pauvres de Paris.* Paris, 1869.

————. *Les Quartiers pauvres de Paris: Le XXᵉ arrondissement.* Paris, 1870.

Lefort, Joseph. "Les Logements ouvriers." Paper presented at the Association française pour l'avancement des sciences, Congrès de Clermont-Ferrand, August 24, 1876.

Lelut, L. F. "De la santé du peuple." *Mémoires de l'Académie des sciences morales et politiques* 7 (1850): 951–87.

Le Play, F. *L'Ecole de la paix sociale: Son histoire, sa méthode, et sa doctrine.* Tours, 1881.

———. *Le Programme des unions de la paix sociale.* Tours, 1876.

Leprince, D. *Les Logements à bon marché: La propriété immobilière rendue accessible aux travailleurs.* Paris, 1888.

Leroy-Beaulieu, Paul. *De l'état moral et intellectuel des populations ouvrières et de son influence sur le taux des salaires.* Paris, 1868.

———. *Essai sur la répartition des richesses et sur la tendance à une moindre inégalité des conditions.* Paris, 1883.

———. *L'Etat moderne et ses fonctions.* Paris, 1891.

———. "Liberty and Property: The Two Main Factors of Human Progress." Paper presented at the Fourteenth Annual Meeting of the Liberty and Property Defense League, March 2, 1897.

———. *La Question ouvrière au XIXe siècle.* Paris, 1899.

Levasseur, E. "Les Populations urbaines en France comparées à celles de l'étranger." *Séances et travaux de l'Académie des sciences morales et politiques* 127 (1887).

Loua, Toussaint. *Les Grands Faits économiques et sociaux, 1878–1883.* Paris, 1883.

Madre, Ct^e Ad. de. *Des ouvriers et des moyens d'améliorer leur condition dans les villes.* Paris, 1863.

Malon, Benoît. *Le Socialisme intégral.* Part 2, *Des réformes possibles et des moyens pratiques.* Paris, 1894.

Marjolin, H. *Etudes sur les causes et les effets des logements insalubres.* Paris, 1881.

Martin, A. J. "Rapport sur des projets de revision de la loi du 13 avril 1850 sur les logements insalubres." *Revue d'hygiène* 4 (1882): 468–88.

———. "Réforme de la législation sanitaire française." *Congrès international d'hygiène et de démographie à Paris en 1889: Comptes-rendus,* 868–85. Paris, 1890.

Mazerolle, Pierre. *La Misère de Paris: Les mauvais gites.* Paris, 1875.

Melun, Armand de. *De l'intervention de la société pour prévenir et soulager la misère.* Paris, 1849.

Monfalcon, J. B., and Polinière, A.P.I. de. *Traité de la salubrité dans les grandes villes suivi de l'hygiène de Lyon.* Paris, 1846.

Monod, Henri. "La Législation sanitaire en France." In *Les Applications sociales de la solidarité: Leçons professées à l'Ecole des hautes études sociales,* ed. P. Budin et al., 81–161. Paris, 1904.

Muller, E., and Du Mesnil, O. "Des habitations à bon marché au point de vue de la construction et de la salubrité." *Annales d'hygiène publique et de médecine légale,* 3rd ser. 22 (1889): 150–60.

Muller, Emile, and Cacheux, Emile. *Les Habitations ouvrières en tous pays.* Paris, 1879.

Napias, H., and Martin, A. J. *L'Etude et les progrès de l'hygiène en France de 1878 à 1882.* Paris, 1882.

Nisard. "Les Classes moyennes en Angleterre et la bourgeoisie en France." *Revue des deux mondes* (1849):968–97.

Pabon, Louis. *Manuel pratique des propriétaires et locataires.* Paris, 1906.

Paris desert: Lamentations d'un Jérémie Haussmannisé. n.d.

Passez, Ernest. "La Désorganisation de la famille et ses conséquences sociales." *La Réforme sociale* 34 (1897).

Pelloutier, Fernand, and Pelloutier, Maurice. *La Vie ouvrière en France.* Paris, 1900.

Petrot, Albert. *Les Conseillers municipaux de Paris et les conseillers généraux de la Seine.* Paris, 1876.

Piart, Georges. *Locataires et propriétaires: Etude sociale sur les abus de la propriété à l'égard de la location.* Paris, 1882.

Picot, Georges. *Conférence sur l'amélioration des petits logements.* Paris, 1894.

———. *Un Devoir social et les logements d'ouvriers.* Paris, 1885.

———. "Les Logements d'ouvriers à Londres." *Séances et travaux de l'Académie des sciences morales et politiques* 124 (1885).

———. *La Lutte contre le socialisme révolutionnaire.* Paris, 1896.

———. "Les Moyens d'améliorer la condition de l'ouvrier." *La Réforme sociale* 21 (1891).

———. *La République: Ses veritables adversaires.* Gien, 1892.

———. "Self-Help for Labor: Some French Solutions of Working-Class Problems." Address delivered to the Liberty and Property Defense League, December 8, 1891.

Poulot, Denis. *Question sociale: Le sublime ou le travailleur comme il est en 1870 et ce qu'il peut être.* Paris, 1872.

Pourquoi des propriétaires à Paris: Dédié aux locataires. Paris, 1857.

Raffalovich, Arthur. *Le Logement de l'ouvrier et du pauvre.* Paris, 1887.

Rémaury, H. *Etudes économiques. Les habitations ouvrières et les petits logements à bon marché.* Paris, 1887.

Reuss, L. M. "Des logements insalubres et de leur influence sur certaines maladies." *Journal de thérapeutique* 9 (1882): 611–21.

———. "Les Maisons ouvrières de la rue de Mouzaia." *Annales d'hygiène publique et de médecine légale,* 3rd ser. 26 (1891): 113–21.

Roberts, Henry. *Des habitations des classes ouvrières.* Translated and published by order of the President of the Republic. Paris, 1850.

Robinet, Dr. *"Finissons Paris!": Observations sur l'édilité moderne.* Paris, 1879.

Roques, François. *Les Logements insalubres: La loi de 1902, le casier sanitaire des maisons.* Toulouse, 1906.

Rostand, Eugène. *Les Questions d'économie sociale dans une grande ville populaire (Marseille).* Paris, 1889.

Roulliet, Antony. *Les Habitations ouvrières à l'Exposition universelle de 1889 à Paris.* Nancy, 1889.

Siegfried, Jules. *Les Cités ouvrières.* Havre, 1877.

———. "Les Habitations à bon marché." In *Les Applications sociales de la solidarité: Leçons professées à l'Ecole des hautes études sociales,* ed. P. Budin et al., 215–36. Paris, 1904.

———. *Quelques Mots sur la misère: Son histoire, ses causes, ses remèdes.* Havre, 1877.

Simon, Jules. *De l'initiative privée et de l'état en matière de réformes sociales.* Paris, 1892.

———. *L'Ouvrière.* Paris, 1861.

———. *Paris aux Parisiens.* Paris, 1869.

———. "Sociétés coopératives de constructions de logements." *Séances et travaux de l'Académie des sciences morales et politiques* 75 (1866).

Simon, P. *Statistique de l'habitation à Paris: Les locaux d'habitation divisés par quartiers et par catégories de loyer.* Paris, 1891.

Strauss, Paul. *Paris ignoré: 550 dessins inédits.* Paris, 1892.

Strauss, Paul, and Fillassier, Alfred. *Loi sur la protection de la santé publique, loi du 15 février 1902: Travaux législatifs, guide pratique et commentaire.* Paris, 1902.

Taillefer, Paul. *Des cités ouvrières et de leur nécessité comme hygiène et tranquillité publiques.* Paris, 1852.

Thillard, Henry. *Rapport sur les habitations économiques.* Havre, 1884.

Trélat, Emile. "Cités ouvrières, maisons ouvrières." *Exposition universelle internationale de 1878 à Paris: Comptes-rendus sténographiques,* no. 10, *Congrès international d'hygiène tenu à Paris 1–10 août 1878,* 538–97. Paris, 1880.

Turot, Henri, and Bellamy, Henri. *Le Surpeuplement et les habitations à bon marché.* Paris, 1907.

Ultor, Jacques. *La Question des loyers, du pain, du travail et le Conseil Municipal de Paris.* Paris, 1884.

Vallin, E. "Hygiènistes et médecins." *Revue de médecine légale* (1902):222.

———. "La Location des maisons insalubres et la responsabilité des propriétaires." *Revue d'hygiène* 13 (1891): 901–7.

———. "La Surveillance sanitaire des maisons." Ibid. 5 (1883): 627–39.

Vauthier, L. L. "De la nécessité de donner, dans les villes populeuses surtout, une base scientifique aux études et travaux d'hygiène publique, et de quelques moyens à prendre pour obtenir ce résultat." *Exposition universelle internationale de 1878 à Paris: Comptes-rendus sténographiques,* no. 10, *Congrès international d'hygiène tenu à Paris 1–10 août 1878,* 2:274–80. Paris, 1880.

Verronneau, F. *Les Logements insalubres: Etude médico-légale.* Paris, 1893.

Veuillot, Louis. *Les Odeurs de Paris.* Paris, 1867.

Villermé, Louis René. *Cités ouvrières.* Paris, 1850.

———. "De la mortalité dans les divers quartiers de la ville de Paris, et des causes qui la rendent très différente dans plusieurs d'entre eux, ainsi que dans les divers quartiers de beaucoup de grandes villes." *Annales d'hygiène publique et de médecine légale* 3 (1830): 294–341.

———. *Tableau de l'état physique et moral des ouvriers employés dans les manufactures de coton, de laine, et de soie.* 2 vols. Paris, 1840.

Weill, Alexandre. *Paris inhabitable: Des loyers de Paris ce que tout le monde pense et que personne ne dit.* Paris, 1860.

———. *Qu'est-ce que le propriétaire d'une maison à Paris: Suite de Paris inhabitable.* Paris, 1860.

SECONDARY WORKS

Ackerknecht, Erwin H. "Anticontagionism between 1821 and 1867." *Bulletin of the History of Medicine* 22 (1948): 562–93.

——. "Broussais; or, A Forgotten Medical Revolution." Ibid. 27 (1953): 320–43.

——. "Hygiene in France, 1815–1848." Ibid. 22 (1948): 117–55.

——. *Medicine at the Paris Hospital, 1794–1848.* Baltimore, 1967.

——. "Villermé and Quetelet." *Bulletin of the History of Medicine* 26 (1952): 317–30.

Anderson, Robert David. *France, 1870–1914: Politics and Society.* London, 1977.

Bastié, Jean. *La Croissance de la banlieue parisienne.* Paris, 1964.

Braudel, Fernand, and Labrousse, Ernest, eds. *Histoire économique et sociale de la France.* Vol. 3, *L'Avènement de l'ère industrielle, 1789–1880.* Paris, 1976.

Briggs, Asa. "Cholera and Society in the Nineteenth Century." In *European Political History, 1815–1870: Aspects of Liberalism,* ed. Eugene C. Black. New York, 1967.

Chapman, J. M., and Chapman, Brian. *The Life and Times of Baron Haussmann: Paris in the Second Empire.* London, 1957.

Chevalier, Louis. *La Formation de la population parisienne au XIXe siècle.* Paris, 1950.

——. *Classes laborieuses et classes dangereuses à Paris pendant la première moitié du XIXe siècle.* Paris, 1958.

——. *Laboring Classes and Dangerous Classes in Paris during the First Half of the Nineteenth Century.* Trans. Frank Jellinek. New York, 1973.

Chevalier, Louis, ed. *Le Choléra: La première épidémie du XIXe siècle.* La Roche-Sur-Yon, 1958.

Coleman, William. *Death Is a Social Disease: Public Health and Political Economy in Early Industrial France.* Madison, 1982.

Corbin, Alain. *Le Miasme et la jonquille: L'odorat et l'imaginaire social, 18e–19e siècles.* Paris, 1982.

Daumard, Adeline. *La Bourgeoisie parisienne de 1815 à 1848.* Paris, 1963.

——. *Maisons de Paris et propriétaires parisiens au XIXe siècle, 1809–1880.* Paris, 1965.

Delabroise, Marcel. *Un Médecin hygièniste et sociologue: Louis-René Villermé (1782–1863).* Paris, 1939.

Duveau, Georges. *La Vie ouvrière en France sous le Second Empire.* Paris, 1946.

Faure, A. "Classe malpropre, classe dangereuse? Quelques remarques à propos des chiffonniers parisiens au XIXe siècle et de leurs cités." *Recherches. L'Haleine des faubourgs: Ville, habitat, et santé au XIXe siècle* (December 1977):79–103.

Flaus, Lucien. "Les Fluctuations de la construction d'habitations urbaines." *Journal de la Société de statistique de Paris,* nos. 5–6 (May–June 1949): 185–221.

Foucault, Michel. *The Birth of the Clinic: An Archaeology of Medical Perception.* Trans. A. M. Sheridan Smith. New York, 1975.

Galdston, Iago. "Social Medicine and the Epidemic Constitution." *Bulletin of the History of Medicine* 25 (1951): 8–21.

Girard, Louis. *La Politique des travaux publics du Second Empire.* Paris, 1952.

Guerrand, Roger H. "Les Conceptions des initiateurs du logement social en France au XIXe siècle." *Affrontement* (January 1962):15–32.

―――. *Les Origines du logement social en France.* Paris, 1967.

Halbwachs, Maurice. *La Population et les tracés de voies à Paris depuis un siècle.* Paris, 1928.

Hayward. J.E.S. "The Official Social Philosophy of the French Third Republic: Léon Bourgeois and Solidarism." *International Review of Social History* 6 (1961): 19–48.

Hausheer, Herman. "Icarian Medicine: Etienne Cabet's Utopia and Its French Medical Background." *Bulletin of the History of Medicine* 9 (1941): 294–310, 401–35, 517–29.

Hugueney, Jeanne. "Un Centenaire oublié: La première loi française d'urbanisme 13 avril 1850." *La Vie urbaine* (1950):241–49.

Humbert, Sylvain. *Les Possibilistes.* Paris, 1911.

Jacquemet, Gérard. "Belleville aux XIXe et XXe siècles: Une méthode d'analyse de la croissance urbaine à Paris." *Annales: Economies, sociétés, civilisations* 30 (July–August 1975): 819–43.

Jones, Gareth Stedman. *Outcast London: A Study in the Relationship between Classes in Victorian Society.* Oxford, 1971.

La Berge, Ann F. "Public Health in France and the French Public Health Movement, 1815–1848." Ph.D. diss., University of Tennessee, 1974.

Lavedan, Pierre. *Histoire de l'urbanisme: Époque contemporaine.* Paris, 1952.

―――. *Nouvelle Histoire de Paris: Histoire de l'urbanisme à Paris.* Paris, 1975.

―――. "Paris à l'arrivée d'Haussmann." *La Vie urbanie,* nos. 3–4 (1953).

―――. *Les Villes françaises.* Paris, 1960.

Lees, Lynn. "Metropolitan Types: London and Paris Compared." In *The Victorian City: Images and Reality,* ed. H. J. Dyos and Michael Wolff. London, 1973.

Legge, Thomas Morison. *Public Health in European Capitals.* London, 1896.

Luria, Daniel D. "Wealth, Capital, and Power: The Social Meaning of Ownership." *Journal of Interdisciplinary History* 7 (Autumn 1976): 261–82.

McKay, John P. *Tramways and Trolleys: The Rise of Urban Mass Transport in Europe.* Princeton, 1976.

Marnata, Françoise. *Les Loyers des bourgeois de Paris, 1860–1958.* Paris, 1961.

Orry, Albert. *Les Socialistes indépendants.* Paris, 1911.

Peter, Jean-Pierre. "Malades et maladies à la fin du XVIIIe siècle: Une enquête de la Société royale de médecine." *Annales: Economies, sociétés, civilisations* 22 (1967): 711–51.

Pinkney, David. *Napoleon III and the Rebuilding of Paris.* Princeton, 1958.

Ponteil, Felix. *Les Institutions de la France de 1814 à 1870.* Paris, 1966.

Rosen, George. "Disease, Debility, and Death." In *The Victorian City: Images and Reality,* ed. H. J. Dyos and Michael Wolff. London, 1973.

―――. *From Medical Police to Social Medicine: Essays on the History of Health Care.* New York, 1974.

―――. *A History of Public Health.* New York, 1958.

———. "The Philosophy of Ideology and the Emergence of Modern Medicine in France." *Bulletin of the History of Medicine* 20 (1946): 328–39.

———. "Political Order and Human Health in Jeffersonian Thought." Ibid. 26 (1952): 32–44.

Rosenberg, Charles E. "Cholera in Nineteenth-Century Europe: A Tool for Social and Economic Analysis." *Comparative Studies in Society and History* 8 (1965–66): 452–63.

———. *The Cholera Years: The United States in 1832, 1849, and 1866.* Chicago, 1962.

Rosenkrantz, Barbara Gutmann. *Public Health and the State: Changing Views in Massachusetts, 1842–1936.* Cambridge, Mass., 1972.

Rouleau, Bernard. *Le Tracé des rues de Paris: Formation, typologie, fonctions.* Paris, 1967.

Saalman, Howard. *Haussman: Paris Transformed.* New York, 1971.

Shryock, Richard Harrison. "Germ Theories in Medicine Prior to 1870: Futher Comments on Continuity in Science." *Clio Medica* 7 (1972): 81–109.

Singer-Kerel, Jeanne. *Le Coût de la vie à Paris de 1840 à 1954.* Paris, 1961.

Stafford, David. *From Anarchism to Reformism: A Study of the Political Activities of Paul Brousse within the First International and the French Socialist Movement, 1870–90.* Toronto, 1971.

Sutcliffe, Anthony. *The Autumn of Central Paris: The Defeat of Town Planning, 1850–1970.* London, 1970.

Temkin, Owsei. "The Philosophical Background of Magendie's Physiology." *Bulletin of the History of Medicine* 20 (1946): 10–35.

Thuillier, Guy. "Hygiène et salubrité en Nivernais au XIXᵉ siècle." *Revue d'histoire économique et sociale,* 1967:305–25.

Vaillard, M. "Rôle de l'Académie de médecine dans l'evolution de l'hygiène publique, 1820–1920." *Bulletin de l'Académie de médecine* 84 (1920): 401–29.

Williams, Roger L. *Gaslight and Shadow: The World of Napoleon III, 1851–1870.* New York, 1957.

Zeldin, Theodore. *France, 1848–1945.* Vol. 1, *Ambition, Love, and Politics.* Oxford, 1973.

Index

DESIGNED BY BILL BOEHM
COMPOSED BY METRICOMP, GRUNDY CENTER, IOWA
MANUFACTURED BY CUSHING MALLOY, INC., ANN ARBOR, MICHIGAN
TEXT AND DISPLAY LINES ARE SET IN SABON

Library of Congress Cataloging in Publication Data
Shapiro, Ann-Louise, 1944–
Housing the poor of Paris, 1850–1902.
Bibliography: pp. 205–217.
Includes index.
1. Public housing—France—Paris—History. 2. Public
health—France—Paris—History. 3. Poor—France—Paris—
History. I. Title.
HD7288.78.F82P357 1984   363.5'8   84-40159
ISBN 0-299-09880-X